Southern Mountain Music

Contributions to Southern Appalachian Studies

1. *Memoirs of Grassy Creek: Growing Up in the Mountains on the Virginia–North Carolina Line.* Zetta Barker Hamby. 1998

2. *The Pond Mountain Chronicle: Self-Portrait of a Southern Appalachian Community.* Edited by Leland R. Cooper and Mary Lee Cooper. 1998

3. *Traditional Musicians of the Central Blue Ridge: Old Time, Early Country, Folk and Bluegrass Label Recording Artists, with Discographies.* Marty McGee. 2000

4. *W.R. Trivett, Appalachian Pictureman: Photographs of a Bygone Time.* Ralph E. Lentz II. 2001

5. *The People of the New River: Oral Histories from the Ashe, Alleghany and Watauga Counties of North Carolina.* Edited by Leland R. Cooper and Mary Lee Cooper. 2001

6. *John Fox, Jr., Appalachian Author.* Bill York. 2003

7. *The Thistle and the Brier: Historical Links and Cultural Parallels Between Scotland and Appalachia.* Richard Blaustein. 2003

8. *Tales from Sacred Wind: Coming of Age in Appalachia. The Cratis Williams Chronicles.* Cratis D. Williams. Edited by David Cratis Williams and Patricia D. Beaver. 2003

9. *Willard Gayheart, Appalachian Artist.* Willard Gayheart and Donia S. Eley. 2003

10. *The Forest City Lynching of 1900: Populism, Racism, and White Supremacy in Rutherford County, North Carolina.* J. Timothy Cole. 2003

11. *The Brevard Rosenwald School: Black Education and Community Building in a Southern Appalachian Town, 1920–1966.* Betty J. Reed. 2004

12. *The Bristol Sessions: Writings About the Big Bang of Country Music.* Edited by Charles K. Wolfe and Ted Olson. 2005

13. *Community and Change in the North Carolina Mountains: Oral Histories and Profiles of People from Western Watauga County.* Compiled by Nannie Greene and Catherine Stokes Sheppard. 2006

14. *Ashe County: A History; A New Edition.* Arthur Lloyd Fletcher. 2009 [2006]

15. *The New River Controversy; A New Edition.* Thomas J. Schoenbaum. Epilogue by R. Seth Woodard. 2007

16. *The Blue Ridge Parkway by Foot: A Park Ranger's Memoir.* Tim Pegram. 2007

17. *James Still: Critical Essays on the Dean of Appalachian Literature.* Edited by Ted Olson and Kathy H. Olson. 2008

18. *Owsley County, Kentucky, and the Perpetuation of Poverty.* John R. Burch, Jr. 2008

19. *Asheville: A History.* Nan K. Chase. 2007

20. *Southern Appalachian Poetry: An Anthology of Works by 37 Poets.* Edited by Marita Garin. 2008

21. *Ball, Bat and Bitumen: A History of Coalfield Baseball in the Appalachian South.* L.M. Sutter. 2009

22. *The Frontier Nursing Service: America's First Rural Nurse-Midwife Service and School.* Marie Bartlett. 2009

23. *James Still in Interviews, Oral Histories and Memoirs.* Edited by Ted Olson. 2009

24. *The Millstone Quarries of Powell County, Kentucky.* Charles D. Hockensmith. 2009

25. *The Bibliography of Appalachia: More Than 4,700 Books, Articles, Monographs and Dissertations, Topically Arranged and Indexed.* Compiled by John R. Burch, Jr. 2009

26. *Appalachian Children's Literature: An Annotated Bibliography.* Compiled by Roberta Teague Herrin and Sheila Quinn Oliver. 2010

27. *Southern Appalachian Storytellers: Interviews with Sixteen Keepers of the Oral Tradition.* Edited by Saundra Gerrell Kelley. 2010

28. *Southern West Virginia and the Struggle for Modernity.* Christopher Dorsey. 2011

29. *George Scarbrough, Appalachian Poet: A Biographical and Literary Study with Unpublished Writings.* Randy Mackin. 2011

30. *The Water-Powered Mills of Floyd County, Virginia: Illustrated Histories, 1770–2010.* Franklin F. Webb and Ricky L. Cox. 2012

31. *School Segregation in Western North Carolina: A History, 1860s–1970s.* Betty Jamerson Reed. 2011

32. *The Ravenscroft School in Asheville: A History of the Institution and Its People and Buildings.* Dale Wayne Slusser. 2014

33. *The Ore Knob Mine Murders: The Crimes, the Investigation and the Trials.* Rose M. Haynes. 2013

34. *New Art of Willard Gayheart.* Willard Gayheart and Donia S. Eley. 2014

35. *Public Health in Appalachia: Essays from the Clinic and the Field.* Edited by Wendy Welch. 2014

36. *The Rhetoric of Appalachian Identity.* Todd Snyder. 2014

37. *African American and Cherokee Nurses in Appalachia: A History, 1900–1965.* Phoebe Ann Pollitt. 2016

38. *A Hospital for Ashe County: Four Generations of Appalachian Community Health Care.* Janet C. Pittard. 2016

39. *Dwight Diller: West Virginia Mountain Musician.* Lewis M. Stern. 2016

40. *The Brown Mountain Lights: History, Science and Human Nature Explain an Appalachian Mystery.* Wade Edward Speer. 2017

41. *Richard L. Davis and the Color Line in Ohio Coal: A Hocking Valley Mine Labor Organizer, 1862–1900.* Frans H. Doppen. 2016

42. *The Silent Appalachian: Wordless Mountaineers in Fiction, Film and Television.* Vicki Sigmon Collins. 2017

43. *The Trees of Ashe County, North Carolina.* Doug Munroe. 2017

44. *Melungeon Portraits: Exploring Kinship and Identity.* Tamara L. Stachowicz. 2018

45. *Always Been a Rambler: G.B. Grayson and Henry Whitter, Country Music Pioneers of Southern Appalachia.* Josh Beckworth. 2018

46. *Tommy Thompson: New-Timey String Band Musician.* Lewis M. Stern. 2019

47. *Appalachian Fiddler Albert Hash: The Last Leaf on the Tree.* Malcolm L. Smith with Edwin Lacy. 2020

48. *Junaluska: Oral Histories of a Black Appalachian Community.* Edited by Susan E. Keefe with the Junaluska Heritage Association. 2020

49. *Boone Before Boone: The Archaeological Record of Northwestern North Carolina Through 1769.* Tom Whyte. 2020

50. *From the Front Lines of the Appalachian Addiction Crisis: Healthcare Providers Discuss Opioids, Meth and Recovery.* Edited by Wendy Welch. 2020

51. *Writers by the River: Reflections on 40+ Years of the Highland Summer Conference.* Edited by Donia S. Eley and Grace Toney Edwards. 2021

52. *Wayne Howard: Old Time Music, the Hammons Family and Mountain Lore.* Lewis M. Stern. 2021

53. *Lost Cove, North Carolina: Portrait of a Vanished Appalachian Community, 1864–1957.* Christy A. Smith. 2022

54. *LeConte Lodge: A Centennial History of a Smoky Mountain Landmark.* Tom Layton and Mike Hembree. 2024

55. *D.D. Dougherty, Lillie Dougherty and the Early Years of Appalachian State.* Doris Perry Stam. 2024

56. *Southern Mountain Music: The Collected Writings of Wayne Erbsen.* Wayne Erbsen. 2025

57. *Appalachian Nursing: A History, 1890–1960.* Sharon Loury. 2025

Southern Mountain Music
The Collected Writings of Wayne Erbsen

WAYNE ERBSEN

Foreword by Tim Stafford

CONTRIBUTIONS TO
SOUTHERN APPALACHIAN STUDIES, 56

McFarland & Company, Inc., Publishers
Jefferson, North Carolina

Some material in this book has previously appeared in *Bluegrass Unlimited* and in *Americana Rhythm Music*.

LIBRARY OF CONGRESS CATALOGUING-IN-PUBLICATION DATA

Names: Erbsen, Wayne, author. | Stafford, Tim, 1960– writer of foreword.
Title: Southern Mountain music : the collected writings of Wayne Erbsen / Wayne Erbsen ; foreword by Tim Stafford.
Description: Jefferson, North Carolina : McFarland & Company, Inc., Publishers, 2025. | Series: Contributions to Southern Appalachian studies; 56 | Includes index.
Identifiers: LCCN 2024056251 | ISBN 9781476696461 (paperback : acid free paper) ∞ ISBN 9781476656205 (ebook)
Subjects: LCSH: Old-time music—Appalachian Region, Southern—History and criticism. | Bluegrass music—Appalachian Region, Southern—History and criticism. | Country musicians—Appalachian Region, Southern—Interviews. | Blugrass musicians—Appalachian Region, Southern—Interviews. | Folk musicians—Appalachian Region, Southern—Interviews. | Country musicians—Appalachian Region, Southern—Humor.
Classification: LCC ML3477.7.A48 E73 2025 | DDC 781.642092/2—dc23/eng/20241211
LC record available at https://lccn.loc.gov/2024056251

BRITISH LIBRARY CATALOGUING DATA ARE AVAILABLE

ISBN (print) 978-1-4766-9646-1
ISBN (ebook) 978-1-4766-5620-5

© 2025 Wayne Erbsen. All rights reserved

No part of this book may be reproduced or transmitted in any form or by any means, electronic or mechanical, including photocopying or recording, or by any information storage and retrieval system, without permission in writing from the publisher.

Front cover images: *(top)* Bill Clifton playing banjo on radio WINA, Charlottesville, Virginia, circa 1953 (courtesy of Bill Clifton); *(middle)* Fiddlin' Arthur Smith and the McGee Bros, *left to right:* Sam McGee, Fiddlin' Arthur Smith, Kirk McGee, circa 1950 (courtesy of Chance Barham); *(bottom)* Maybelle Carter, ca. 1930 (John Edwards Memorial Foundation Records [20001], Southern Folklife Collection at Wilson Special Collections Library, University of North Carolina at Chapel Hill). *Background* © michelangeloop/iStock.

Printed in the United States of America

McFarland & Company, Inc., Publishers
Box 611, Jefferson, North Carolina 28640
www.mcfarlandpub.com

Table of Contents

Acknowledgments — ix
Foreword by Tim Stafford — 1
Introduction — 3

Mountain Music Pioneers, Foreshadowing Bluegrass — 7
Bluegrass Roots in Western North Carolina 7 • Vernon Dalhart 11 • Henry Whitter 12 • Ernest "Pop" Stoneman 14 • Uncle Eck Dunford and "Angeline the Baker" 15 • The Carter Family 20 • The Lesley Riddle Story 23 • Dock Walsh and the Carolina Tarheels 25 • Charlie Poole and the North Carolina Ramblers 26 • Wade and J.E. Mainer 29

Brother Duets — 33
Wiley and Zeke, the Morris Brothers 33 • The Callahan Brothers 43 • The Blue Sky Boys 46 • Curly and Jack, the Shelton Brothers 47

Fiddling — 51
Thicker'n Fiddlers in Hell 51 • Eck Robertson—Master Fiddler 54 • Fiddlin' John Carson 57 • Fiddlin' Arthur Smith 58 • Jim Shumate 62 • Lester Woodie—Coming Up the Hard Road 71 • Aynsley Porchak, Fiddler 79 • Fiddles, Fangs, and Folklore 84 • The Hanging of Fiddlin' Joe Coleman 87

Banjo Picking — 89
Walter Davis—Fist and Skull Banjo 89 • Snuffy Jenkins 94 • Earl Scruggs 96 • Raymond Fairchild—Making His Own Way 99 • Why Are There So Many Banjo Jokes? 104

More Bluegrass Pioneers — 107
Cleo Davis—The Original Blue Grass Boy 107 • Tommy Millard—Blackface Comedian and Blue Grass Boy 118 • Clarence White and the Roots of Bluegrass Guitar 123 • Bill Clifton 125

Songwriters and Songs — 128
The Great American Tearjerker 128 • Gussie L. Davis—Tin Pan Alley/Bluegrass Songwriter 130 • William Shakespeare Who? 131 • Johnny Bond 134 • "Wildwood Flower" 136 • "Jimmie Brown, the Newsboy" 138 • "Otto Wood, the Bandit" 143 • "Stagolee" 145 • "Diamond Joe" 145 • "Run Mountain" 148 • "Fox on the Run" 150 •

"I've Just Seen the Rock of Ages" 152 • "I'm a Little Teapot" 153 • Other Songs with Quirky Stories 154
"Banks of the Ohio" 154 • "Buffalo Gals" 154 • "Cumberland Mountain Deer Chase" 154 • "Old Joe Clark" 154 • "Roll on Buddy" 155 • "Poor Ellen Smith" 155 • "Red River Valley" 156 • "My Rough and Rowdy Ways" 157 • "Please Pardon Me" 157

Appendix I. Miscellaneous   159

Cowboys in Bluegrass Music? 159 • Two Meatballs in the Sand and Other Mondegreens 162 • The Secret Signals of Bluegrass 163 • The Lester Flatt G Run 166 • We Almost Played on the Grand Ole Opry 167 • Charlie Cline, Powerful Snorer 169 • Hoss Cartwright's Hat 169 • "Winning" the Folk Song Completion at Galax 170 • Jamming with David Grisman 171 • Bigfoot's Gone Away 172 • Arthur "Guitar Boogie" Smith 174 • Jim Bob Tinsley—Cowboy Singer and Mountain Lion Hunter 175 • The Ghost of Scotty Stoneman 176 • My Radio Career 176 • Gods and Generals 177

Appendix II. Quickies   179

Jethro Burns 179 • On Their Tippy Toes 179 • Give Me a Break! 179 • Ralph and Stanley Carter 179 • Septic Music 179 • Making Stuff Up 180 • Hank Williams Said 180 • Playing Pool 180 • Dimwits 180 • "Wee Wee" 180 • Fresh Picks 180 • Ernest Tubb 180 • Marshmallows 180 • The Smoggy Mountain Boys 180 • As Long as Yarn 180 • Bagels Ain't Sweet 181 • Bill Monroe on the Railroad Tracks 181 • The Stanley Brothers in Florida 181 • The Stanley Brothers' Bass Fiddle 182 • You Ain't Comin' Back 182 • Bluegrass Motels 182 • Leave Now! 182 • Laying Out Pants 182 • Willie Nelson Look-Alike 182 • Senator Wayne Erbsen 182 • Nothing to Eat 183 • Bill Monroe and Frank Sinatra 183 • Runnin' Out of Memory 183 • Jimmy Martin 183 • Chicken Necks 184 • Discovering Clarence Ashley 184 • Showmanship of Mac Wiseman and Lester Flatt 185 • "Lee Highway Blues" 185 • Joe Maphis' Flatpick 186 • Charlie Poole 187 • Brad Keith 187 • Professor Wayne Erbsen 187 • Dog Bit 188 • Lost Cassette Covers 189 • How I Bought My Martin Guitar 189 • Ry Cooder and Donna Stoneman 189 • No Such Thing as Time 190 • Outrageous Old-Time Band Names 190 • Don't Touch My Suit! 191 • Water Bottle 191 • Strange Names 192 • Is Hair Here? 192 • Thornton Spencer 192 • White Bread and Cold Beans 192 • Zeke Morris, the Body Shop Man 193 • Wiley Morris, Another Body Shop Man 193 • Bill Monroe's Mandolin 193 • The Biggest Bull in the World 194 • Playing for a Mobster's Funeral 194

Index   197

Acknowledgments

Thanks to all those friends and colleagues who have mentored me over the past fifty years: Guthrie T. Meade, Jr.; Dick Spottswood; Neil Rosenberg; Norm Cohen; Charles K. Wolfe; Loyal Jones; Kinny Rorrer; Tom Ewing; Tom Mindte; Bill C. Malone; Wayne W. Daniel; Dave Freeman; Thomas A. Adler; Penny Parsons; Natalya Weinstein; Wayne Seymour; Pete Peterson; Darren Moore; Ken Landreth; Ernie Hill; Brody Hunt; Charles Pennell; Stephanie P. Ledgin; Chandler Marburg; Jordan L. Laney; Barry Mazor; Judy Muldawer; Charlie Walden; Dana Ward; David Davis; Annie Erbsen; Barbara Swell; Tim O'Brien; Thomas Goldsmith; Fred Bartenstein; Bruce Ziff; Marc Horowitz; Jamie Hooper; Ira Gitlin; and Tater Tate.

Foreword

By Tim Stafford

I first met Wayne Erbsen after he called me about filling in with his band at the Grayson County Fiddlers' Convention in Elk Creek, Virginia, back in 2022. I had heard of Wayne and actually had some of his books, but we had never met. He, Tom Mindte, Eddie Ray Buzzini, Fred Mock, and I had a great time playing music over at Grayson but also re-telling and listening to all the wonderful stories about this music that add a special dimension to it all.

It only makes sense that stories like those—and many more—are collected in *Southern Mountain Music*. Wayne Erbsen is one of the most prolific writers about bluegrass, old-time country, and gospel music, and he's been doing it since the 1970s. His books and articles have always been ground zero for enthusiasts and scholars who want to know more about roots music and how it serves as a cultural backbone of the Southern Appalachians.

His is a personal style that feels like an old friend relating a story, and I can practically hear Wayne talking about his trip to see Uncle Eck Dunford's old house and instruments, or the Carter Family; their important African American friend Lesley Riddle; and the groundbreaking music of Charlie Poole, Pop Stoneman, Henry Whitter, and Dock Walsh and the Carolina Tarheels and even the first "citybilly" bluegrass musician and ambassador, Bill Clifton.

Focusing on the fertile ground of Western North Carolina, Wayne has compiled a number of his previous articles into this fine book. You can almost *hear* the old-time brother duets in these pages. That's partly because of the invaluable interviews Wayne was able to conduct in the 1970s with figures like Wade Mainer, Wiley and Zeke Morris, Homer Callahan, Bill Bolick, and Jack Shelton. These great sources make the stories and music come alive.

When Wayne goes on to trace the influence of instruments like the fiddle and banjo through brilliant players and pioneers like Eck Robertson, Fiddlin' John Carson, Fiddlin' Arthur Smith, Jim Shumate, Lester Woodie, Walter Davis, Aynsley Porchak, Snuffy Jenkins, Earl Scruggs, and Raymond Fairchild, he's aided again by original interviews with many of the subjects.

I'm so glad Erbsen also gives us a unique, clear picture of the first version of Bill Monroe's Blue Grass Boys through interviews he conducted with Cleo Davis, the original Blue Grass Boy, and Tommy Millard the comedian. Again, these first-hand accounts make this book truly valuable, and Wayne has a few of his own here, including remembering watching young Clarence White blaze a new trail on acoustic guitar in Southern California in the early 1960s.

Not content to recount stories about musicians, he traces the roots of country sentimental and tearjerker songwriting through characters nearly lost to time like Gussie Davis, the African American tunesmith who wrote songs that were recorded by nearly every act in old-time country and bluegrass music, and the riverboat captain and brilliant nineteenth-century songwriter William Shakespeare Hays, who produced an incredibly varied catalog of popular songs, including standards like "Little Old Log Cabin in the Lane" and "I'll Remember You Love in My Prayers." Wayne traces the origins of songs like "Wildwood Flower"; "Jimmie Brown, the Newsboy" (another of Hays' songs); "Otto Wood, the Bandit"; "Stagolee"; "Diamond Joe"; "Run Mountain"; "Fox on the Run"; "I've Just Seen the Rock of Ages"; and many more. This is one of my favorite parts of the book.

Along the way, he repeats those funny anecdotes and personal stories, explores lore and muses about things like putting rattlesnake rattles inside fiddles, banjo jokes, cowboys in bluegrass music, mangled lyrics, jam etiquette, and the "Lester Flatt G run." His penchant for storytelling also runs over into great little asides, experiences, quotes, and observations gathered over the years and collected at the end of the book. The man is a living history of this kind of music. I'm glad to know him, and I'm sure you're going to enjoy *Southern Mountain Music*.

Tim Stafford is an artist in residence with the Bluegrass, Old-Time and Roots Music Program, Appalachian Studies, at East Tennessee State University.

Introduction

As a boy of nine, I wrote my first story. It told of a little boy who ran away from home by jumping in an empty boxcar as the train passed by his family's farm. Soon growing homesick, he was befriended by a kind hobo who was riding in the same boxcar. Of course, the hobo escorted the boy back to his overjoyed parents. To the boy, home never looked so good before. As a reward, the father hired the hobo to work on their farm, and everybody lived happily ever after.

Not all my stories have had happy endings. In the 1960s I studied at the University of California, Berkeley, and majored in American history. I wrote my senior thesis on Gerald L.K. Smith, an Arkansas preacher and a fascist who preached the hatred of Jews, minorities, intellectuals, and everyone who dared to disagree with his way of thinking. In graduate school at the University of Wisconsin, I again studied American history and wrote my master's thesis on the first hippies: "the beat generation" of the 1950s and early 1960s.

Wyoming ghost town, ca. 1996 (photograph by the author).

Introduction

Over the last fifty years I've been involved in old-time and bluegrass music as a performer, teacher, radio broadcaster, publisher, and author. In fact, it was bluegrass music that first lured me from my home in California to North Carolina, where I knew the music first started. I originally landed in Charlotte, where I was hired in 1972 as an assistant professor of music and history at Central Piedmont Community College.

Around that time, the movie *Deliverance* became a smash hit, and soon there were scores of people standing in line to register for my bluegrass banjo classes. Out of these classes came my first book, *A Manual on How to Play the 5-String Banjo for the Complete Ignoramus*. As time allowed, I began researching the roots of bluegrass and discovered that Charlotte was the place where Bill and Charlie Monroe made their first recordings back in 1936. It had also been the home of the 50,000-watt WBT radio, which hosted the *Crazy Water Barn Dance*. It was on the *Barn Dance* that many of the predecessors of bluegrass music played.

It wasn't long after moving to North Carolina that I began interviewing some of the older musicians who were playing early strands of bluegrass music but didn't call it that. I soon realized that many of the musicians I spoke with about their music careers had been largely ignored or forgotten by country music scholars. Looking back, I am grateful that I was able to capture the warmth and humor of these musicians, so that future generations will know the role they played in the roots of old-time country and bluegrass music.

Soon after I left Charlotte in 1973, I landed a job as professor of southern Appalachian music at Warren Wilson College in Swannanoa, North Carolina, where I stayed for thirty-eight years. After retiring from Warren Wilson, I accepted a teaching position at the University of North Carolina Asheville, where I currently coach the university's

UNCA Bluegrass Band, ca. 2023. From left: Emelyn Scales, Shaelyn Dossett, Cole Pilgrim, Colson Combs, Matt Files, Clayton Hutchinson, Wayne Erbsen, Chun Si Lee (photograph by Isabella Giambuso).

bluegrass band. Over these many years I've kept my hand in writing, producing some thirty-eight books and seventy articles, many of which have appeared in various bluegrass magazines as well as online and printed newsletters for bluegrass associations.

This book is a compilation of many of the articles I've written over the last forty-plus years. Through blind luck, I've had the great fortune to have met and made friends with many of the legends of old-time and bluegrass music. These friendships have allowed me to interview the folks whose stories populate this book. In many cases, I was the first and sometimes the *only* one to ever interview them. These unsung heroes of old-time and bluegrass music truly have a tale to tell, and I am honored to bring their voices to future generations, who I am counting on to give them the credit they so richly deserve.

In these pages you'll read about Appalachian pioneers, free and enslaved, who faced the wilderness of rugged mountains and erected sturdy log cabins using nothing more than an axe. Old World ballads and tunes helped them keep a bond with their ancestral homelands. There is also information on early songsmiths from busy cities, whose sentimental ballads could draw tears from a glass eye.

The fiddle has always been at the heart of old-time music, so I included write-ups on some of the legendary fiddlers whose impact is still felt today. Not far behind the fiddle was the banjo, at the core of mountain music. I've always loved to sing, so I am glad I was also able to include my research of such songs as "Wildwood Flower"; "Jimmie Brown, the Newsboy"; "Run Mountain"; and "Diamond Joe."

I'm also happy to share several light-hearted sections, like "Two Meatballs in the Sand and Other Bluegrass Mondegreens," "Why Are There So Many Banjo Jokes?" and "The Secret Signals of Bluegrass."

Finally, near the end of the book you'll find a number of "Quickies," which are short and punchy jokes, stories, and pieces of lore about many of your favorite bluegrass stars.

I hope you'll enjoy getting to know some of these legends of old-time and bluegrass music.

Mountain Music Pioneers, Foreshadowing Bluegrass

Bluegrass Roots in Western North Carolina

Western North Carolina was fertile ground for the birth of bluegrass music. In fact, no other region or state has contributed so much to its development.

For many people, the appeal of bluegrass music is that it is a relatively new form of music that sounds old. Most scholars agree that bluegrass first gained national attention when a classic edition of Bill Monroe and His Blue Grass Boys appeared on the Grand Ole Opry between 1945 and 1948. In addition to Bill Monroe himself, this legendary band consisted of Lester Flatt (guitar), Earl Scruggs (banjo), Chubby Wise (fiddle) and Cedric Rainwater (bass).

The reason that bluegrass music sounds old is that it is a synthesis of many older

Log cabin with unknown woman, Hart Square, Hickory, North Carolina, ca. 2012 (photograph by the author).

styles of music. Many of the earliest settlers in western North Carolina were Scots-Irish. These early pioneers brought with them a wealth of vocal and instrumental music traditions that originated in the British Isles. It was mainly the pioneer women who carried on the strong vocal traditions. Often barred by local custom from playing the more raucous instruments such as the banjo or the fiddle, most women preferred to sing. They sang the old ballads that had been passed down from mother to daughter for generations. These ballads were carefully preserved by a culture that was bent on keeping intact the traditions of their ancestors. They preserved these ancient ballads so well that, during the years 1916 to 1918, English folksong collector Cecil Sharp visited western North Carolina for the sole purpose of collecting English ballads in their purest form, because in England these ballads had long been forgotten.

Ballad singing in western North Carolina had a strong impact on what later became known as bluegrass music. The subject matter of most of the ballads was either murder or lost love. This leant a somber tone to the music. The way the old ballads were sung also affected the singing styles of later bluegrass singers. The women who sang the old Scots-Irish and English ballads normally sang with a tight voice that produced a high, shrill tone. Today this is referred to as bluegrass music's "high lonesome sound." In contrast, singers from African traditions sang with a looser voice that produced lower and more relaxed tones. Bill Monroe, who later became known as "the father of bluegrass music," is the perfect example of someone who sang with the tight vocal style of his Scots-Irish ancestors. He was able to emulate the vocal styles of female ballad singers because he naturally had a high vocal range.

While the women's musical role in early pioneer life in western North Carolina was in singing the old ballads and songs, the men favored playing instruments. In particular, the fiddle was among the few treasured possessions that Scots-Irish immigrants brought with them when they first came to America. Even more important than the instrument itself was a deep well of ancient melodies from Scotland, England, and Ireland. Many of these fiddlers could play for days without repeating a tune. This was handy, because fiddlers often provided the only music for the many all-night dances that

Samantha Bumgarner from Dillsboro, North Carolina, ca. 1940 (courtesy Mars Hill University).

took place in backwoods communities. Because of their ability to provide much needed entertainment, fiddlers were often held in higher esteem than doctors, lawyers, or politicians. The dance tunes as played by Scots-Irish fiddlers certainly had a strong impact on the music of this area.

Not lagging far behind the fiddle in providing music for rural communities was the banjo. The origins of the banjo can be traced back nearly 4,500 years to ancient Egypt. From there, ancestors of the instrument spread to the Middle East and to Africa. Slaves from West Africa eventually brought forerunners of the instrument to the American South and to the Caribbean, where the banjo as we know it was first created, using gourds for the body and hides for the head. From there it took hold and spread. In North Carolina the banjo became a deeply ingrained part of everyday life. Both Blacks and whites frequently played the banjo, along with the fiddle and later the guitar, for rural dances and frolics.

In the mountains of western North Carolina, the banjo changed to adapt to local conditions. Mountain craftsmen built smaller and softer-sounding banjos using a groundhog hide for the "head" or "skin" of the banjo. These banjos were normally fretless and had wooden tuning pegs. In contrast to these homemade wooden instruments, factory-made banjos began to be produced as early as the 1870s in cities of the Northeast. These banjos often featured mechanical tuning pegs and tone rings and brackets made of metal. Produced in large quantities, they were sold in Sears and Montgomery Ward mail order catalogs and soon found their way into the parlors and front porches of musicians in western North Carolina.

There were other modern influences that were bringing change to the mountains of western North Carolina. The first radio station in the area was WWNC, which began broadcasting in 1927. Its first location was in the Flat Iron Building in downtown Asheville. Up the marble steps trooped local musicians carrying banjos, fiddles, mandolins, and guitars. Among the popular shows was *The Farm Hour.*

Radio made it possible for some dedicated musicians to go professional, because it allowed them to advertise and promote show dates in rural schoolhouses. These local shows became popular at the same time that rural roads were improved to accommodate increasing numbers of cars and trucks. Bands that played the schoolhouses often mixed old-time fiddle tunes, banjo picking, and harmony singing with humor and skits from the minstrel and vaudeville show traditions.

In North Carolina, it seemed that practically every family played string music. Thus, it is not surprising that many bands that performed in western North Carolina during the 1930s and '40s were brother duets. Local musicians like Wiley and Zeke Morris, Wade and J.E. Mainer, Jack and Curly Shelton, Homer and Walter Callahan, and Bill and Earl Bolick are a few of the best-known brother acts from western North Carolina. These men established a strong tradition of instrumental virtuosity mixed with closely blended harmony singing.

In the mid–1930s, two brothers from Kentucky came to North Carolina to actively participate in the vibrant musical scene there. Bill and Charlie Monroe, performing as the Monroe Brothers, maintained a hectic schedule, playing nearly every night in venues that ranged from one-room schoolhouses to county fairs. To promote their shows, they appeared on numerous radio stations, including Asheville's WWNC, Charlotte's WBT, and Raleigh's WPTF. They were so busy performing and burning up the rubber on their Hudson Terraplane that they dismissed an invitation to record for Bluebird, a

Asheville, North Carolina, skyline with WWNC radio tower atop the Citizen-Times Building, ca. 1942.

subsidiary of RCA Victor Records, because they didn't have time for it. They also didn't realize the impact that being on a major record label could have on their performing career. At last, RCA's Eli Oberstein convinced them to record, which they did in 1936, in a makeshift rented studio in Charlotte. In that crowded warehouse the Monroe Brothers waxed ten sides, including "My Long Journey Home," "Nine Pound Hammer Is Too Heavy," and "On Some Foggy Mountain Top." On those first recordings they established the style that would mark their entire recorded efforts: tight vocal harmonies, often played at lightning speeds with spellbinding instrumental virtuosity.

The professional musical partnership of the Monroe Brothers was not to last. As Charlie Monroe once admitted, "We were mean as snakes." The brothers' notorious fiery tempers doomed them to go their separate ways in 1938. Both went on to form their own bands. Charlie moved to the Winston-Salem area and formed the Kentucky Pardners. Bill Monroe first formed a band in Arkansas and then moved to Atlanta, Georgia. There he placed an ad in the local newspaper, looking for someone to sing old folk songs. Answering the ad was a young Cleo Davis, who played guitar and sang. Monroe hired Davis on the spot and spent several months teaching him his brother Charlie's guitar runs and vocal style. By the time Monroe had finished training Davis, their sound was practically identical to that of the Monroe Brothers.

After unsuccessfully auditioning at several radio stations, Bill Monroe and Cleo Davis came back to North Carolina, landing a radio program on Asheville's WWNC. While Monroe and his wife lived out of a small travel trailer, Davis stayed nearby at a boarding house. Not satisfied with their current sound, Monroe began searching for other musicians. He eventually hired Art Wooten from Piney Creek, North Carolina, to play fiddle; Tommy "Snowball" Millard to do blackface comedy and play jug; and Amos Garren to play the string bass. Before long the band sought greener pastures and moved to Greenville, South Carolina. Monroe tirelessly rehearsed the band in a converted gas station until he thought they were ready for bigger things. In 1939, after the departure of Millard, the band successfully auditioned for the Grand Ole Opry. The rest, as they say, is history. Monroe's band was now known as "the Blue Grass Boys." Members came and went, but the sound was evolving to become what we now call bluegrass music.

Vernon Dalhart

His real name was Marion Try Slaughter II and he was born in Jefferson, Texas, on April 6, 1883. Before he died on September 14, 1948, he had used at least one hundred pseudonyms. The best remembered is "Vernon Dalhart," from two Texas towns where he had worked as a child cowhand. His grandfather, Marion Try Slaughter I, had been a Confederate soldier who joined the KKK after the Civil War. While Dalhart was still a boy, Dalhart's father was killed by his brother-in-law in a barroom knife fight. By the time he was twelve or thirteen, Dalhart showed a strong interest in music and started singing and taking piano lessons. He soon became proficient on the harmonica, Jew's harp, and kazoo, and he was an excellent whistler.

In 1910 Dalhart moved to New York, possibly with the hope of being part of the booming music industry there. At first, he had to settle for working in a music store, selling and moving pianos. Meanwhile he studied opera and moonlighted as a featured vocalist in churches and singing for funerals. Eventually, he landed vocal roles in several operas, including *The Girl of the Golden West* and *Madama Butterfly*.

Down on his luck and nearly broke, Dalhart saw an ad in the newspaper: "Wanted: Singers for Recording Sessions." He spent what little money he had getting to the audition in East Orange, New Jersey. When he arrived, the room was packed with some of the best-known opera singers in the area, and Dalhart figured he was outgunned. When his turn finally came, he sang "Can't Yo' Heah Me Callin' Carolina." At

Carson J. Robison (left) and Vernon Dalhart, ca. 1919.

the end of the audition, all the singers were dismissed but, to his surprise, Dalhart was invited to a private audition with none other than Thomas Edison! By this time Edison was nearly deaf and asked Dalhart to sing the same song into his ear trumpet. When he finished singing, Edison told him, "You are the man for me."

Dalhart's recording career may have started with Edison, but he eventually went on to record with practically every record label in America. The material he recorded covered a wide range, including light opera, fox trots, Hawaiian songs, racist coon songs, and World War I patriotic songs. By 1924 Dalhart's popularity was on the decline, and he approached Victor Talking Machine Company with the idea of recording two country songs, "The Wreck of the Old 97" and "The Prisoner's Song." With Victor's national sales in a slump, they initially resisted but finally they gave in. The success of "The Prisoner's Song" was stunning. It became the first million-seller in country music history and went on to sell almost six million copies. The song not only boosted Victor out of the doldrums but also helped make Vernon Dalhart a household name and showed the vast commercial potential for country music.

Henry Whitter

No one ever stands up for Henry Whitter anymore. And they never did! Recent scholars have scoffed at his meager guitar skills and at his "rustic" singing. He is given credit for little more than inspiring others to become recording artists, because they knew they could sing and play rings around old Henry. And they were right! He was no guitar virtuoso, and he was not endowed with a great voice. But he was clever or persistent enough to get himself a recording contract in New York. Among those who heard his 1924 recording of "The Wreck of the Old 97" was Ernest V. "Pop" Stoneman, who complained that Henry "sang through his nose so bad … everybody's going to think we all sing through the nose." After hearing Henry, Stoneman set his sights on signing his own record deal.

Henry Whitter in pinstriped suit playing a 1919 L-1 Gibson guitar with a harmonica rack around his neck, ca. 1924 (John Edwards Memorial Foundation Records [20001], Southern Folklife Collection at Wilson Special Collections Library, University of North Carolina at Chapel Hill).

Although Henry Whitter was no great shakes as a singer or a musician, he did do a number of things right. His 1923 recording of "The Wreck of the Old 97," which he learned from a fellow mill worker in his hometown of Fries, Virginia, inspired Vernon Dalhart to copy down the words from his record and record it in 1924, first for Edison and then for Victor. Backed with "The Prisoners Song," the Victor recording was the first million-seller in country music. With the money that Whitter earned, he soon bought himself a brand-new Model T Ford—not bad for someone with a mediocre voice who was limited on the guitar! In 1925 Whitter made records with Kelly Harrell and with Roba Stanley. Later he also recorded as a member of a group with one of the greatest names in old-time music: Fisher Hendley and His Aristocratic Pigs.

Perhaps Henry Whitter's smartest move was teaming up with blind fiddler G.B. Grayson, from Laurel Bloomery, Tennessee, which even today is but a wide spot in the road. Grayson was an expert fiddler and singer who could sing and play at the same time—no mean feat! Together, Grayson and Whitter started recording in 1927, and they produced a string of forty recordings that have become an important part of the repertoire of bluegrass musicians. Ralph Stanley, for one, has paid homage to Grayson and Whitter by recording an entire CD of their songs.

The numbers waxed by Grayson and Whitter read like a set list for any of hundreds of traditional bluegrass and old-time bands: "Train 45," "Short Life of Trouble," "Handsome Molly," "Little Maggie," "Don't Go Out Tonight My Darling," "Rose Conley,"

The Greer Sisters, Henry Whitter (standing), and G.B. Grayson in Boone, North Carolina, 1927.

"Omie Wise," "Nine Pound Hammer," and "Going Down the Lee Highway." Not bad for old Henry, whose fellow mill workers laughed at his first efforts to leave the mill and become a recording artist!

Ernest "Pop" Stoneman

We couldn't quite figure out who he was. As the lights were dimmed and the audience hushed, my sister Bonnie and I sat in suspense at the West Hollywood club known as the Ash Grove. All at once the band started to play and, even as our attention became riveted on the spectacle unfolding before us, we wondered about the little old man sitting on stage in a hard-backed chair with an autoharp flat on his lap and a little black hat stuck on his head. We got a hint when members of the Stoneman Family eventually introduced him as the patriarch of the clan, Pop Stoneman. When his time came to sing, the old gentleman forcefully launched into the old-time song "The Titanic," which he had recorded way back in 1924.

While we thought his performance quaint, we were frankly more awed by the bigger spectacle of the younger Stonemans' show. There was Roni, whose hard-edged banjo playing was tempered by her goofy stage persona; pretty Donna, who danced while her fingers fairly flew over the mandolin; big Van on guitar; and Jimmy on bass fiddle. But what really caught my attention was the fiddler, Scotty. He played with a wild abandon

From left: Iver Edwards, George Stoneman, Eck Dunford, Ernest Stoneman, Hattie Stoneman, and Balen Frost, Galax, Virginia, 1928 (John Edwards Memorial Foundation Records [20001], Southern Folklife Collection at Wilson Special Collections Library, University of North Carolina at Chapel Hill).

that made me think he was being chased by the headless horseman from "The Legend of Sleepy Hollow." It was almost like he was possessed by the devil himself. Only later did I find out that wasn't so far from the truth.

Looking back on that memorable evening in 1964, I'm embarrassed to admit that I didn't pay more attention to Pop Stoneman. Now that I've researched his career, there are so many questions I'd like to ask him. Luckily, folklorist Archie Green had the forethought to interview him back in 1962.

Although he was known in later years as "Pop," his given name was Ernest V. Stoneman. He grew up in the tradition-rich region of southwestern Virginia, in Carroll County. His great-great-grandfather had been shanghaied from England when he was only twelve years old and put off in North Carolina to fend for himself. As young Ernest was growing up near Iron Ridge, Virginia, he was surrounded by the music of family and neighbors.

In early 1924 the thirty-one-year-old Stoneman was in the Warwick Furniture Store in Bluefield, West Virginia, when he heard a phonograph record that caught his attention. He recognized the voice of Henry Whitter singing "The Wreck of the Old 97." Stoneman knew Whitter from way back, when they both worked at a cotton mill in Fries, Virginia. Knowing he could outdo Whitter in singing and playing, Stoneman determined to make his own phonograph records.

Without delay he wrote both Columbia and Okeh. He soon received positive replies, with Columbia setting a September 2 audition and Okeh inviting him to "come up any time." That was the beginning of a career that would span more than four decades. In that time, he recorded hundreds of songs in every available medium: cylinders, 78s, LPs, radio, and TV. Through his performances and recordings, he helped to perpetuate old-time music for future generations.

Ironically, his biggest contribution may have been by accident. During Stoneman's Victor recording session in late July of 1927 in Bristol, Tennessee, Ralph Peer let it slip to a newspaper reporter that Stoneman's royalties amounted to $3,600 in the previous year alone. Once that story hit the paper, droves of old-time musicians came out of the hills to audition for Victor. Included in that number were Jimmie Rodgers and a group calling themselves the Carter Family. The rest, as they say, is history.

Uncle Eck Dunford and "Angeline the Baker"

It all started in San Francisco. It was there that the leader of the band I was playing guitar with tricked me into learning to play the fiddle. The year was 1970 and our band sorely needed a fiddler. Our leader, Stan Vincent, said he'd sell me a fiddle, case and bow for ten bucks, which was too good to pass up. It was only later that I found out that he paid a lot more for it than that, but he needed a fiddler more than he needed the money. He knew I was either too cheap or too poor to buy a decent fiddle.

One of the first tunes I learned was "Angeline the Baker." I picked it up from the legendary blind mandolin player Kenny Hall, who never used a pick to play his bowl-back mandolin. Instead, he plucked the strings with a beak-like nail on his right index finger. The only words that Kenny ever sang were "Angeline the Baker, Angeline the Baker, Angeline the Baker, Angeline the Baker." That tune was so popular back in those days that at every old-time jam there was "Angeline the Baker."

When I moved to the Southeast in 1972, I carried "Angeline the Baker" along with me. It helped me win the 1st place old-time fiddle ribbon at the fiddler's convention in Chilhowie, Virginia, and also the blue ribbon for clawhammer banjo at the Galax Old Fiddler's Convention in 1973. There was a set of lyrics going around for "Angeline the Baker" beyond the few that Kenny Hall had sung. I never learned them because I figured it must have been written by some folkie during the folk revival of the early 1960s.

In 1980 I edited two songbooks for the Carl Fischer company, *The Backpocket Old-Time Songbook* and *The Backpocket Bluegrass Songbook*. For those books I did some research on "Angeline the Baker" and discovered that the song was written by Stephen Foster in 1850 as "Angelina Baker." For his efforts, Foster realized a grand total of $16.87. The melody of the fiddle tune

Uncle Eck Dunford, self-portrait, 1927 (courtesy Doris Brown).

was almost identical to Foster's melody, but the lyrics were completely different. Foster's song told the story of a young slave girl (Angelina Baker) who was sold and taken from her true love, who pinned away by playing his old banjo. It was Foster's arrangement of the song that I included in *The Backpocket Old-Time Songbook*.

Recently, I was working with my friend Ted Parrish on our second ukulele instruction book, *Ukulele—Tunes, Tips & Jamming*. For "Angeline the Baker," I wanted to use Stephen Foster's lyrics, but Ted preferred the words that most people were singing, the same ones I assumed were written by some long-haired folkie. Boy, was I wrong!

With some digging, I traced the tune back to an old-time fiddler and guitar player by the name of Uncle Eck Dunford from Galax, Virginia. In the mid-twenties, Dunford performed and recorded alongside Ernest V. Stoneman, whose legendary recordings laid the foundation of modern country music. Dunford fiddled and sang lead on "Angeline the Baker" for Victor records in 1928, which was the first recording of the song. Could it be that Uncle Eck composed the lyrics? From my study of old-time music traditions, I knew that most old-time songs and tunes were handed down from family or friends. Rare was a musician who composed lyrics to older melodies. A tune that sprouted a full set of gray whiskers was always welcomed over a new-fangled composition that still had the bark on it. That's why I wondered if Dunford could have

Ballard Branch Bogtrotters, ca. 1927. From left: Doc Davis, Crockett Ward, Uncle Eck Dunford, Fields Ward, and Wade Ward, ca. 1927 (John Edwards Memorial Foundation Records [20001], Southern Folklife Collection at Wilson Special Collections Library, University of North Carolina at Chapel Hill).

written the lyrics of "Angeline the Baker." I immediately started digging into the life of Uncle Eck Dunford.

It didn't take me long to figure out that Uncle Eck was as quirky as a three-sided nickel. Starting in 1927, Dunford recorded a series of tall tales and leg-pulling stories for Victor Records such as "My First Bicycle Ride," "The Savingest Man on Earth," and "The Taffy Pulling Party." One listen to these monologues firmly convinced me that Uncle Eck was crazy or creative enough to easily have come up with the new set of lyrics of "Angeline the Baker." I *had* to find out more about ole Uncle Eck.

The trail leading to Uncle Eck Dunford got considerably warmer when I mentioned to my friend Ken Landreth that it seemed that all the fingers were pointing to Eck Dunford as the creator of the lyrics of "Angeline the Baker." Ken has deep roots in the area near Galax, Virginia, and his eyes lit up when he said that he knew Oscar Hall, who had been Dunford's neighbor. After many years of attending the Galax Old Fiddler's Convention, I knew Oscar as the man who ran the festival. Ken revealed that Dunford's old cabin is perched right behind where Oscar still lives on Ballard Branch Lane, about two miles from the town of Galax. We decided to go see Oscar as soon as we could find a time.

A few days later I went to the Fries Fiddlers Convention, just up the road from Galax, Virginia. While I was on stage fiddling "Cherokee Shuffle" in the fiddle bluegrass fiddle contest, I looked out in the audience and there was Oscar Hall sitting in the stands. As soon as I put my fiddle away, I went over to Oscar to introduce myself. Even with my Covid mask on, 94-year-old Oscar Hall remembered me, even though I hadn't seen him in more than twenty-five years. When I told him I was looking for information about Uncle Eck Dunford, he invited me to come see him. So, a week or two later, Ken Landreth and I trooped over to Oscar's house on Ballard Branch Lane. That name rang a bell because I knew that Eck Dunford had been a member of the Ballard Branch Bogtrotters. That legendary old-time band consisted of Crockett Ward and his brother Wade along with Fields Ward (Crockett's son), Doc Davis, and Uncle Eck Dunford. As we left Galax and drove down Ballard Branch Lane toward Oscar's house, I was getting the eerie feeling that we were passing through the area where the fires of old-time music once raged in the early 1920s, and I could almost taste the smoke.

Oscar Hall greeted us at the door of his small country home, and he made us feel right welcome as we came in and sat down. After we shook howdy, the first thing I did was to thank him for his many years of putting on the Galax Old Fiddler's Convention. As I plied him with questions about his former neighbor, Eck Dunford, I quickly realized that Oscar is a man of few words. But he certainly helped me to get a measure of Dunford when he admitted that Uncle Eck was rather peculiar, to say the least. Oscar said Dunford had his own peculiar way of speaking that resembled an Irish brogue. His slow way of talking was unlike anyone else's way of speaking of folks who lived around there. Oscar went on to explain that Eck wore a heavy wool overcoat all year round, even in the hottest summer months. Eck never owned a car, so he walked the two miles to the town of Galax and back for groceries wearing that heavy coat. I remembered reading that Uncle Eck wore a pair of pink earmuffs when the weather was cold.

Oscar then asked me if I wanted to see Eck's cabin, and I practically leaped out of my chair in anticipation. As I walked behind Oscar's house, I looked up the hill and there was a dilapidated old shack with blackberry vines hanging all over the front porch. As I made my way up the rickety steps, I munched on a few of the ripe blackberries and went inside. As I looked around, I could see that the small cabin was filled with old junk from Oscar's family that had been piled there over the years. Lawn chairs, old Christmas tree ornaments, you name it. I had heard that Eck had been a cobbler, and there in the corner was his old black sewing machine. Hanging on the wall of the back porch was a one-man crosscut saw and a carpenter's square. Inside was Uncle Eck's rusty wind-up alarm clock and a crooked blue sign that said, "Have Faith in God."

After I took photos of Eck's cabin, I returned to Oscar's house to find him sitting on his front porch. He asked me if I wanted to see several of Uncle Eck's instruments, and of course I said, "Yes!" Oscar's daughter had just walked over from her house next door, so she went back to get the instruments which were kept at her house. She soon returned, toting a guitar and a fiddle. When I saw the guitar, my jaw practically dropped to the floor. This was the very same 1912 Sears Roebuck guitar that I had seen in several of the old photos of Uncle Eck. The old decals were still on the top of the guitar. As I held it, my hands were almost shaking, because here was an historical instrument if there ever was one! It was light as a snowflake. Then I examined Eck's fiddle, and I even rosined his bow with the very same rosin that he had used until his death in 1953. I realized that the fiddle he held in some of the earliest photographs was a blonde fiddle, but this one was brown. When I looked through some of the old photos that Oscar soon showed me, I did see Uncle Eck holding a brown fiddle, so the one I had held must have been the fiddle he used in his later years.

When the sun was starting to sink low in the sky, Ken and I decided it was time to get out of Oscar's hair and leave. As we said our goodbyes, Oscar suggested we might want to stop by and see Crockett Ward's house, which was only a short distance on the road back to Galax. We both knew that Crockett was a legendary fiddler who had fronted the old-time band The Ballard Branch Bogtrotters, which included Uncle Eck Dunford. And just as Oscar had said, there on the next corner was cream-colored farmhouse where the Bogtrotters used to practice for their many Victor recordings.

Now that I had interviewed Oscar Hall and learned all I could about Uncle Eck Dunford, the only thing left for me to do was to listen to all of Uncle Eck's recordings. For that, I thought of Joe Bussard, who had practically all the old-time 78s that were ever released and a lot that weren't! I managed to get Joe's number, and in our phone conversation, Joe said he had once been to Eck's cabin in Galax. A week or two later, Joe's CD showed up in my mailbox; it contained most or all of Uncle Eck Dunford's recordings. As I listened to Joe's compilation and thought back over my recent visit to Eck's forlorn

Crockett Ward's house, 2022 (photograph by the author).

cabin on Ballard Branch Lane, I could almost imagine Uncle Eck walking down Ballard Branch Lane on the road toward Galax on a hot summer day, humming an old fiddle tune, and wearing his heavy wool overcoat. So long, Uncle Eck!

The Carter Family

Yesterday [May 15, 2003], I heard that June Carter Cash had died. It was not a total surprise, as she had been in ill health for some time. Still, it was a shock that yet another of the legends of country music had passed away. On the evening news, there was a nice little memorial with an old photo of June with her family as they appeared in the 1930s while performing on border radio station XERA in Del Rio, Texas. They even played a short clip of June belting out her rendition of "The FFV" (also known as "Engine 143"). She couldn't have been more than about eight years old at the time. By the time you read this, June Carter Cash's passing will be old news, no longer featured on the front page of the daily newspaper. But for fans of country music and bluegrass, her passing is just another reminder of the critical role the Carter Family played in the roots not just of bluegrass but all of country music.

From left: Maybelle, A.P., and Sara, the Carter Family, ca. 1935 (John Edwards Memorial Foundation Records [20001], Southern Folklife Collection at Wilson Special Collections Library, University of North Carolina at Chapel Hill).

It all started when someone told A.P. Carter about an ad in the Sunday, July 24, 1927, issue of the Bristol, Virginia/Tennessee newspaper, *The Bristol News Bulletin.* Victor Talking Machine Company was looking for people to make records. For A.P., this opportunity was too good to pass up. In a borrowed Model A Ford, he loaded his wife, Sara; their eight-year-old daughter, Gladys; and their fussy seven-month-old son, Joe. Traveling with them was Sara's cousin, Maybelle, who was eight months pregnant.

The trip to Bristol would be no smooth ride. Traveling on primitive mountain roads, they forded several creeks and had three flat tires, with each succeeding patch melting off in the sultry July heat. When they finally arrived at 408 State Street on the morning of August 1, 1927, they found the building that had once been a furniture store. With A.P. dressed in overalls and the women wearing their best calico dresses, they were thankfully granted an audition with Ralph Peer, who later described them as looking very much "like hillbillies."

Liking what he heard, Peer invited them back to record that evening at 6:30. The first song they recorded was "Bury Me Beneath the Willow," with Sara singing lead, Maybelle the tenor, and A.P. chiming in at random on bass. Peer was beaming. He knew he had found what he was looking for. In Sara, he heard the clear mountain voice that would translate well over the new "talking machines."

Always a shrewd businessman, Peer also knew that the Carters' reworkings of the older songs was prime material he could copyright. This was, after all, a business. Peer's arrangement with Victor was that he would work without a salary in exchange for the publishing rights to any song that was fair game. This meant

The Carter Family, from left: Maybelle, A.P., and Sara, ca. 1934 (John Edwards Memorial Foundation Records [20001], Southern Folklife Collection at Wilson Special Collections Library, University of North Carolina at Chapel Hill).

he would receive a royalty on every copyrighted song that was sold. For the previous quarter alone, Peer reportedly had raked in $250,000, a tidy sum, even now!

With "Bury Me Beneath the Willow" for a starter, the Carters were now on a roll. That evening they recorded three more songs and were invited back the following morning to record two more. This was the start of a musical career that would make an indelible mark on country music. The heart of the Carter sound was the voice of Sara and the harmony vocals and guitar stylings of Maybelle. A.P.'s uneven bass vocals were, more than anything, an afterthought.

June Carter Cash later described her mother Maybelle's guitar style, which eventually became known as the "Carter scratch." "She'd hook that right thumb under that big bass string and just like magic, the other fingers moved fast like a threshing machine." In this way Maybelle was able to play the melody on the bass strings with her right thumb, while her index finger strummed the treble strings which provided the accompaniment. Over the years, untold thousands of would-be guitar pickers have tried to copy Maybelle's guitar style, especially on her signature tune, "Wildwood Flower," which was actually an old tune called "I'll Twine 'Mid the Ringlets."

Before the long career of the Carter Family finally ended as a recording entity in 1943, they had amassed a recording catalog approaching some 350 songs—no small legacy. Their songs were gathered from a wide variety of sources. In fact, it was A.P.'s role in the group to gather the material. This he did by collecting songs from friends and neighbors in the area near his home of Maces Spring in southwestern Virginia. Often accompanied by the Black North Carolina guitarist Lesley Riddle, who served as a kind of "walking tape recorder," A.P. visited countless homes to collect and learn new songs. These he rearranged and rewrote to suit the Carter Family style. Many of the songs he gathered were fragments of old ballads, while others were sentimental pieces that were once penned by popular Tin Pan Alley songwriters.

One of these songsmiths who provided many of the Carter Family songs was William S. Hays, who had once spent time in prison for writing a "seditious" song about President Lincoln. His early hits included "The Drummer Boy of Shiloh." His later songs, while popular in the 1870s and '80s, reached their full potential when recorded by emerging country music artists. Hays's 1871 song, "Little Log Cabin in the Lane," was recorded by Fiddlin' John Carson in his landmark June 14, 1923, session that proved to be the spark that ignited the entire country music industry's new interest in old-time music. The Carter Family recorded several of Hays's songs, including "Mollie Darling"; "Jimmie Brown, the Newsboy"; and "I'll Remember You in My Prayers."

The body of material recorded by the Carter Family is now affectionately referred to as "Carter Family songs." I can't tell you how many times I've bonded with another musician when we sat down to play for the first time and discovered that we both knew many Carter Family songs. These songs have helped to form the core of the bluegrass repertoire, with scores of them being performed and recorded in bluegrass style.

But even more than the songs themselves, the verse and chorus structure of the Carter Family songs has endured in bluegrass style. The Carters' preference for the sentimental songs of longing to return to the cabin in the pines also made a strong mark on bluegrass musicians as they chose songs to perform or compose.

Not to be forgotten is the harmony singing of the Carter Family. These church-inspired harmonies were not only an essential part of the Carter sound but they also helped to inspire the first generation of bluegrass singers to include harmony in their music. For all these reasons and more, both the Carter Family style and their songs have affected bluegrass in a fundamental way. It would not be a stretch to say that, without the Carter Family, bluegrass as we know it would not exist.

The Lesley Riddle Story

On a cool, crisp, fall day several years ago, I drove from Asheville up to Celo, North Carolina, passing through the rugged mountains of Yancey County on Highway 19E. As I drove past Burnsville, I couldn't help but notice a highway marker that said, "Lesley Riddle—Old-Time Musician and Song Collector." Seeing it made me smile because the name Lesley Riddle was no stranger to me. From my study of the Carter Family, I knew that Riddle had traveled the backroads of southwest Virginia and east Tennessee with A.P. Carter collecting songs for the Carter Family to record.

Returning home, I began researching the life of Lesley Riddle. I found out he was born on June 13, 1905, in the Silvers Gap community of Yancey County, which was northwest of Burnsville, North Carolina. While he was in his teens, Lesley's parents separated, and his mother moved Lesley and his two siblings to Kingsport, Tennessee.

In about 1920, when Lesley was about fifteen, he went to visit a friend who worked nearby at the Clinchfield Cement plant. While there, his foot slipped into an auger on the floor, which took off part of his right leg. Over many months of recovery from this tragic accident, Lesley decided to take up the guitar. He received valuable instruction from Ed Martin, his mother's brother, who played blues and gospel music on the guitar.

Not long after learning to play the guitar, Lesley and Uncle Ed got into an argument and Lesley tried to wrestle a shotgun away from him. During their tussle, Lesley grabbed the barrel of the weapon when it suddenly discharged, taking with it the middle and ring fingers of Lesley's right hand. When he recovered from yet another tragic accident, he had to relearn the guitar using only his thumb and index and pinky fingers.

In the late twenties, after Lesley adjusted his guitar style to account for the missing fingers, Uncle Ed introduced him to some of the local Black musicians around Kingsport, Tennessee. On almost any night of the week you could find Lesley at the home of John Henry Lyons. These front porch sessions often included such legendary musicians as Brownie McGee, Steve Tarter, Harry Gay, and Blind Lemon Jefferson, who gathered to jam and trade licks.

Word of these jam sessions eventually spread northeast to Maces Spring, Virginia, the home of the Carter Family. After their successful recording session on August 1, 1927, the Carters needed additional songs to record. The task of adding to their repertoire fell to A.P. Carter, the patriarch of the group, who immediately started collecting old songs from friends and neighbors in Poor Valley, Virginia. In 1928, A.P. got wind that some African American musicians frequently gathered on the front porch of John Henry Lyons' house, in Kingsport, Tennessee, to jam and trade licks. When A.P. arrived at Lyons' house, a lively blues jam session was in full swing. Minutes later, A.P. was introduced to Lesley Riddle, who played several songs for him. A.P. was so impressed that he invited Lesley to come back to Maces Spring to meet Sara and Maybelle, the other members of the Carter Family.

A.P. Carter soon realized that Lesley had exactly what he lacked: the ability to remember the melody of many songs. Even during this era of segregation, A.P. and

Lesley took off for weeks at a time, driving the backroads of southwest Virginia, western North Carolina, and east Tennessee looking for old songs to collect. Typically, A.P. would copy down the lyrics in his notebook, and Lesley would commit the melodies to memory. When the pair had gathered a number of songs, they would return to Maces Spring, where they would share them with Sara and Maybelle. The four musicians would make necessary changes to the songs to fit the Carter Family's style.

In addition to helping A.P. collect songs, Lesley also taught the Carter Family old blues and gospel numbers that he had composed or picked up around Kingsport, Tennessee. These included "The Cannonball," "Lonesome for You," "The Storms Are on the Ocean," "If You See My Savior," "One Kind Favor," "Working on a Building," "Let the Church Roll On," "On a Hill Lone and Grey," "Motherless Children," "Wouldn't Mind Dying," and "On Jordan's Stormy Banks." Unfortunately, Lesley never received composer credit for the songs he composed. That's mainly because Ralph Peer, the Carters' record producer and manager, was intent on recording only Carter Family originals or songs in the public domain.

Ralph Peer played a prominent role not only in the career of the Carter Family but also in much of commercial country music. A shrewd businessman, Peer negotiated a deal with Victor records where his yearly salary would be one dollar. In exchange for this princely sum, Peer would find and record talent, and Victor would press the records and distribute the

Brownie McGee (left) and Lesley Riddle, ca. 1926. As a prank, the musicians held their instruments with the necks pointing the opposite way. The photographer then reversed the film when he printed it. Notice that Lesley's mandolin pickguard is on top of the sound hole, instead of below it. Lesley's *right* hand was disfigured, but in the photograph, it appears that his *left* hand was deformed. Finally, Lesley was originally sitting on the left before the photograph was flipped.

music. In return, Peer was allowed to copyright the songs under his own imprint, Peer International, aka Southern Music. With this arrangement, Peer practically invented the idea of publishing songs. The only catch was that Peer would have to exclusively record artists who composed their own songs or arranged music that was in the public domain. This is what made the Carter Family so appealing to Peer. Their repertoire was entirely made up of old songs they had learned in their childhood, public domain songs that A.P. and Lesley had collected, original numbers by members of the Carter Family, or songs Lesley Riddle composed.

Besides strongly influencing the repertoire of the Carter Family, Maybelle gave Lesley credit for teaching her Piedmont-style fingerpicking guitar which she used on such songs as "The Cannonball," "Hello Stranger," and "I'm Lonesome for You." She also learned from him how to play bottleneck style guitar using a pocketknife for a slide. Her slide guitar can be heard on "Little Darling Pal of Mine" and "Meet Me by the Moonlight Alone." Riddle once told Mike Seeger, "You don't have to give Maybelle any lessons. You let her see you playing something, she'll get it—you better believe it."

By teaching the Carter Family songs from his own repertoire, plus helping them find and arrange songs they were able to record, Lesley Riddle had a powerful role in shaping the music of the Carter Family. They, in turn, changed the course of country music with their songs, harmonies and rhythms and the guitar wizardry of Maybelle Carter. She would be the first to tell you how much she learned from Lesley Riddle. If there's a place next to the Carter Family in the Country Music Hall of Fame, that place should certainly be filled by Lesley Riddle.

Dock Walsh and the Carolina Tarheels

Standing tall among the early pioneers of the roots of bluegrass music was Dock Walsh. Born and

Dock Walsh, Wilkes County, North Carolina, 1929 (John Edwards Memorial Foundation Records [20001], Southern Folklife Collection at Wilson Special Collections Library, University of North Carolina at Chapel Hill).

raised on a farm in Wilkes County, North Carolina, on July 23, 1901, Dock was one of eight children who all played music from an early age. His first banjo was presented to him by an older brother who made it out of an axle grease can. Dock eventually outgrew this first instrument in favor of a fancy "store-bought" Bruno banjo.

In 1924 twenty-three-year-old Dock heard Henry Whitter's recording of "Lonesome Road Blues" and "Wreck of the Southern Old 97" on Okeh Records. Wanting to quit his job as a schoolteacher, Dock saw music as his ticket to freedom. He contacted Okeh but received no response. He next tried getting in touch with Columbia Records but again came up empty handed. Not easily discouraged, he traveled unannounced to Atlanta, Georgia. There, after six months, he managed to be auditioned by Columbia's William Brown. On October 3, 1925, he recorded four songs under the supervision of Frank Walker, who put pillows under Walsh's feet to "stop the racket." These recordings make Dock one of the earliest musicians to record three-finger banjo picking. After his triumphant initial recording session, Dock actually walked home from Atlanta to Wilkes County, North Carolina, a distance of some 300 miles!

On February 19, 1927, Dock, along with harmonica wizard Gwen Foster, traveled back to Atlanta to record. On that date they recorded "Going to Georgia," "There Ain't No Use Working So Hard," "Her Name Was Hula Lou" and "Bring Me a Leaf from the Sea." The latter song featured Dock's solid three-finger banjo picking, which was common in North Carolina during this period. Dock's lead vocals were seconded by Gwen's high harmony vocals, in much the way modern bluegrass vocalists would approach the song.

In some ways, the most interesting aspect of the Carolina Tar Heels' recording of "Going to Georgia" is the harmonica playing of Gwen Foster, who can be called one of the greatest harmonica players who ever lived. His playing on this recording combines blues, slides, and wild improvising that smacks of swing and early jazz. While the harmonica is not an instrument that is normally associated with bluegrass, Foster's choice of notes would make many a bluegrass fiddler drool.

Charlie Poole and the North Carolina Ramblers

There are so many stories about Charlie Poole and the North Carolina Ramblers that it's hard to know where to begin. As one of nine kids, Charlie dropped out of school so early that he only learned to read and write as an adult. Growing up in the Haw River area of North Carolina, he was known as a prankster and a scrapper who never shied away from a fight. He was arrested so many times for his wild drinking and fighting that he was on a first-name basis with the local police. Many times, when the police would arrive to arrest him, his affable personality would convince them to take him home with them, where they often shared their private stash of hooch.

Charlie's fascination with the banjo apparently started when he was eight or nine years old and made his first banjo out of a gourd. After he started working at the Granite Cotton Mill of Haw River, North Carolina, he purchased a store-bought banjo for the princely sum of $1.50. It is likely that Charlie's role model for the banjo was his cousin Daner Johnson, who played in a three-finger style. Daner had in turn come under the spell of the classical style of banjo playing that was popular in the Northeast around the turn of the century. No slouch on the banjo, he once beat the legendary Fred Van

Eps at a banjo contest held in St. Louis in 1904, winning a gold-plated S.S. Stewart banjo, which was soon stolen. Like Charlie, Daner had itchy feet and constantly rambled from place to place. Later in life his behavior became quite strange. Once known for his snappy attire, he grew a long white beard and dressed in old, tattered clothes. He refused to sleep in his house and could frequently be found sleeping out in the woods with his banjo and his dog. Penniless, he would show up at someone's back door, offering to play his banjo for something to eat.

In addition to working at Granite Cotton Mill, in Haw River, North Carolina, Charlie often made and delivered moonshine. Among his clientele were local judges and attorneys. He made moonshine with fiddler Posey Rorer, and the pair would often play their banjo and fiddle with Charlie singing "Don't Let Your Brew Run Down." One time while he was playing music at a bootleggers' joint, the place

From left: Posey Rorer, Charlie Poole, and Roy Harvey, the North Carolina Ramblers, ca. 1926 (John Edwards Memorial Foundation Records [20001], Southern Folklife Collection at Wilson Special Collections Library, University of North Carolina at Chapel Hill).

was raided by the police. In the wild fight that followed, Charlie came down on an officer's head with his banjo. The banjo neck reportedly hung down the officer's chest like a necktie. Coming to the first officer's rescue, another officer attempted to shoot Charlie, and the two wrestled with the revolver. When the gun went off, Charlie moved his head at the last second, and instead of killing him, the bullet chipped several of his front teeth. No wonder Charlie's later publicity photos do not show him smiling!

By June of 1925 Charlie and two co-workers, fiddler Posey Rorer and guitarist Norman Woodlieff, were determined to advance their music careers by making records. They quit their jobs at the mill and, when they went down to pick up their last paycheck, they brought their instruments and performed "Don't Let Your Deal Go Down" for their fellow mill workers. Arriving in New York nearly broke, the trio got jobs while Charlie sought recording opportunities. When they finally auditioned for Columbia's Frank

Walker, they played "Don't Let Your Deal Go Down." Even before they had finished the song, Walker interrupted them with an offer to record.

Their first session was on July 27, 1925, when they recorded "The Girl I Left in Sunny Tennessee," "I'm the Man That Rode the Mule 'Round the World," "Can I Sleep in Your Barn Tonight, Mister" and "Don't Let Your Deal Go Down." For their efforts, the trio was paid a total of $75, which was nothing to sneeze at in 1925, and it sure beat working in the cotton mill! Released in September of 1925, "Deal," as it was called, became a huge hit, eventually selling an astonishing 102,000 copies—no small potatoes, even now. Unfortunately, the band received no royalties for these first recordings.

The success of Charlie Poole's records did more than make him a star in his hometown of Spray (now Eden), North Carolina. He had a strong impact on untold numbers of rural musicians who widely copied not only his three-finger banjo style but also learned many of the sentimental songs that he recorded. Most of these sad laments originated in New York's Tin Pan Alley around the turn of the century.

Charlie's musical arrangements also had an influence on what would become bluegrass music. As opposed to the wild and woolly string band style of Gid Tanner and His Skillet Lickers or Earl Johnson's Clodhoppers, Charlie's band was a tightly controlled performing unit where every note was perfectly in place. In contrast to Gid Tanner or

North Carolina Ramblers, Charlie Poole (left), Posey Rorrer (center), and Roy Harvey, ca. 1926 (John Edwards Memorial Foundation Records [20001], Southern Folklife Collection at Wilson Special Collections Library, University of North Carolina at Chapel Hill).

Earl Johnson's style of sawing out rough-hewn hoedowns on the fiddle, Charlie's fiddlers, including Poser Rorer, Lonnie Austin, and Odell Smith, all played with a smooth bow arm that set the style for later bluegrass fiddlers.

Wade and J.E. Mainer

It was the oddest thing. While researching old-time music in North Carolina back in 2003, I was listening to an RCA Victor LP titled *Early Bluegrass*, which included the old song "Going to Georgia." I looked at the liner notes to the album and saw that it was recorded February 14, 1936, by Wade Mainer and Zeke Morris in Charlotte, North Carolina. About midway through this song, I couldn't quite make out some of the words that Wade Mainer was singing. While pondering how I was going to decipher those mysterious words, it dawned on me that, if memory served me correctly, Wade Mainer was still living! Although he and his brother J.E. grew up in Weaverville, North Carolina, which is only a short distance from where I live in Asheville, I remembered that J.E. had passed away in 1971 but that Wade still lived in Michigan.

Wade Mainer and the Sons of the Mountaineers, WWNC Radio, Asheville, North Carolina, ca. 1940s. Back row, from left: Jack Shelton, Tiny Dotson, Howard Dixon; front row, from left: Curley Shelton and Wade Mainer.

Right then I called *Bluegrass Unlimited* and immediately got Wade's phone number. Almost in disbelief, I stared at that number for a moment, and then I dialed it. After a few rings, Julia Mainer answered the phone and then passed the receiver to her husband, Wade. After I introduced myself and we exchanged "how do's," I found out that he was ninety-six years old and in fairly good health. We conversed for more than an hour, and this wonderfully cordial man shared many stories of his early days as a professional musician, beginning in the 1930s. After I hung up, I was exhilarated at having talked with this living legend but remembered that, in my excitement, I had forgotten to ask about those mysterious lyrics!

That conversation with Wade Mainer only deepened my conviction that he and his brother, J.E., had played a vital role in the early roots of bluegrass music. Determined to dig deeper, I eventually unearthed some important information about the Mainer brothers. The older brother was Joseph Emmette Mainer (1899–1971). His younger brother, Wade Eckhart Mainer, was born in 1907 and died in 2011 at the age of 104.

Both brothers were born in a one-room log cabin near Asheville, North Carolina. Like most rustic cabins in that area, it had no electricity or running water. On Saturday nights the boys would take their baths in a galvanized tub. At the age of nine, J.E. began playing the banjo with the help of his older brother-in-law, Roscoe Banks. Banks played left-handed, and even as a lad, J.E. accompanied him on the banjo for dances. Before long, J.E. took up the fiddle and eventually became known as a skilled but rough and ready hoedown fiddler who seemed to follow in the footsteps of Gid Tanner and Fiddlin' John Carson.

When J.E. was only twelve years old, he went with his father W.J. (William Joseph) Mainer (1850–1947) to live in Glendale, South Carolina, where he worked in a cotton mill long before child labor laws were even seriously considered. Eventually, J.E. moved to the rolling hills of Concord, North Carolina, to work in the Gibson Cotton Mill and play music on the side. His pay was about $5.50 per week and his weekly board was $1.75.

Wade started on the banjo when he was twelve or fourteen years old. He explained that he'd go with Roscoe Banks and his brother Will to square dances. When Will would lay down his banjo between dances, Wade would be right there, picking it up, trying to figure out how to play it. Even though Will played in a drop-thumb clawhammer style, Wade was trying to pick the banjo with two fingers. Some people who heard him scoffed at his efforts, saying, "You can't pick a banjo like that!" Strong-minded, Wade persisted. One time he picked across the strings and it went "bing, bong, bong," he explained to me on the phone. Before long, he had mastered his own two-finger style of picking the banjo and often played for dances when Will couldn't go.

In 1923 Wade moved to Concord and got a job in the same mill where J.E. worked. Wade remembered that "we would play music in our spare time, for parties, corn shuckings, lassy pullings [molasses making] bean stringings, and fiddlers conventions," where they often went home with the blue ribbon. In 1932 the brothers formed a band with Howard and Lester Lay, who both played guitar. They were soon playing on radio WSOC in Gastonia, North Carolina, and their reputation began to spread.

In 1934 banjo player Fisher Hendley encouraged the two pairs of brothers to audition for J.W. Fincher's *Crazy Water Barn Dance* on WBT radio in Charlotte, North Carolina. WBT beamed a strong signal to much of western North Carolina. Sponsoring the show was Crazy Water Crystals, a compound that promised relief from constipation. Fincher was delighted with the sound of the group and named the band The Crazy

Mountaineers. This powerhouse radio show had the financial moxie to ensure that the Mainer brothers could leave the security of working at the mill and become professional musicians.

Eventually both Mainers grew homesick for the mountains and returned to Weaverville, where they immediately began looking for a guitar player who could sing tenor. Wade explained, "At a shindig in Marion, North Carolina, we got together with George Morris, Gwen Foster, Walt Davis, and the Carolina Tar Heels." Impressed with Morris's guitar style, J.E. and Wade went back to Morris's home to talk to him about working with their band.

At the time George was not at home, but his younger brother, Wiley, told the Mainers that a third brother, Zeke, could outplay George on guitar. As Wade explained it, "We took Zeke and his guitar on the side of a mountain, and we sat and played a few numbers together and tried to harmonize on some songs that we knew. He sounded pretty good, so we took Zeke in the band instead of George."

By the time of their first recordings, in August of 1935 for the Bluebird label, the band consisted of J.E. on fiddle, Wade on banjo, Claude Edward "Zeke" Morris on guitar, and Daddy John Love on guitar. Boyden Carpenter soon replaced Love. In addition to the Saturday night *Crazy Water Barn Dance*, the Mountaineers played early morning radio shows on WBT. This widespread radio exposure ensured that they played to capacity crowds who filled up rural Grange halls and schoolhouses. Admission was normally fifteen to twenty-five cents. The band moved briefly to WWL in New Orleans and then to WPTF in Raleigh, North Carolina. In 1937 Wade and Zeke Morris had a bitter dispute with J.W. Fincher over money and they left and formed a band known as Buck and Buddy, the Little Smilin' Rangers.

J.E. moved back to Concord, where he eventually joined forces with three-finger banjo pioneer DeWitt "Snuffy" Jenkins, George "Sambo" Morris on guitar, and Leonard "Handsome" Stokes on mandolin. Together they played on radio WSOC in Charlotte, WSPA in Spartanburg, South Carolina, and WIS in Columbia, South Carolina.

Before long, Wade and Zeke Morris were back in Asheville performing on WWNC radio, where they announced shows in local schoolhouses. As Wade said back in 2003, "We played most anywhere we could get 50, 75, or 100 people in the building. A lot of times it was them old one-room schoolhouses that wouldn't hold over 100 or 150 people. People would come and stand outside and listen to the music. After we did our first show, we'd dismiss those people and open the door and do another show for the crowd that came and stood around outside to get in. A lot of times the same ones who come in to the first show would turn around and pay another fifteen or twenty cents and come back and sit in on the second show."

Wade and Zeke knew a good thing when they had it, so they stayed together and on August 6, 1935, recorded an old Gussie L. Davis song titled "Maple on the Hill," which became a huge hit. On the flip side was "Take Me in a Lifeboat," which was later recorded by Flatt and Scruggs. In 1980 Zeke told me that they were paid a half cent for each record sold.

In live shows, the duo of Wade and Zeke was occasionally joined by fiddlers Homer Sherrill, Tiny Dotson, or Steve Ledford. When Zeke's younger brother Wiley got old enough, he joined the band on guitar and vocals. With Wiley on guitar, Zeke switched from guitar to mandolin.

Despite the band's popularity around the Asheville, North Carolina, area, they eventually decided to seek greener pastures and moved to 5,000-watt radio station

WPTF in Raleigh, North Carolina. Following them on their 7:15 to 7:30 a.m. radio show were Bill and Charlie, the Monroe Brothers. Working closely together every morning, the Morris Brothers and the Monroe Brothers became good friends. Zeke fondly remembers that back in those days "I had a '37 Ford V8, and Charlie had a '37 Hudson Terraplane. We'd always take off and see who could outrun the other. The cops weren't bad back then. We always respected each other as musicians, you know. We got along perfect because they done their thing and we done ours. We never would try to copy another musician's music."

Although neither band copied the other, it is very likely that Bill Monroe was deeply affected by Wade Mainer's banjo playing, noting how much it added to the music. He also could not help but notice how well the whole band fit together, with two-finger banjo, mandolin, guitar, and fiddle, plus lead and tenor vocals. In time, he would recreate this kind of band, and it would eventually be called "bluegrass."

The Morris Brothers (Zeke, left, and Wiley), with Fiddler Tiny Dotson, ca. 1935 (courtesy the Morris Brothers).

My hat's off to Wade and J.E. Mainer, whose music prefigured the original sound of bluegrass music long before it was called that. These North Carolina musicians combined the excitement of the old-time string band with banjo, mandolin, guitar, and fiddle, as well as solos, duets, and quartets. Listen, if you will, to their 1935 recording of "Lights in the Valley" on YouTube. You'll hear what sounds like a traditional bluegrass gospel quartet with two-finger banjo, fiddle, and two guitars. The 1935 date is important because this was four years before Bill Monroe and His Blue Grass Boys made their historic performances on the Grand Ole Opry and five years before their first legendary recordings.

Wade Mainer put it this way: "I believe we were doing bluegrass and didn't know it." He went on to say, "We sung by the letter method. We opened our mouths and let 'er fly!"

The above is partially based on several personal interviews I had with Wade Mainer in 1977–1980.

Brother Duets

Wiley and Zeke, the Morris Brothers

It all started with Georgia Ellen Morris, mother of the musical Morris brothers. It seemed like she could make music on about anything with strings on it and some things that didn't, like the French harp (harmonica). There never was enough time for her to play, what with raising six rambunctious sons. But often on Saturday nights she would put her work aside and get together with her two brothers, Rome and Joe, to make music.

Joe played banjo in the old clawhammer style, and Rome played the fiddle. In addition to the hoedown square dance tunes, Rome played some beautiful waltzes, like "Over the Waves" and "Wednesday Night Waltz." According to his many admirers, when Rome played the fiddle, every note was right where it was supposed to be. He did have one quirk that amused some and distracted others. Rome tended to grunt and moan while he played, all the while puffing on his big pipe stuffed full of tobacco.

It seemed like all the music came from Georgia's side of the family. Her husband, Russell Morris, could do little more than keep time with his foot. So it was she who passed on music to her sons. It wasn't too long before their fingers started

Zeke Morris (left) and Wiley Morris, ca. 1940s (courtesy the Morris Brothers).

to make chords on the guitar. It was brother George who first got his hands around the neck of the instrument. He spotted an ad in a farm catalog advertising a free guitar to any boy who could sell enough seeds, so George worked hard and, before long, the postman hauled a large box out of his trunk. The guitar was a Stella. Not long after the guitar was unwrapped, George was able to tune it like a Hawaiian guitar. By barring his finger across all the strings, he was able to play chords. The first tune he played was "Go Feather, Go Feather Your Nest."

Even though Georgia passed away before she could teach George the rudiments of the guitar, there were plenty of people around to get George on his way. On Saturday evenings a group of local musicians gathered at Lackey's hardware store in nearby Old Fort, North Carolina. Sitting on the front porch of the store could be found Walter Davis on guitar and French harp and Clarence Greene on fiddle. These musicians would play the old hoedowns and waltz tunes. As people would pass by, some would gather around to listen and there was always a hat where a penny might be pitched.

More than any of the other musicians it was Walter Davis who really took a liking to young George Morris. The two could often be found playing together at church suppers and, of course, out front of Lackey's hardware store. Davis had been earning his living as a street musician for several years, playing with Clarence Greene, Gwen Foster, and occasionally Clarence Ashley. He recorded with Foster as the Carolina Twins and with Foster and fiddler Greene as the Carolina Tar Heels and the Blue Ridge Mountain Entertainers. Their recordings for the American Recording Company included "Corrina" and "Bring Me a Leaf from the Sea." Davis played the guitar with two fingers; he had picked up this style by standing spellbound in front of an old Black street singer who often played in Johnson City, Tennessee. That guitarist was none other than Blind Lemon Jefferson, now a legendary figure in blues guitar history. It was this style that George Morris emulated.

For quite some time after their mother died, George thought he was the only one in the family who cared anything about string music. But soon he discovered that his younger brother Zeke had been sneaking the guitar out from under the bed while George was at school or out working with his father in the fields. Worse yet, Zeke was getting good at it. George didn't take too kindly to his younger brother messing with his guitar while he was away and forbade Zeke to touch it. This, of course, instilled in Zeke an even greater desire to learn the instrument. The youngest brother, Wiley, learned in the same fashion, by sneaking Zeke's guitar out of the case while Zeke was gone.

It wasn't too many years before the two older brothers, George and Zeke, began performing together with their guitars. They had heard there was prize money to be won at a fiddlers convention in nearby Marion, so they threw their guitars on their backs and caught a freight train down there. "That was the only way we had to travel back then," Zeke remembers. "We didn't have cars. And if we did, we had no money to buy gas. We'd hobo down there and win every time. We never did lose."

"We both played guitar. One of us would play lead and the other would chord it. We entered in the duet singing competition and won on the spirituals every time. We didn't have a special song we played for all the contests. We'd just sing the first one that came to us. We'd make 'em up as we went along. As long as I've got the tune in my head, I can make up the words. I've been before a microphone many a time, forgot the words, and made it up and went right on. I've seen some people forget the words and their britches would almost shake off. But I've never had stage fright. The bigger the crowd, the better I can do."

In 1933 J.E. and Wade Mainer, two brothers from nearby Weaverville, North Carolina, were putting together a string band to go on the road. Wade played banjo in a two-finger style and his brother J.E. played the fiddle. They needed a guitarist to round out their band and had heard of a young one in Old Fort by the name of George Morris. One day they came looking for George.

They first located George's younger brother, Wiley, who was only a small boy at the time. He directed the Mainers to his father's house, where George lived. Arriving to find George gone, Wiley suggested that his brother Zeke could play just as good as George, so they auditioned Zeke on the front porch of the house. Liking what they heard, they hired Zeke on the spot, and together they moved to Charlotte, North Carolina, where they played as J.E. Mainer and His Crazy Mountaineers and were sponsored by the Crazy Water Crystal Company. They soon headed back to Asheville, and then once again to Charlotte, where the band consisted of J. E., Wade, Zeke, and Daddy John Love. Love was a blues singer and yodeler in the style of Jimmie Rodgers.

Soon after the group started working in Charlotte, they were contacted by RCA Victor to make records for the Bluebird label subsidiary. In early 1934 they traveled to Atlanta where they cut "Maple on the Hill" and "Take Me in a Lifeboat." Zeke recalls that RCA told him that "Maple on the Hill" outsold anything up to that time, even above Jimmie Rodgers. "Of course, you had to sell a million records before you made any money at all. They paid a half cent on every record sold, and it takes a lot of records to amount to some money, but I did draw some pretty big checks off of that thing."

While traveling with the Mainers, Zeke recalled that his weekly salary for a seven-day week was $26. "I told J.E. and Wade that I can't work for those wages. They couldn't understand why I couldn't because I was single and all. I told them yes, I was single, but I was doing a lot of courtin' and I had to have money.

"I said, 'Let's hit old man Fincher up for a percentage basis.' He was our boss. We were on a straight salary, and they were collecting all the money at our show dates. Mr. Fincher's boy, Hubert, was our emcee. He went out with us on our shows and sold tickets. I said, 'Let's tell him to forget the salary and we'll advertise for him for free and we'll collect the money at the show dates.' So we got together and put it to him and that's what we done. We told him it was either that or we was going to quit. So then we really started making the money, plenty of it for those days, and that was at fifteen and twenty-five cents a head. We'd have to put on two or three shows a night just to get 'em all in."

After working with J.E. and Wade Mainer for about three years, Zeke decided that his brother Wiley was good enough to join him. In 1937 Zeke and Wade left J.E. and came to Old Fort, where they picked up Wiley. Zeke and Wiley (on guitars) and Wade (on banjo) then started on WWNC in Asheville, broadcasting a fifteen-minute show every day from 3:15 until 3:30.

It wasn't long before Zeke started playing the mandolin on the program. He had begun playing the mandolin some years before and now decided it would give the band more variety. Zeke remembers that his first mandolin was a little flat-back instrument, similar to a Martin. He later got a 1906 Gibson A-1 mandolin, which he continued to play for the rest of his career.

In learning the mandolin, Zeke had to develop his own style of playing, because mandolin players back in the mountains were very few indeed. The early mandolins were often referred to as "tater bugs" and had round backs. These instruments were extremely awkward to hold; doubtless the shape of the instrument had a lot to do with its lack of popularity.

Zeke remembers that he started out playing breakdowns on the mandolin, like you would on the fiddle. "I played 'Sally Goodin,' 'Red Wing,' the old tunes. I probably did more with intros to my singing than anything else. Of course, I'd take a break now and then to give us a chance to swallow a time or two, and maybe get some fresh air in our lungs. When I'm singing, I more or less stay in the background with it, and maybe hit a note or two at the end of each chorus."

As was the custom in those days, musicians did not usually stay long on any one radio station. The programs were used to advertise local dates in schoolhouses and theaters in the winter and county fairs in the summer. After "playing out" one area, it was necessary to switch stations and find new audiences. In the later part of 1937, the Morris Brothers and Wade Mainer moved to 5,000-watt station WPTF in Raleigh, North Carolina. Sponsored by the Zebulon Supply Company, they played every morning from 7:15 to 7:30. Following them on the air was another brother act that was starting to raise quite a stir in the Carolinas: Bill and Charlie, the Monroe Brothers.

As with most bands, the Morris Brothers and Wade Mainer didn't stay together very long. During the period that Zeke played with J.E. and/or Wade Mainer, they recorded more than sixty sides for Bluebird. Most of them were old love songs and ballads, and others were composed by members of the band. Zeke had been writing songs since he was a boy and it was his songs, in fact, that were to prove the most popular of any the band recorded.

At the beginning of 1938 Homer Sherill joined Zeke and Wiley Morris on fiddle. Homer had been playing with Bill and Earl Bolick, the Blue Sky Boys, over radio WGST in Atlanta. With the addition of the new member, the band changed their name to the Smiling Rangers. By April they were ready to move on, and their next stop was radio WBTM in Danville, Virginia. Joining the Smiling Rangers was Joel Martin, who played banjo in a three-finger style. Together they played a program called the *Farm Bulletin Program*. With the addition of Joel Martin, the band had the basic instrumentation that would later go by the name of bluegrass—banjo, guitar, mandolin, and fiddle.

According to Zeke, Martin was a fine banjo player and one of several who deserves credit for helping to develop three-finger style banjo playing. Zeke remembers that Mack Crow, who was billed as the "King of the Five-String Banjo," was the first three-finger style banjo player he ever heard. Crow was originally from Hickory, North Carolina, but spent most of his life in nearby Marion. Zeke also praises both Snuffy Jenkins and his nephew Hoke Jenkins as unheralded pioneers of the banjo. Hoke later worked with the Morris Brothers and later went on to record with Jim and Jesse.

When the Smiling Rangers made their move to Danville, Zeke recalls that they were practically broke. "I was the only one with a little money in my pocket. I did have a new car, which I owed for. We didn't have a place to stay, so we found a rooming house and the lady said she thought I had an honest face by looking at me and by talking to me. So she let us stay without paying a cent. That lady and her daughter fixed meals for us and it didn't cost us to eat for several days. I went out and booked a school at Schoolfield, Virginia, a suburb of Danville. I managed to borrow another $6 from that lady to get the advertising out. We put up posters and announced it on the station, and when we went out there to play, we had packed the house crammed full and running over. That got us started and gave us a little bit of money, so I paid the lady back. I tried to give her some extra off the money we made, but she wouldn't take it. I told her she saved our lives, and she said she was only glad to do it. So that got us started and from there we swept that country."

By the end of 1938 Zeke had become disenchanted with the music business. He quit the band and moved to Gastonia, North Carolina, where he worked in a cotton mill. Wiley kept the band together by hiring a musician named Wellon from Danville to sing tenor. It didn't take Zeke very long to decide that the music business, for all its faults, was still better than the long hours and short pay he was making in the cotton mill. So Zeke, wanting to get back in the band, met resistance from the members who didn't want to divide the already meager earnings another way. Wiley and Zeke then decided to form their own act, just the two of them. They came back to Asheville and started a program on WWNC radio sponsored by JFG Coffee, calling themselves Wiley and Zeke, the Morris Brothers.

While the Morris Brothers were working at WWNC, an old friend dropped by to see them. It was Bill Monroe. Monroe explained that he and Charlie had just broken up and Bill was getting together his own band. Bill wanted help in getting a program started over WWNC, so the Morris Brothers put him in touch with Israel McIntosh, the station manager. With this help from the Morris Brothers, Bill Monroe first formed the Blue Grass Boys in Asheville in 1939.

Joining Monroe were Cleo Davis on guitar, Art Wooten on fiddle, and Tommy Millard, who played blackface comedian and played spoons and bones. The stay in Asheville was short lived, however, when Bill became dissatisfied with his band. Wiley recalls the members couldn't sing high enough lead vocals for Monroe to harmonize to, so Monroe went to South Carolina, where he formed a new band and began working at station WFBC. In the later part of 1939, the Morris Brothers received a postcard from Bill Monroe saying he was going to do an audition at the Grand Ole Opry the following Saturday night and for them to tune in. He requested that they drop him a postcard telling him how he sounded.

It wasn't long before the Morris Brothers themselves had the chance to join the Grand Ole Opry. Wiley had taken an audition record to Nashville when he heard that the Delmore Brothers were leaving and that WSM was looking for another brother act. Wiley made contact with Jack Stapp, who played the record for "the Solemn Old Judge," announcer George D. Hay. Hay and Stapp were to take the record to the board of directors who decided which acts would play on the Opry.

Within a week the Morris Brothers received a telegram asking them to appear backstage at the Grand Ole Opry the following Saturday night. Zeke, however, firmly stated that he wasn't going. He said that he didn't want to go to Nashville, that he was doing all right where he was. Wiley tried to convince him, but there was no changing Zeke's mind. Unable to get the Morris Brothers, the Opry hired the Wilburn Children instead. Zeke later admitted his mistake, but the Wilburn Children (later the Wilburn Brothers) were seemingly there to stay, and there wasn't room for another family act.

Meanwhile, the Morris Brothers continued playing to standing-room-only crowds who paid their fifteen and twenty-five cents to watch them perform in schoolhouses and theaters throughout the Carolinas. Their group at times included brother George Morris and banjo player Hoke Jenkins. Zeke recalls, "We really had an outfit back then. Wiley, George, and I could really do those spirituals. We often sang spirituals such as 'Get on

Board Little Children' and 'Walking in Jerusalem Just Like John.' We used to tear 'em all to pieces. Of course, we were brothers and had an advantage over most other groups. We always knew exactly what the other one was going to do. Back then there were no amplifiers, but our voices were so strong that they could hear us way in the back of the auditorium. We usually tuned our instruments high to make our voices come out better. We couldn't sing soft like a lot of people. Later on, we found that we could tone it down. I believe that when you get older, you can't sing as loud as you could when you're younger, although you may actually be able to harmonize better."

In addition to their singing, the Morris Brothers featured a blackface act. Zeke recalls, "George was a big heavy-set guy, so he played the man's part. Because I was smaller, I always got stuck with the part of the Black mama. Hoke Jenkins, our banjo player, played the little child. We'd often have it that George would pretend to aggravate the child and I would come out and chase George off the stage with a broom. Of course, we'd rehearse all the time and kept adding new stuff to our program because many of the same people came to see us time after time. But we always had a good wholesome program, and it was a good show too. It was for the entire family, something that any and everybody could enjoy. We never would allow anything dirty or vulgar in our program."

"We respected people. In fact, we learned a lot about spiritual singing from colored people themselves. I used to sing and play at the Black people's church over at Old Fort, North Carolina. Back in those days, we didn't know what segregation was, because we was raised up around Black people. We worked together, played together, and often ate at each other's houses. That's the way it was back in those days. I've seen many a time when Black people would come to the white church. So I went to the Black church to learn their spiritual singing. They really could do that. Later on, people quit that, and you couldn't mix like that, because there would be trouble. But back in those days, there was no trouble between the Blacks and whites."

On January 26, 1938, the recording career of the Morris Brothers began. On that date Wiley and Zeke along with fiddler Homer Sherrill traveled to Charlotte, North Carolina, and recorded eight sides for Bluebird under the supervision of Eli Oberstein. In September of 1938 Victor moved its portable equipment to the Andrew Jackson Hotel in Rock Hill, South Carolina. This time they recorded nine sides. Wiley vividly remembers how it happened.

"They had two rooms rented for the recording. They used one of them as a studio and in the other they had the machinery to do the recording. They had one big machine in there which turned a bunch of stuff and there was a big cake of wax with a needle sticking in it. It cut the grooves right then. They let you hear the first song you recorded—and that was it. You didn't get to hear no more 'til it came out as a record. I guess the reason was that, when you recorded, you put the sound in that cake of wax, and when they played it back it took the sound back out. Later on, they changed all that. So if you made a mistake it was a mistake, 'cause they couldn't let you do it over. That cost them money. If you really messed up I guess they'd let you do it over, but they didn't like that. I remember they had one mic which was right between me and Zeke. It stood in the middle of the room. We stood side by side and both sang into the same side of that mic. It was a big mic. They had a red light down at the bottom to tell you when to play. They also had speakers so you could talk back and forth. They told us not to play longer than three minutes. I never will forget that big cake of wax. When that needle was cutting the grooves, it sounded like grinding an axe on a grindstone."

During the recording session in Rock Hill, South Carolina, the Morris Brothers recorded the song that was their all-time hit, "Let Me Be Your Salty Dog." The song was first recorded in 1924 by African American bluesman Papa Charlie Jackson. His version was covered in 1927 by the Allen Brothers, Sam and Kirk McGee, and the Booker Orchestra. Zeke apparently took the older song, rearranged it, and added some verses, mainly from the public domain.

Wiley explained, "I have a different definition of a salty dog than Zeke has. Back when we were kids down in Old Fort, we would see a girl we liked and say, 'I'd like to be her salty dog.' There also used to be a drink you could get up in Michigan. All you had to do was say, 'Let me have a Salty Dog,' and they'd pour you one."

Zeke remembers, "I got the idea when we went to a little old honky-tonk just outside of Canton, which is in North Carolina. We went to play at a school out beyond Waynesville somewhere and we stopped at this place. They sold beer and had slot machines—at that time they were legal in North Carolina. We got in there after the show and got to drinking that beer and playing the slot machines with nickels, dimes, and quarters. I think we hit three or four jackpots. Boy, here it would come! You know you had a pile of money when you had two handfuls of change. The name of that place was 'The Salty Dog,' and that's where I got the idea for the song. There are actually more verses to it than me and Wiley sing, a lot more verses."

There is little doubt that "Salty Dog" is the most popular number the Morris Brothers ever recorded. According to Wiley, "Everybody uses it in the bluegrass field, just about. We're making more money off it now on copyright royalties than we ever did on our record, with other people using it. I reckon that song is known all over the world. When I get my statement every six months, it's being played in every nation under the sun. That song is even popular in Japan! 'Salty Dog' ain't one that's gone up to high heaven and then fell completely down. It's just one that's considered a standard. It's our biggest song 'cause it's a good five-string banjo number played bluegrass style."

In early 1944 the Morris Brothers moved to Knoxville, Tennessee, in search of new audiences. Before long, however, Zeke got into a fight with one of the local musicians over a crap game and decided to leave. He went to Asheville, North Carolina; picked up "Little" Red Rector, A.L. "Red" Smiley, and Fred Smith; and took them to WJHL in Johnson City, Tennessee.

Wiley stayed in Knoxville and did a radio program every Saturday morning on WIRL called the *Tennessee Valley Network*. Wiley explained, "I done all the singing, and Chet Atkins, John Gallaher, and Harry Nitus furnished the music. Chet could play the guitar as good then as he can now. We also played together on the *Midday Merry-Go-Round*. He sat back there while we were at the *Merry-Go-Round* and played that guitar for days on end. Chet would tell you today that the most important part of music is staying with it and practicing to get it down to perfection."

Although the Morris Brothers were no longer playing together, their record sales were substantial enough that in November of 1945 RCA Victor Records requested another session for their Bluebird subsidiary. Wiley explained, "When we made our last session of records for Victor, Zeke and I weren't even playing together. I was with a band in Knoxville playing for the Cas Walker family of stores and Zeke was in Johnson City. But Victor wanted me and Zeke, the Morris Brothers, to record. So I came by Johnson City and picked up Zeke and together we went to Charlotte to record. We hadn't even played together for several years, but we knew our stuff so well we didn't need to practice.

"So we went to Charlotte, to the Charlotte Hotel. Eli Oberstein was the recording manager. He said, 'Now boys, I want you to do this "Salty Dog" again. Now since you play the mandolin, Zeke, mandolin and guitar is all I want on it.' He said, 'I also want the title shortened. I don't want it to be "Let Me Be Your Salty Dog."' And Zeke said, 'Well, how about changing it to "Salty Dog Blues"?' And Eli said that was fine, so that's what it was."

In addition to the "Salty Dog Blues," they recorded three other songs that they had written: "Grave Upon the Green Hillside," "Tragic Romance," and "Somebody Loves You Darling." Wiley explained that Zeke wrote "Somebody Loves You Darling." "I wrote 'Grave Upon the Green Hillside' and 'Tragic Romance.'" Here's how Wiley explained the origin of "Tragic Romance":

"Somewhere along the line somebody wrote this poem and sent it to me. I don't know who it was, but naturally, anyone who would write a poem with good words would send it to me and I would use it if I could. So I got this poem, rearranged it, titled it, and had it copyrighted. But in the forties, there was a big uproar about it. Pee Wee King wanted to use it and Cowboy Copas had recorded it on King Records. But Grandpa Jones had put his name on it as the writer, although he had no proof that he owned the song."

"Well, Pee Wee King found out that I had an unpublished copyright there in my briefcase, from the Library of Congress in Washington. He paid my expenses up to Nashville. So there I was standing in the hall at WSM talking with Eddy Arnold and Pee Wee King when up comes the Bailes Brothers and Grandpa Jones. Eddy called Grandpa over, because I didn't know Grandpa at the time. He called him over there and says, 'Grandpa, I want you to meet the boy who owns "Tragic Romance,"' and that guy turned every color under God's heaven. Eddy said, 'He owns the song, him and his brother, and I know them both.' And I said, 'Yes, and I've turned this thing over to a lawyer.'"

"I asked him how much money he had made from King Records off of the song, and he said, 'Nothing to speak of.' And I said, 'How come you gave your name as the writer of that song?' Well, he said, 'I wrote it.' I said, 'You couldn't have wrote it. When did you write it?' He gave me the date and I asked him why didn't he have it copyrighted, and he said, 'I couldn't; they wouldn't copyright it.' I said, 'You know why, don't you? There's already one copyright there and they won't copyright two.' Then Pee Wee butted in and said, 'I'm not here to start an argument, I'm here to buy the rights from the Morris Brothers to use Copas's picture on one side and the words on the other.' That was my reason for being there, but Zeke decided not to sign, so they couldn't use it."

Wiley also remembered how he wrote "Grave Upon the Green Hillside." "I believe the Carter Family had one called 'Grave on the Green Hillside,' but mine was altogether different from theirs, but I did get the title from that record." Zeke admitted that he didn't know the song until he walked into the studio to record it in November of 1945. "I never sang the song before and didn't even know the tune to it. I put that song on the music stand and sang along with Wiley one time. One time is all it took me in those days."

In their long association with country music, the Morris Brothers certainly deserve credit for helping to establish the sound that would later be called bluegrass. "Of course, we didn't call it bluegrass then," remembers Zeke. "We referred to it as country music, although others snarled their noses at it and called it hillbilly music. Back then, the college people looked down on it, but today they eat it up. There's something in it that everyone can be proud of. You don't have to be ashamed of country music. When you listen to it played by the right ones, you know it's for real."

Zeke insists, "When we were coming up, there was no such a thing as bluegrass music. But we helped to build it into what it is today. If we hadn't come along, I doubt very seriously if there would have been this particular type of music. A lot of people think bluegrass music's got to have a fiddle. Well, we had good fiddlers like Tiny Dodson and Benny Sims. Benny later played fiddle with Flatt and Scruggs and recorded 'Foggy Mountain Breakdown' with them. They also say that bluegrass has to have a banjo and that it ain't bluegrass without a banjo. Well, we had a banjo, several of them. Take Don Reno and Earl Scruggs. They both played with us. In fact, we gave them the first job they ever had. Don worked with us before Scruggs and then after. Don came to Asheville when he was but a boy and started playing with us. He was playing guitar then. We liked him so we hired him. That was in '41. We hired him to play guitar and then found out he played the banjo too. Don could really play that banjo. He played with three fingers, but it was his own style. He could play in any key and not use a capo or anything."

Wiley remembers the night they met Earl Scruggs for the first time. "We were playing a high school in Chesney, South Carolina, and had a terrible big crowd that night. George and I were selling tickets and I left George to sell the tickets while I went back to tune my guitar with Zeke's mandolin. Then I heard somebody knock on the back door to the auditorium, where the stage entrance was. I opened it and standing there was Grady Wilkie and Earl Scruggs. Of course, I didn't know either one of them at the time. They had both driven up to Chesney in a model A Ford coupe, and both were wearing blue shirts and overalls. Grady said, 'I got a guy out here I wish you boys would listen to on the five-string banjo.' Well, we were needing one at the time because Hoke Jenkins had been called into the service, so I said, 'Bring him in here. Let's tune him up and hear how he sounds.' So he came in and tuned his banjo to my guitar and he could play as good that night as he can now, if not better. He was just shaky and nervous then. He's always been nervous, and I'd have thought he'd have missed everything on the banjo, but he didn't miss a string.

"So we hired him that night and paid him $20 a week. We took him back to Spartanburg, South Carolina, with us and he stayed with us for about eight months, until he got his draft notice to report for his induction or examination. He left us and went back and got a deferment 'cause his daddy was dead and he had to keep his mother up. The next thing I knew he was with Bill Monroe at the Grand Ole Opry playing his five-string."

"When he went with Bill, Lester Flatt was also in the band. Bill had Lester singing lead for him and playing guitar, so he hired Earl and they stayed with him for, I don't know, two or three years. Then Lester and Earl pulled out and formed their own outfit, the Foggy Mountain Boys. They came to WCYB in Bristol, Virginia, on the *Farm and Fun Time*."

"I did a show at a horse arena in Lexington, Kentucky, with Curley and Jack Shelton, Benny Sims, and myself. We doubled-showed it with Flatt and Scruggs. It was that night that they asked Benny about working with them. He later got them to record 'Salty Dog Blues.' [Lester] should have known it, but he didn't, so Benny sang lead on the record that Flatt and Scruggs made. He played the fiddle too. That was for Mercury Records. When it came out on Columbia [in 1963] it was Lester and Earl doing the singing with their group. It didn't do any good for us when Benny sang it, but when Lester and Earl put it on Columbia, it skyrocketed."

More than anything else, it was the war that made Wiley and Zeke turn away from music as a profession. Zeke explained, "You couldn't get tires, you couldn't get gas to travel, and the war took our best musicians. Hoke got called in the first draft, and then they got Wiley. I was lucky. I got to go to a defense job. When the war was over, Wiley and I got into the auto repair business. We also quit 'cause of our families. We both raised big families, and any time you go to raising a family it takes money."

"Of course, we still play together some. Always have, and always will. I don't say that we're the best in the country to get along, but we do stick together. If one needs the other, he's always there. Although we do disagree on some things, we don't let that interfere. Not all brothers are like that. But me and Wiley's always lived pretty close together all our lives. Of course, if any of us needs any help from the other, he knows where he can find it."

Even though the Morris Brothers hadn't recorded together in many years, a young record company bent on presenting and preserving the old music approached them to record again in 1973. Wiley remembers, "This little record company out of Somerville, Massachusetts, Rounder Records, came down here and wanted to make an album of me and Zeke and Homer Sherrill. They wanted it just as it was in the beginning, or just as close as we could get it."

"So Homer came up from selling cars in Columbia, South Carolina. He came up with his wife and spent two weekends with me and my wife. We rehearsed and then went down to the Owen High School band room to record. They had a soundproof room there, you see. We put sixteen numbers on it. That is the last record we've made, and the only album we ever made."

In looking back over a career that has spanned more than forty years, Wiley admits, "We didn't go out for the big time. We didn't see it then because we had no manager. Most of these groups now have a front man that do all the publicity for them and that counts. Elvis Presley would never have gotten where he did without Colonel Parker. He put him on the map. You have to have

Wiley Morris, Black Mountain, North Carolina, ca. 1960 (courtesy Wiley Morris).

somebody to sell you. It's hard to sell yourself. Where you sell yourself is out on the stage to the audience. But now, selling you to a television show or booking, you need a front man for that, and you've got to pay him a percentage or a flat salary."

"The type of stuff that me and Zeke does will draw a bigger crowd in New York State than it will in North Carolina. But I never knowed that. I never had time to take advantage of it, because I thought if you got out of North Carolina or Virginia that you were out of the world. Being an old country codger, I never got to know the modern generation. People down here like what we do, but it's nothing like it is up north. Down here we sign a few autographs, but not many. But up there, when we got off the stage after doing our thing, they'll want to crowd back on you and ask you all kinds of questions about it. They want to know, and they're entitled to know if they paid their money to see you. I never would shun nobody, never have."

"I guess if I would've made a million dollars at it, I guess I would be the same as I am today sitting here. I don't believe I would have changed. I can't tell that Earl Scruggs has changed and he's worth over a million dollars. But that's the way I look at it. I figure that life is life, people is people, and I've always liked people. So I've always worked for people in one capacity or the other. I've served people. They feed me. They pay me, and therefore I try to be in their good graces the best I can. Why shun them? Why big hat them? You're no better than they are, just because you're up there performing to them and they're paying to see you. Actually, if you want to turn it around, they're better than you are. They're paying to see you and hear you. You got something they want to hear. Zeke will probably tell you the same thing. It's the truth, I tell you, and if you tell the truth you ain't got no flyback."

This section is based on numerous personal interviews I had with each of the Morris Brothers at their respective auto body shops in Black Mountain in 1979–80. It originally appeared in Bluegrass Unlimited, *August 1980.*

The Callahan Brothers

We stood there for a moment, staring at the watermelon-sized hole in the floor. "That's where the groundhog made his entrance. He chewed a hole right through the floor." I turned toward the speaker, spry eighty-one-year-old Homer Callahan, and said, "He must have wanted to get in awful bad." "Maybe so," Homer joked, "but he sure was disappointed when he got inside. There's not a crumb to eat in here!"

We laughed and went out on the front porch of the old Callahan homeplace in Bear Branch, North Carolina. No one had lived in the house for many years, and the weeds were knee high in the yard. As I turned on my portable tape recorder, Homer kept me in stitches for several hours as he told me tales of growing up in rural Madison County.

"My brother Walter was two years older than I am. My parents were both musically inclined, and Walter learned guitar as a young kid. When he was ten and I was eight, we'd go down to the tobacco warehouse in Asheville and perform for the farmers. Walter would play guitar, and I would dance. The farmers would pitch us dimes, which seemed like big money to us back then in 1920."

Homer explained that by the time they were in their teens Walter had perfected his skills on the guitar and he had taken up not only the mandolin and the guitar but also the banjo, fiddle, ukulele, harmonica, and bass. I learned that they worked especially

Bill (left) and Joe, the Callahan Brothers, ca. 1936 (John Edwards Memorial Foundation Records [20001], Southern Folklife Collection at Wilson Special Collections Library, University of North Carolina at Chapel Hill).

hard on their harmony singing and virtually invented the duet yodel. While performing at Asheville's Rhododendron Festival, they were heard by the manager of a Knoxville radio station and hired to perform on the radio for $4 a week, sponsored by the JFG Coffee Company.

In 1934 an Asheville furniture dealer was so impressed with their singing and playing that he contacted W.R. Callaway of the American Record Company, who offered the brothers a chance to record in New York. Homer recalled that they stayed in the Wilson Hotel and the guests were so fascinated with their appearance and mountain speech that they bought them "eats" just to hear them talk. With ARC's Art Satherley looking on, the Callahan Brothers cut thirteen sides beginning on January 2, 1934. Among the songs recorded that day was "She's My Curly Headed Baby," a song which the brothers wrote and made famous.

With the success of these first recordings, the Callahan Brothers were called back to the studio on August 16, 1934, where they recorded fifteen more songs, including "Little Poplar Log House on the Hill," which was later covered by the Carter Family in 1940. I was shocked when Homer suddenly stood up and pointed a short way up the hill from where we were sitting, saying, "Right up there, that's where the poplar log house used to stand." I couldn't believe what I was hearing! To be able to trace this song to a particular Madison County hillside was nothing less than amazing.

As the lazy afternoon sun started to dip below the tall mountains behind the Callahan homeplace, Homer regaled me with yet more stories of a musical career that spanned more than seven decades. He told me that by the time their first records hit the market they were hired by radio WHAS in Louisville, Kentucky, where they earned the whopping sum of $4 a day. The trail then led them to WWVA in Wheeling, West Virginia, and then to WLS in Cincinnati, Ohio, where they performed with Red Foley and the Coon Creek Girls until 1938. After stops at several radio stations in Oklahoma and Missouri, they ended up in Texas, which became their base of operations throughout much of the 1940s. It was during this period that Walter and Homer changed their names to Joe and Bill. Homer wisecracked that their given names were too hard to pronounce.

The Callahan Brothers, Bill (left) and Joe, ca. 1950 (courtesy Homer Callahan).

In 1945 the Callahan Brothers traveled to Hollywood to appear with Jimmy Wakely in several B movies, including *Springtime in Texas*, which Homer referred to as a "shoot-'em-up." In 1951 they toured with Lefty Frizzell, who Homer even managed for a time. Eventually, Walter decided to retire and move back to Asheville, where he passed away in 1971. At the time of our interview in about 1980, Homer was in good health, and he went on to live to the ripe old age of ninety.

Before the afternoon was over, Homer and I dragged out our instruments and played and sang several of the songs that he and his brother had written and made famous, including "They're at Rest Together"; "Sweet Thing"; and, of course, "Curly Headed Baby." I found out quickly that Homer still had an incredibly powerful voice, and even at sixty-eight, he could yodel the paint off a barn door. When I called his house in Dallas, Texas, in the fall of 2003 to chat with him about a book that I was working on, I found out from his son, Buddy, that he had passed away in September 2002. I'm just glad I got to know him and share a lot of laughs with him.

The above is based on several personal interviews I had with Homer Callahan in 1983–84.

The Blue Sky Boys

It all began with a misunderstanding. It was early June 1936, and the teenaged brother duet of Bill and Earl Bolick had abruptly ended a three-month stint at radio WGST in Atlanta over a dispute with the sponsor, J.W. Fincher's Crazy Water Crystals. Within a matter of days, they traveled to the RCA Victor studio in Charlotte, North Carolina, to fulfill a contract to make their first recordings for the Bluebird subsidiary. Perhaps out of spite, Fincher passed on to RCA Victor the erroneous information that the brothers had broken up their act.

So Eli Oberstein at Victor was surprised and annoyed when he discovered that the two young men who had been impatiently sitting in the waiting room for three hours were Bill and Earl, the Bolick brothers. Once Oberstein found out who they were, things went from bad to worse. He curtly asked, "You're the boys who copy the Monroe Brothers, aren't you?" The brothers prickled at the charge that they copied anyone. True, they had taken over the spot vacated by the Monroe Brothers on radio WGST in Atlanta, but as of yet, they had never even heard the Monroe Brothers!

When things calmed down, Oberstein relented and invited the Bolicks to audition. The first number they tried was "Sunny Side of Life," a song they had sung on the radio for more than a year. After little more than a verse and chorus, Oberstein burst into the

The Blue Sky Boys, Earl Bolick (left) and Bill Bolick, 1962 (John Edwards Memorial Foundation Records [20001], Southern Folklife Collection at Wilson Special Collections Library, University of North Carolina at Chapel Hill).

studio and interrupted them, admitting that their sound was "nothing like the Monroes" and adding, "I think it's something that will sell." He then proceeded to record them, right on the spot. In addition to "Sunny Side of Life," they waxed nine other songs which would help write a new chapter in the history of recorded country music.

After the brothers finished recording, they had to come up with a name to use on the records. The most recent name they had used was the Blue Ridge Hillbillies, which was given to them by J.W. Fincher of Crazy Water Crystals, their sponsor at WGST in Atlanta. Since Homer Sherrill, along with Shorty and Mack, had assumed that name when they took over the Bolicks' slot on the radio, it was no longer available. They suggested the Bolick Brothers, but Oberstein said there were already too many names with the word "brothers" in it. As a compromise, they took the name Blue Sky Boys, after "The Land of the Sky," which refers to the area in and around Asheville, North Carolina. Although born and raised in Hickory, some seventy-five miles east of Asheville, they had played the year before over Asheville radio WWNC, along with Homer Sherrill and the Good Coffee Boys, when they were sponsored by the J.F. Goodson Coffee Company.

Just as Eli Oberstein had predicted, the close harmony singing and the Bolicks' uncanny ability to blend their voices made these first Bluebird records a success. By October 1936 they were called back by Victor to record twelve more sides. With their first royalty check, in November 1936, they were able to purchase an automobile, which they used to travel to numerous radio stations and shows.

Just as their career was really taking off, the Blue Sky Boys had the rug pulled out from under them when they were both drafted for World War II. It was almost five years before they could resume their music career. By then country music had changed and the Bolick brothers' plaintive style of singing old songs and ballads with just mandolin and guitar was no longer in fashion. In 1951, with RCA pushing solo acts like Eddy Arnold, the Bolick brothers decided to retire from music.

Although they later reunited to play for a limited number of folk and bluegrass festivals and to record on several occasions in the late 1950s and early '60s, the career of the Blue Sky Boys was essentially over. But far from over was the impact their music would have on old-time country and bluegrass music for years to come. Many careful listeners point to the Blue Sky Boys as among the finest harmony singers the music has ever produced.

Their recordings preserved a body of songs that would likely otherwise have been lost. These songs included a large number of gospel hymns, as well as sentimental songs derived from English ballads, mountain folk songs, and Tin Pan Alley tunes like their 1938 theme song, "Are You from Dixie," which was written in 1915 by Jack Yellen and George L. Cobb. By anyone's count, scores of songs recorded by the Blue Sky Boys have been sung by countless bluegrass musicians. Their legacy will stand as long as people revere the songs of the tragic side of life.

The above is partly based on a personal interview I had with Bill Bolick at his home in Hickory, North Carolina, in 1977.

Curly and Jack, the Shelton Brothers

Among the favorite pastimes in the mountains of North Carolina was music. They say fiddlers and banjo players were so numerous they practically fell out of the trees when it rained. Although banjos and fiddles were common, it is said that a guitar was a rare and precious commodity in the early days. Anyone who could play one was awarded the respect due only to a preacher or a moonshiner.

Accordingly, it was a special day in the Shelton household when Charlie Pack came to visit. Charlie always brought with him a black Stella guitar. In the evenings Charlie would chord the Stella and sing the old-time songs, sometimes accompanied by Manly Shelton on fiddle. These special evenings of music making did not go unnoticed by the young Shelton boys, Manly Jr. and Carson. They watched Charlie with an intense fascination, as if a miracle was unfolding before their eyes.

By copying the chords that Charlie played, the Shelton boys began learning on their father's beat-up guitar that had been left abandoned in the corner. This guitar proved more of an obstacle than an aid, as the strings were "this high" off the fretboard. Noting their interest, Manly Shelton finally ordered his sons a better guitar from Sears Roebuck.

The Shelton Brothers, Jack (left) and Curly, undated but likely 1940s (courtesy Jack Shelton).

Soon the Shelton home was filled with guitar music, and before long the boys tried their luck at harmony singing. After school they could be found with their ears glued to the family radio listening to WWNC (Wonderful Western North Carolina). Among their favorite groups was the JFG Coffee Boys, which included Bill and Earl Bolick. From recordings of the Sons of the Pioneers they learned "Way Out There," which contained a difficult harmony yodel.

Excited by the progress they were making with their music, the Shelton boys entered and won an amateur contest at White Rock School, in nearby Madison County. Also entertaining that evening were cowboy-style singer and guitarist Fred Kirby and fiddler Tiny Dodson. As part of the prize for winning the contest, the Shelton brothers were given the chance to play over WWNC in Asheville. As luck would have it, Kirby and Dodson, who were also performing over WWNC, were breaking up, so Dodson joined forces with the Sheltons. Tiny, a robust and jovial man and a nimble fiddler, renamed both brothers. Manly became "Jack" and Carson "Curly." Their new names stuck.

Before going their separate ways in 1938, Kirby and Dodson did a final recording session for Decca in Charlotte as Fred Kirby's Carolina Boys. The Shelton brothers, who were invited along, had recently traded instrumental and vocal parts. With their young voices changing, Jack went down to lead and Curly up to tenor. Curly switched to mandolin and Jack to guitar. It was with this arrangement that they held a successful audition for Decca.

Among the six sides they recorded in a hotel room with two microphones were "Two Little Rosebuds," "Unfriendly World," and "I'd Rather Have Jesus." The recordings came out under the name Tiny Dodson's Circle-B Boys. The fact that their names weren't featured did not seem to bother Jack or Curly, as they were just beginning their career and were still teenagers. A probable explanation is that Decca already had a successful act billed as the Shelton Brothers (Bob and Joe). Those brothers recorded extensively between 1935 and the late 1940s. Born in Texas and having changed their stage name from Attlesey, they were initially teamed with fiddler Curly Fox.

In late 1939 or early 1940, Tiny Dodson, Curly, and Jack moved to radio WFBC in Greenville, South Carolina, and worked there for some time. After "playing out" the Greenville area they relocated to WOPI, a 250-watt station in Bristol, Virginia. Playing on the radio barn dance held on Saturday night, they used the broadcasts to advertise shows in schoolhouses throughout the area. The station was not powerful enough to reach a wide audience, so their stay in Bristol lasted only six to eight months. The Shelton brothers moved back to Flag Pond and Tiny to his home in Walnut Cove, North Carolina.

Before long, however, Tiny contacted the Sheltons with the news that Wade Mainer and Zeke Morris had parted company and that Wade was looking to start another band. They auditioned for Wade in Winston-Salem, North Carolina; were promptly hired; and played that area with him and Tiny.

From there the band, now known as Wade Mainer and the Sons of the Mountaineers, moved to Asheville and WWNC. They were soon packing schoolhouses and theaters. A typical show included Wade singing lead and playing the banjo in a two-finger style, Tiny on fiddle and singing bass, Curly playing mandolin and singing tenor, and Jack on guitar and baritone. The Sheltons also did duets, and Tiny and Wade did a comedy routine. Note that this band had the exact vocal harmony and instrumentation (minus the bass) that would later be called bluegrass music.

In early 1941 folklorist Alan Lomax invited Wade Mainer and the Sons of the Mountaineers to Washington to play for President Roosevelt. Billed as a concert of old-time music, the program also included Burl Ives and the Golden Gate Quartet. In September of that year Jack and Curly journeyed to Atlanta, Georgia, with Wade to record four sides on Victor's Bluebird series. Among them was a duet with Jack and Curly singing "The Precious Jewel," a cover of a song Roy Acuff had recorded in 1940.

Just before the U.S. entered World War II in December 1941, the band moved to WNOX in Knoxville, Tennessee. After Pearl Harbor, Wade quit and returned to North Carolina. Wade's older brother had earlier taken Tiny Dodson's place on fiddle, so the band was renamed J.E. Mainer and the Sons of the Mountaineers. It was then that Curly, the oldest of the Shelton brothers, was ordered to report for induction. With Curly's departure, the band members went their separate ways.

Jack moved back to Asheville and WWNC, joining Carl Story and the Rambling Mountaineers, who had taken over the spot left open when Wade Mainer and the Sheltons moved to Knoxville. Story's guitar player, Ed McMahan, had just been called into the service, so Jack Shelton took his place. Also in the band at that time were Dudley Watson, singing tenor and playing guitar, and Johnnie Whisnant, who was known as "Half Pint," playing five-string banjo. Jack stayed with Carl for about a year, until he too was called to the war.

Jack served in the army until 1946. Carl Story wrote to Jack several times while Jack was overseas about forming a band after the war. When it was finally over, Carl landed a spot on WNOX in Knoxville, Jack Shelton's old stomping grounds. Joining Carl were Jack and Curly Shelton, Claude Boone on guitar, and Hoke Jenkins on banjo; Carl played fiddle. Maintaining a heavy schedule, the band played every day in schoolhouses and theaters and on the Saturday night radio barn dance. By this time the band members were each receiving a salary of $40 a week for playing on the *Mid-Day Merry-Go-Round*.

After playing with Carl Story for about a year, the band broke up. Jack and Curly and Hoke Jenkins went to Raleigh, North Carolina. Joining them there was Lonnie Glosson on harmonica. After a short stay in Raleigh, the Sheltons returned to Asheville and got a program started on WWNC. A young fiddler by the name of Benny Sims came to the radio station to meet the Sheltons and persuaded them to hire him on as fiddler. Also playing with the band was Chuck Henderson on banjo and Carl Smith (later to become a legendary country music singer) playing bass and singing solos.

In 1949 the band moved to WCYB in Bristol, with Wiley Morris taking Carl Smith's place. The band worked out of Bristol for about a year, until a knee injury put Jack in the hospital, breaking up the band. Disgruntled with the music business, Curly followed many Southerners to Detroit to work in the automobile industry.

When Jack got out of the hospital, he received a call from Benny Sims, who had been playing fiddle with Flatt and Scruggs. Tired of the road, Sims persuaded Jack to take over as bandleader on the *Mid-Day Merry-Go-Round*, along with Fred Smith on guitar, Speedy Krise on Dobro, and Sims on fiddle. Calling themselves Jack Shelton and the Greene County Boys, the band stayed in Knoxville for four years. After it became apparent that they had once again "played out" the territory, the band decided to call it quits for good.

Jack, especially, was tired of moving to yet another station and could see "the handwriting on the wall," as he tells it. Unable to secure a major recording contract, the band was dependent on radio to advertise their shows and spread their name. With TV coming into prominence and live radio shows on the decline, it seemed like an uphill struggle to keep a band together and working.

Faced with these changes in the entertainment world, and relishing some stability, Jack returned to Asheville to take a regular job at WLOS-TV. Curly died of a heart attack in 1968 at the age of fifty-two, having returned from Detroit to Asheville. Unlike many performers who were forced out of professional music by the changes in the music industry, Jack was not bitter about the way his career turned out. He still keeps his guitar under the bed and promises one day to get his fingers toughened up enough to where he can get back to singing and playing again. I, for one, am going to hold him to that promise. [After working for thirty-seven years for WLOS-TV, Jack died in Asheville in 2016 at the age of ninety-five.]

The above is based on a personal interview with Jack Shelton at his home in Asheville, North Carolina, in 1983. It originally appeared in Bluegrass Unlimited, *May 1984.*

Fiddling

Thicker'n Fiddlers in Hell

Throughout its long and spicy history, the fiddle has been both loved and loathed. It was a lone fiddler who held sway at community dances, the most popular form of entertainment in early America. Without the fiddler, there simply was no dance. A pioneer community that could boast of a fiddler was the envy of all, and a skilled fiddler was always in demand for community gatherings such as barn dances, log rollings, cornshuckings and bean stringings. Fiddle contests existed as early as 1736, when fiddlers in Hanover County, Virginia, competed against each other, with the winner taking home a fine violin. In some frontier communities, fiddlers were held in higher esteem than doctors, lawyers, and politicians.

But in a strange twist of fate, fiddle players were also among the most despised members of society. Fire-and-brimstone preachers accused fiddlers of walking hand in hand with the devil himself. From many a Sunday morning pulpit, congregations were warned that "the devil rides the fiddle bow" and that the fiddle was "the devil's stalking horse." Faced with banishment from the church, some distraught fiddlers were driven to burn their fiddles or bust them over a white oak stump.

Even in death it was said that fiddlers were seldom allowed to enter either heaven or hell but were instead sent to a place called Fiddlers Green. According to Ozark folklorist Vance Randolph, Fiddlers Green was to be found seven miles on the other side of Hell and originally reserved for fiddlers, but later, sailors, peddlers, tinkers, a few cowpokes, and even a thin smattering of old soldiers were admitted.

A fiddle came to be called "the devil's box." In some ways, fiddlers had only themselves to blame for their sullied reputation. Their penchant for strong drink while playing for rowdy dances certainly didn't help their standing in the community. Nor did their superstition of keeping a rattlesnake rattle inside their fiddle make them popular with the genteel set. Even worse, some fiddlers defied America's work ethic and "fiddled their time away." A casual look at some common and not so common expressions will show you that fiddlers have had a somewhat sullied reputation:

The devil's riding horse (a fiddle)
To fiddle (to trifle or make mindless hand movements)
Fiddle on a broomstick (nonsense)
Fiddlededee (nonsense)
Those who dance must pay the fiddler (suffer the consequence)
Drunk as a fiddler's clerk
Drunk as a fiddler's bitch (even drunker)

Wayne Erbsen and Barbara Swell at the Zebulon B. Vance Birthplace, Weaverville, North Carolina, ca. 1995 (photograph by Martin Fox).

Adding to the fiddler's unsavory reputation is his long association with the devil. In the book *Popular Beliefs and Superstitions of North Carolina*, we discover the best method of learning the fiddle: "Before sunrise on five mornings, take a fiddle and go into the country until you come to one of the main roads or to a crossroads. On the fifth morning you will meet a man also carrying a fiddle. He will teach you to play. He is the devil."

If you lived in Illinois and wanted to play the fiddle, here's what you would do: "If you

Doc Hoppas, ca. 1945 (John Edwards Memorial Foundation Records [20001], Southern Folklife Collection at Wilson Special Collections Library, University of North Carolina at Chapel Hill).

want to learn to play the fiddle, go on a dark night at 12:00 o'clock to the forks of a road. Sit down with your fiddle over your shoulder just like you were going to play. While you are sitting there, a big black snake will crawl by you with his head up in the air. Don't get scared. The snake will go up the road and turn around and a big man with a fiddle will come back down the road and stand by you and play three or four pieces on his fiddle. Then he will disappear, and you can go home and play any piece on the fiddle you want. I knew a man in Missouri that did this, and he was the best fiddler in the state."

The popular fiddle tune "Devil's Dream" was supposedly taught to a fiddler by the devil himself. We can only guess at the origin of such American fiddle tunes as "Devil in the Strawstack."

Throughout history, fiddlers not only cavorted with the devil but also had numerous unpleasant encounters with the hangman. Folklorist Alan Lomax wrote that Wilkes County, North Carolina, native Tom Dula apparently played his fiddle while sitting on his coffin on the way to the gallows, while singing the ballad that was later called "Tom Dooley."

Going back in history, we find many references to fiddlers who played their last tune just before the hangman clinched the knot around their neck. In a 1965 article titled "Fiddler's Farewell," folklorist D.K. Wilgus describes how numerous fiddlers played their last tune on the gallows. The first in a long line of hanged fiddlers was a Scottish gypsy named James McPherson, who was executed on November 16, 1700. Just before his execution he played a "rant" or dirge on his favorite violin and offered it to anyone in the crowd that would think well of him. Since there were no takers, McPherson busted the fiddle and tossed it into the freshly dug grave that was waiting next to the gallows. A similar tale says that the condemned man who played the tune now known as "McPherson's Farewell" promised to give his fiddle to anyone who would play the tune at his funeral. When no one came forward, he dashed the fiddle over the hangman's head.

For many years I've been playing a tune called "Hangman's Reel," which I learned from the late fiddler Albert Hash, of Whitetop, Virginia. According to legend, a fiddler was about to be hanged. While waiting for his execution, he could see workers constructing the gallows outside his jailhouse cell. Just then the prisoner noticed an old fiddle hanging on the jailhouse wall. He called the jailer over and claimed to be the best fiddler in those parts. After a heated argument, they made a wager. If the condemned man would get up on the gallows before his execution and prove beyond a shadow of a doubt that he was the best fiddler, he would be set free. Otherwise, he would get the noose. The jailer gave the prisoner a fiddle to practice on and left him alone in his cell.

Unbeknownst to the jailer, the condemned man had never touched a fiddle in his life. Deciding this was his best chance at freedom, he practiced all night. When morning came, the prisoner was escorted to the gallows where he expertly played the tune now known as "Hangman's Reel." Unfortunately, history forgot to record if he was set free or instead received the "suspended sentence" he so richly deserved. Nevertheless, it makes a damn good story!

Eck Robertson—Master Fiddler

In 1877 Thomas Edison invented the phonograph. By the next year he had established the Edison Speaking Phonograph Company to sell record players in furniture

Eck Robertson, Amarillo, Texas, ca. 1924 (John Edwards Memorial Foundation Records [20001], Southern Folklife Collection at Wilson Special Collections Library, University of North Carolina at Chapel Hill).

stores across America. Improvements by such inventors as Alexander Graham Bell and Emile Berliner helped to make "gramophones" coveted items for home entertainment. Sales of records went to four million units in 1900, up to thirty million in 1909, and more than one hundred million by 1920. By 1922 consumers could purchase such hit records as "Way Down Yonder in New Orleans," "Carolina in the Morning," "I Wish I Could Shimmy Like My Sister Kate" and "Somebody Stole My Gal."

But in the early years of the twentieth century, people who liked their music on the rustic side found it impossible to purchase phonograph records of old-time fiddling or stringband music. This was because in those days record companies were mainly located in New York City, and they simply did not realize there was a market for the music of rural America. All this changed in 1922, when into the New York City offices of Victor Talking Machine Records walked Eck Robertson and Henry Gilliland. But wait; we're getting ahead of ourselves.

The story actually begins in the late 1880s, when Alexander Campbell "Eck" Robertson was growing up in north central Texas. Every one of his five brothers and two sisters played music and sang. Both of his grandfathers, his uncles, and his father competed at local and regional fiddlers conventions in the late nineteenth and early twentieth century.

Eck later claimed that he taught himself to play the fiddle before he ever saw one. As a kid he killed a tomcat, tanned its hide, and stretched the skin over a long-necked gourd to make himself a fiddle. One of his brothers traded a pig for a genuine factory-made fiddle, and Eck was soon playing that. Eck later recounted his innate ability to play tunes on the fiddle. "It was just natural with me to play them. I didn't have to learn them.... I already knew them. I mostly improved every old hoedown tune that was ever put out. I generally played better than anyone else, [and had] better arrangements of the tunes" (Earl V. Spielman, "An Interview with Eck Robertson," *JEMF Quarterly* 28, Winter 1972).

In 1903 sixteen-year-old Eck decided to become a professional musician. He soon left home and joined a traveling medicine show. Over the next several years he worked with a half dozen different medicine shows. In 1906 Eck and his new wife, Netty, started traveling around Texas and adjacent states, playing fiddle and piano in silent-movie houses. Never shy about promoting himself, Eck was a superb showman who billed himself as "The Cowboy Fiddler" and outfitted himself from head to toe in the style of a western cowpuncher.

When interviewed in the mid–1960s by Earl Spielman, Eck remembered, "I was the most popular dang fiddler ever was on the road. I could book every dang town I came to; it didn't make any difference where it was. There were lots of places where they turned musicians down, but I came right along and booked them."

After honing his fiddle chops to a fine edge, Eck started winning the fiddlers conventions that were held all over the Southwest. Competition at these fiddle contests was notoriously fierce, and winning was no mean trick. One story had Eck in a showdown playoff with John Wills, the father of legendary fiddler Bob Wills. Legend has it that in a last-ditch effort to give himself an edge, Eck broke off a piece of a wooden match and stuck it under one of his strings, so that he could bow three strings at once. The trick worked and Eck was victorious.

At another popular fiddlers convention held in Munday, Texas, John Wills and Eck were running neck and neck, so the judges decided that the pair should play a run-off. This was a prestigious convention, and a lot of prize money was at stake. Eck was up first, and he likely played "Beaumont Rag," a number he often performed when competition was stiff. John Wills got up next and played "Lost Indian," his lucky tune that had helped him win many fiddle competitions. When John reached a certain point in the tune, he let out a high-pitched cry that he held for what seemed like several minutes. Of course, when he finished fiddling, the audience went wild, and the judges awarded him first prize. When Eck was leaving the festival grounds someone hollered out to him, "Eck, did John out-fiddle you?" Eck shot right back with "Hell, no! He didn't out-fiddle me. That damned old man Wills out-hollered me."

In addition to competing at fiddlers conventions, by 1919 Eck started attending reunions of Confederate veterans. In June of 1922 Eck traveled to a Confederate reunion in Richmond, Virginia. It was perhaps there that he met, or was reacquainted with, seventy-six-year-old Henry Gilliland (1845–1924), who had fought in the Civil War and was later an Indian fighter and justice of the peace. The pair decided to travel to New York to try to convince Victor to let them make records. They were apparently undaunted by the fact that no record company had ever shown the slightest interest in recording old-time fiddle music.

Part of the reason that Eck and Henry decided to make the trip to New York was that Henry was acquainted with a lawyer named Martin W. Littleton, who did occasional legal work for Victor. He invited the musicians to stay with him after they arrived in New York and promised to introduce them to the people at the office of Victor Records. And that's exactly what happened.

The staff at Victor must have been flabbergasted when Eck and Henry showed up unannounced at their Manhattan office, with Robertson and Gilliland both dressed head to toe in full cowboy regalia. Trying to dispatch the pair with impunity, one of the Victor officials bustled into the waiting room and said to Eck, "Young man, get your fiddle out and start off a tune." Eck responded by breaking into a rousing version of "Sallie Gooden," a tune he had used to win many a fiddle contest in Texas. He later recalled, "I didn't get to play half of 'Sallie Gooden; he just threw up his hands and stopped me. He said, 'By Ned, that's fine! Come back in the morning at 9:00 o'clock and we'll make a test record.'"

The next day, June 30, 1922, Eck and Henry returned and recorded "Arkansaw Traveler," "Turkey in the Straw," "Forked Deer" and "Apple Blossom." Eck alone returned the next day and recorded "Sallie Gooden" and several other tunes. With the September 1, 1922, two-sided issue of "Sallie Gooden" and "Arkansaw [sic] Traveler," Eck and Henry had truly broken new ground. The release marked the initial foray into country music by a reluctant record company.

In retrospect, Eck's performance of "Sallie Gooden" justly deserves credit for being not only one of the first recordings in country music but also one of the very best. Even today, some one hundred years later, few fiddlers have come up to the level of Eck's fiddling. Bill Monroe himself paid homage to Eck's skill when he rushed ace Oklahoma fiddler Byron Berline into the studio in 1967 and recorded "Sally Goodin." Himself a renowned contest fiddler, Byron showed his own debt to Eck by playing a slightly souped-up rendition of the original 1922 version. Even today, virtually every fiddler who plays this standard fiddle piece in some way owes a debt to Eck Robertson. But even more than his influence on the tune itself, Eck set an extremely high standard that fiddlers ever since have tried to follow.

The stories behind "Sally Goodin" are almost as good as the tune itself. Eck Robertson once recalled, "Long ago there lived a beautiful maiden. She sent word to all the lands around about for fiddlers to come together and have a big fiddlers contest. And to the one who played the tune that suited her the best, she'd give her heart and hand. One young man won the contest; his name was Gooden. And the tune thereafter was called 'Sallie Gooden.'"

North Carolina musician Bruce Green collected a different story about "Sally Goodin" from Hiram Stamper, a fiddler from Knott County, Kentucky. Hiram was born in 1893 and learned to play from several Civil War veterans, who told him the story. The tune originally had several names, including "Boatin' Up Sandy" and "The Old Bell Ewe and the Little Speckled Wether." The name was changed during the Civil War by several soldiers who were attached to John Hunt Morgan's unit of irregulars. Apparently, the company set up camp on the Big Sandy River in Pike County, Kentucky. Nearby was a boarding house that was run by a kindhearted woman named Sally Goodin. She went out of her way to be kind to the soldiers by allowing them to camp and play their fiddles on her property. In appreciation of her hospitality, the solders renamed the tune "Sally Goodin" in her honor.

Even though the origin of the name of "Sally Goodin" may be hotly debated, one thing is crystal clear. The powerful way that Eck Robertson fiddled it on Victor Records in 1922 will endure for all time.

Fiddlin' John Carson

It wasn't the popcorn at New York's Palace Theater that spring day in 1923 that got Atlanta businessman Polk Brockman thinking. Instead, it was the newsreel he watched of a Virginia fiddlers convention that made him scribble this note on a piece of paper: "Record Fiddlin' John Carson." Seconds before he reached in his pocket for his pen, Brockman recalled why he had come to New York on this most recent trip.

As the owner of several furniture stores in the Atlanta area, Brockman also sold what were then called "race" records (featuring Black artists) as well as the phonographs to play them on. He was visiting New York to work out the details with Okeh Records to distribute their recordings. While he was in the Okeh offices, the manager asked if there was enough talent in the Atlanta area to justify bringing down a mobile recording unit. For the moment Brockman couldn't think of anyone but promised to think about it. When he saw the rolling footage of the fiddlers convention, things clicked in Brockman's mind and he remembered Atlanta's well-known fiddler, Fiddlin' John Carson.

Fiddlin' John was certainly an unforgettable character. By the time he was eleven years old he was fiddling for tips on the streets of Coopertown, Tennessee. As an adult, he could be counted on to be at the big Atlanta fiddlers convention that was held once a year. In 1922 Fiddlin' John added to his regional fame when he started to broadcast over the South's first radio station, WSB in Atlanta.

On the strength of Brockman's suggestion, Okeh Records sent Ralph Peer and several engineers to Atlanta in June of 1923. They transformed a vacant building on Nassau Street into an impromptu recording studio. During an audition before Peer, Carson did his trick of playing fiddle and singing at the same time. Peer was not impressed. He liked Fiddlin' John's fiddling well enough but thought his singing sounded "pluperfect awful" (Peer may have been referring to the recording quality).

Brockman persuaded Peer that Carson's singing would go over just as well on record as it did in person. The clincher was Brockman's order of 500 records on the spot, even before Fiddlin' John struck a lick. For his recording Carson chose Will S. Hays's "Little Old Log Cabin in the Lane" and "The Old Hen Cackled and the Rooster's Going to Crow." Still having his doubts, Peer had the 500 records shipped to Brockman without even bothering to give them a catalog number.

On the day the records arrived, Fiddlin' John was to attend a local fiddlers convention. In a stroke of genius, Brockman loaded the records into his car; with Fiddlin' John hawking records from the stage, he managed to sell the entire box in short order. When Brockman placed another order for records the next day, Peer promptly gave the releases a number and invited Carson to record more songs in their New York studio that coming November. Fiddlin' John was now on his way.

The success of Fiddlin' John's initial release was a milestone in country music. Up until that point, it was possible to purchase a phonograph of light classical, marching bands, minstrel performers, and comedy.

Fiddlin' John Carson, ca. 1924 (John Edwards Memorial Foundation Records [20001], Southern Folklife Collection at Wilson Special Collections Library, University of North Carolina at Chapel Hill).

What you could not buy were records of down-to-earth, old-time music. It remained for Fiddlin' John to demonstrate the potential market for that. Once the floodgates were open, there was no shutting them. For this, Fiddlin' John's legacy is assured.

Fiddlin' Arthur Smith

Thunderstruck. What better word can be used to describe the reaction of fans of old-time fiddle music when they first tuned into the Grand Ole Opry and heard the fiddling of Arthur Smith coming out of their radios? From the time he first stepped up to the WSM microphone in December 1927, the world of Southern fiddling would never be the same.

Fiddling

From left: Sam McGee, Fiddlin' Arthur Smith, and Kirk McGee, ca. 1950 (courtesy Chance Barham).

Who was this man that set fiddling so much on its ear? Born April 10, 1898, near Bold Springs, Tennessee, Arthur Smith got his first fiddle when his young wife, Nettie, sold enough chickens to buy him a Sears Roebuck mail-order instrument for $6.50. After his initial solo performance on the Opry, he went on to become a regular on the show, first with his cousin, Homer Smith, and then with Sam and Kirk McGee as Fiddlin' Arthur Smith and His Dixieliners. Eventually Smith played and recorded with the Delmore Brothers and toured widely with country-western star Jimmy Wakely.

Perhaps it was Jim Shumate, who was Flatt and Scruggs's first fiddler, who best described the impact of Smith's fiddling: "He was a genius, a flat genius, when it comes to playing the fiddle. He fiddled stuff like nobody else you ever heard. Smooth ... he didn't fiddle a whole lot of fancy stuff; he was flat down to earth. He didn't do a lot of fancy, show-off, kick-up-the-dust stuff, but when he fiddled a tune, it was fiddled just like it ought to be."

Jim Shumate was far from the only fiddler to come under Arthur Smith's spell. In fact, Smith single-handedly changed the style of countless fiddlers who faithfully tuned in to his Saturday night performances on the Grand Ole Opry, bought his RCA Bluebird records, or were lucky enough to see him in live performance.

Before Arthur Smith came along, a country fiddler's main role in old-time music was playing for square dances. Except for playing a few waltzes, fiddlers mainly played what were called "hoedowns." Their fiddling was propelled along with a rhythmic bow stroke known as the "shuffle." To play this shuffle, the fiddler would make his bow go long-short-short or ONE, two, three, with the accent on the one. This heavy, rhythmic accent played by the bow arm goes back to the early days of frontier fiddling, when the fiddler literally played the entire night for a square dance, backed up (or fortified) by nothing more than a jug of moonshine. By the time other instruments like guitar, banjo, and bass began providing rhythm behind the fiddle, the shuffle was so embedded in the tunes themselves that most old-time fiddlers maintained it in their music.

Arthur Smith changed all that. He let the back-up instruments provide the basic rhythm, while he simply glided along on top with the melody. Although it sounds simple enough, this was a revolutionary new approach to fiddling. It meant that Smith's music

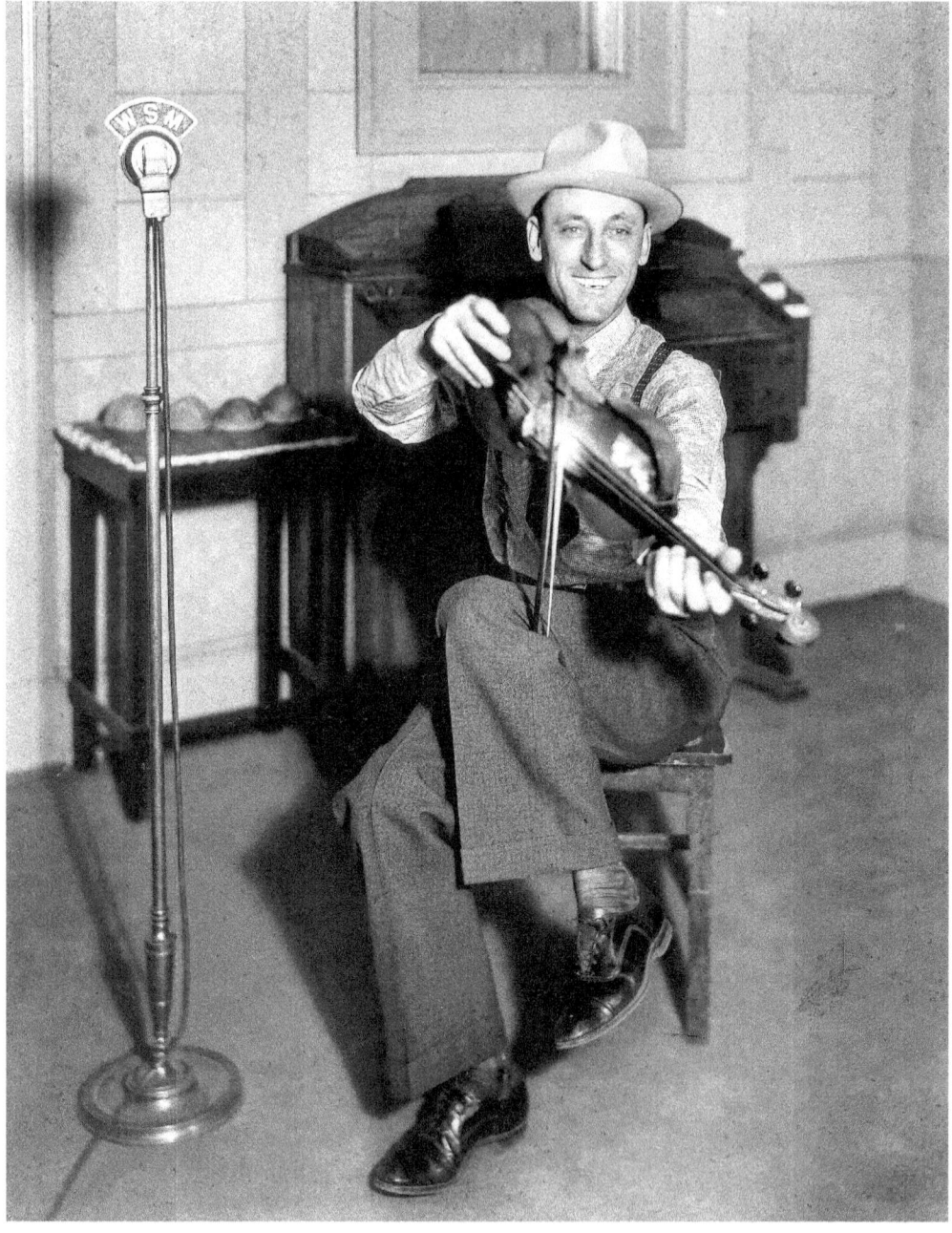

Fiddlin' Arthur Smith, ca. 1940 (courtesy County Records).

was designed not for dancing but for listening. His tunes became known as "breakdowns" rather than "hoedowns."

Smith's left hand was another key to his unique approach. Whereas most old-time fiddlers pumped out the tunes with their bow arm, often using a separate bow stroke for each note, Smith developed what has been called the "longbow style." This meant that he used the full length of his bow to play a series of cascading notes, with the fingers of his left hand doing most of the work rather than his bow arm.

Even as country fiddlers were reeling from the impact of hearing Smith's music, he was introducing yet more techniques that changed fiddling. Along with African American fiddlers, he was among the first to include blues in his fiddling. He accomplished this by using frequent slides, both up and down. He combined single notes with chords, which fiddlers call "double stops." He even introduced the technique of moving or sliding these chords from one position to another. Smith's impact on Southern fiddling was profound. Few players escaped his influence or wanted to. Bluegrass fiddlers owe a special debt to Smith. Without exception, all credit Smith as a major stylistic influence.

It's an interesting coincidence that Smith was indirectly involved in Bill Monroe's first recording session with the Blue Grass Boys. On October 7, 1940, Smith's last session

From left: Sam McGee, Fiddlin' Arthur Smith, and Kirk McGee, ca. 1942. Smith looked sullen because he hated the idea that old-time music was played by hillbillies. He was trying to elevate fiddlers to a higher level (John Edwards Memorial Foundation Records [20001], Southern Folklife Collection at Wilson Special Collections Library, University of North Carolina at Chapel Hill).

for RCA Victor's Bluebird subsidiary was set up in Atlanta, but he had no musicians to back him. Bill Monroe and his new band, the Blue Grass Boys, were there to record the same day. With Bill's permission, Smith used Clyde Moody on guitar, Bill "Cousin Wilbur" Wesbrooks on bass, and Tommy Magness on second fiddle to produce eight classics, including "K.C. Stomp," "Smith's Rag," "Peacock Rag," "Crazy Blues," and "Bill Cheatham."

Besides fiddling, Fiddlin' Arthur Smith loved to fish. One time while fishing on Trace Creek, about five miles out of Waverly, Tennessee, he got a little impatient and decided to get his limit quick by using a stick of dynamite. To mask the sound of the explosion, he tried to time it so the charge would go off at the same time that a big freight train rumbled over the huge trestle. As luck would have it, the charge didn't go off as planned, and the train was long gone by the time the dynamite finally exploded, announcing to everybody in the county that Fiddlin' Arthur Smith was fishing again.

Note that a perennial source of confusion to country music history buffs is the existence of three influential Arthur Smiths: "Fiddlin' Arthur Smith" (1898–1971), songwriter Arthur Q. Smith (1909–1963), and Arthur "Guitar Boogie" Smith (1921–2014).

Although I never did meet Fiddlin' Arthur Smith, I was able to interview his son, Ernest Smith, who played and sang on my Country Roots *radio show in the 1980s. As Ernest sang, I attempted to play fiddle in the style of his legendary father. Good luck with that!*

Jim Shumate

It's a long drive from Raleigh, North Carolina, to Nashville, Tennessee. Before Interstate 40, driving west from Raleigh meant winding through such towns as Siler City, Mocksville, Statesville, Hickory, and Old Fort. Bill Monroe is no stranger to that road. [This article was written in 1978. Monroe died in 1996.] In the forty-odd years he has been performing, he has worn out many a set of tires driving that road. Being a bluegrass musician means accepting show dates spread out all over the country; it never seems to matter how many miles lie between. To pass the time, Monroe often tunes to the nearest radio outlet in hopes of catching some good country music.

One day in early 1943 Monroe chanced to pick up WHKY, broadcasting from downtown Hickory, North Carolina. It was noontime, and Don Walker was doing a live show with his Blue Ridge Boys. Typical of many country bands during that period there were two guitars, a mandolin, a fiddle, and a banjo. Along with the usual comedy routines and skits, the show featured both sacred and secular songs, interspersed with fiddle tunes like "Katy Hill" and "Grey Eagle." It was the fiddling that especially caught Monroe's ear.

Before the program was over, Walker had introduced all the band members, and Monroe did not forget the name of the fiddler: Jim Shumate. Not long after Monroe reached Nashville, he put in a call to the twenty-year-old musician. Howdy Forrester, who had been Monroe's fiddler, had just given his notice. It was wartime, and the navy had plans for Forrester. Suddenly needing a fiddle player, Monroe chose Shumate.

"One day I got a call from Bill Monroe. 'Course all my life I'd always wanted to be at the Grand Ole Opry. That was my idol. I'd listened to those guys ever since I first

From left: Jim Turner, Ralph Pennington, Jim Shumate, and Don Walker, WHKY Radio, Hickory, North Carolina, ca. 1943.

started playing the fiddle but never dreamed I'd ever be there. So the telephone rang, and a voice said, 'This is Bill Monroe.' That shook me up, you know. He said, 'Now you play the fiddle, don't you? You've got Howdy Forrester, Tommy Magness, and three or four others all mixed up together. If you play that type of fiddle, that's what I want.'"

That's how Monroe, in his typically indirect way, offered Shumate the job as fiddler with the Blue Grass Boys. Within days, Shumate packed his bags, tucked his fiddle under his arm, and caught the bus to Nashville.

Monroe had only heard Shumate fiddle a few tunes over the radio before hiring him, and he was mistaken in thinking that Shumate had learned from Howdy Forrester or Tommy Magness. Shumate's real influence was Fiddlin' Arthur Smith. "I learned off of Arthur Smith and the Dixieliners, the king of the fiddlers. He was what enthused me to want to play the fiddle. I fiddle a lot of his tunes today; I never have gotten away from it."

"I never got to see Smith in person but one time. It was at the Grand Ole Opry when he was playing fiddle with Jimmy Wakely. I admired him all my life, from the time I was a little shaver on up. He was considerably older than I was. I didn't even get to talk to him. The dressing room was so full, so many people crowding around. Jimmy Wakely was a pretty big movie star at that time, and I just got close enough to see Smith."

"He was a genius, a flat genius, when it comes to playing the fiddle. He fiddled stuff like nobody else, like nobody you ever heard. Smooth … he didn't fiddle a whole lot of fancy stuff; he was flat down to earth. Like Earl [Scruggs] on the five-string. Earl don't play a lot of fancy banjo, but what he plays is right; it's there. And that's the way Smith's fiddling' was. He didn't do a lot of fancy, show-off, kick-up-the-dust stuff, but when he fiddled a tune, it was fiddled just like it ought to be."

"When I got to the Opry [with Monroe], Curly Fox helped me a lot too. Curly was a real good fiddler, one of the best. Curly Fox and Texas Ruby had a program in Nashville at the same time we did. We had a program on the *Checkerboard Jamboree*; it was a network thing. He and Forrester and myself, we'd all work together, and naturally one would show the other what we knew. I learned a lot from Fox. Anything like 'Buckin' Mule' or 'Lee Highway Blues' and stuff like that that I needed to know, why, during the program I'd say, 'Get back here, Fox, I want you to show me something.' And he was very gracious to do it. He's a splendid fellow, and he'd help you in any way he could. Now some people will, and some won't. Some of them say, 'Now I'm Mr. Big, and you can learn like I did, the hard way.' But not Fox, he is a splendid fellow. That's what it's all about, one helpin' another. I don't care who you are, somebody can fiddle stuff that you can't fiddle."

In addition to Bill Monroe on mandolin and Jim Shumate on fiddle, there was a comedian and banjo player in the Blue Grass Boys named Stringbean; his real name was David Akeman. "When I sang bass on the gospel numbers," Shumate recalls, "String would sing the baritone. String and me also did a comedy act together. I worked [as the] straight man. People used

Jim Shumate, ca. 1960 (courtesy the Shumate Family).

to come up to Stringbean after he'd left Monroe and say, 'You know, that Earl Scruggs can really pick a banjo.' String would say, 'Yeah, but you ought to hear both me and him play at the same time.' He never would let himself down, and he never would say that Earl could pick."

"String and I used to room together in the hotel. We buddied around together quite a bit. He was a card. We used to rib him about being stingy. I came in one day, and I guess he'd heard me coming. There was a trash can sittin' there beside the door. Just as I opened the door he had his pocketbook out, shuffling $1 bills out into this trashcan. He said. 'How in the dickens did all them ones get in there?' As I started walking toward the trash can, he dived in there to get 'em."

Playing guitar with the Blue Grass Boys was a young musician and singer from Tennessee by the name of Lester Flatt. Shumate recalls, "Lester had just started working with Bill when I joined the band. He'd been with Bill two or three weeks. He'd been singing tenor with Charlie Monroe. So he left Charlie and went with Bill at the Grand Ole Opry. I had met Lester when he was working with Charlie, so I was glad he was with Bill. We were both rookies."

The fifth member of the Blue Grass "Boys" was Sally Forrester, Howdy's wife, on accordion. Shumate remembers, "We always called her 'Sally Ann.' She did a solo sketch on each program as well as doing the books for us … she was the bookkeeper. Everybody thought that Sally Ann and me were brother and sister. Wherever we went, old boys would get to aggravating us, and she'd say, 'I'll call my brother and straighten you out.' I remember walking in one night and some old guy was harassing her, and she said, 'Here comes my brother, and you better level off, hear?' He came running over, and man, you shoulda heard him apologize. I said, 'I suggest you stay just as far away from her as you can, old friend,' and that was the end of it."

Rounding out the Blue Grass Boys was Andy Boyett, from Florida, on bass. Boyett, whose nickname was "Bijou," was a comedian and worked a blackface act along with Stringbean.

Like many fiddlers before him, Jim Shumate was surprised to discover that Bill Monroe often sang in keys most musicians aren't used to playing. While most singers stick to G, A, D, and C, Monroe prefers B, Bb, and E. Shumate recalls his experiences playing with Monroe: "Oh my! That was the first time I'd ever hit B, Bb, and I'd never played anything in E 'til I got on the stage of the Opry. The one thing about Monroe, you didn't know what to expect. Sometimes when we was getting ready to play a tune, he'd whisper over to me, 'This is going to be in Bb or B natural.'

"With Monroe, you had to be set and ready for anything. But one thing about him, he'd never let me down. He'd always kick it off with the mandolin, which gave me a chance to feel out the first verse and be ready, 'cause he'd always expect me to come in to kick off the second break. I had to do the second break, always. If there was any doubt in my mind, why, there was a look I'd give him, and he'd take it himself, because he knew I wasn't ready. On some of those ones I'd never played, me being a rookie to start with, why, sometimes he'd have to make two rounds before I'd have it figured out."

"I'll never forget the time when I was a rookie with Monroe, new at the job. After we finished the Opry, we was going to play a show in Evansville, Indiana. We loaded up and started out from Nashville. Bill had one of those twelve-passenger buses, a '41 Chevrolet. It would really run. We were sailing along down the road and had a flat tire, so we got out to fix it. It was dark as the dickens. We didn't have a flashlight. I got the extra tire out of the trunk and started to roll it around the bus, and it was heavy. There was some trees chopped down there where we had pulled off the road. And I thought it was a log that I rolled the wheel up against. I pushed and pushed, and that old wheel was heavy. I finally got it on over the log and, just as it got on the other side, Bill yelled from under the bus, 'Who in the dickens is that rollin' that wheel over me?'"

"The one thing about it is you didn't practice with Bill. He'd check you out, I reckon, before he hired you. The only practicing we did that I can remember was one time when there was this particular tune that we were going to do on the Opry on Saturday night. He and Lester worked one out one night. Ernest Tubb had a record that was going pretty good during the war, 'Are You Waiting Just for Me.' Bill and Lester did it on the program one night out on a show, they kicked it up bluegrass style. And it was real good, real pretty. So we went to the hotel room to brush that one up a little bit and use it on the Opry on Saturday night." After Bill Monroe and His Blue Grass Boys' success with "Are You Waiting Just for Me" on the Opry, it wasn't long before other Opry performers started doing the song too.

In addition to introducing new arrangements of country songs to Opry audiences, the Blue Grass Boys also added new techniques in playing the songs. It was Jim Shumate who introduced what is now the standard fiddle kickoff to songs. "Nobody kicked off a tune with the fiddle 'til I started doing it. Lester Flatt got me to kick 'em off with the fiddle. I remember the first one I kicked off, 'Daisy Mae.' That was one of Ernest Tubb's numbers too. So I kicked it off with the fiddle, and from then on, everybody started kickin' off solo songs with the fiddle. I guess I must be the originator of that fiddle kickoff. I never heard nobody do it before. Flatt said he never had either, and after we did it, everybody started doing it. I was talking to Sonny Osborne not long ago, and he said, 'You boys were the originator of that; I never heard nobody do it before.'"

It was in one of the rare practice sessions that Shumate came up with the fiddle kickoff. "Lester had a funny lick on the guitar. Bill would kick it off with the mandolin, but he couldn't turn him in. When Lester would come in to pick up the rhythm to sing, somehow or another they'd miss a beat. I kept standing and listening, and I knew right off the bat what was happening, 'cause one of them was coming in a lick ahead of the other. Flatt turned around and said, 'Jim, see if you can kick that thing off with the fiddle.' He'd been hearing me in the background, I was kinda kickin' it off a little. So I just kicked if off and when I wound it up and turned him in, he hit that thing right on the button. So we kicked it off three more times before we hit the stage, and man, it was right."

"From then on, if Monroe had something that he wanted to kick off, he did. If Lester had one he wanted to sing, Monroe left it usually up to the guys. If he thought we could handle one better the way we wanted to do it, why, that's the way he let us do it. After all, if [one of us] flubbed, he was the one that took the rap."

The life of a Blue Grass Boy in the 1940s often meant being out on the road all week and getting back to Nashville just in

Jim Shumate in the studio of radio WSKY, Hickory, North Carolina, ca. 1948.

time to play the Opry on Saturday night. On one trip, Shumate borrowed Bill's violin while his was being fixed.

Shumate explained, "When we were packing up after a show, we'd take turns loading up the music [instruments] in the bus. My fiddle was small, and it was the last thing to be put in. I'd always just lay it on the bumper. When Bill stuck in his mandolin, he'd always lay my fiddle in with his mandolin on top. He had a little compartment there on the side just for those instruments. I laid Bill's fiddle on the bumper as usual, and Bill was busy doing something else. We got loaded and started to leave. I got in the bus to drive and seesawed around. We had a short place to turn, and I had to back up a little."

"When I backed up, I felt the bus hit something and then I heard it. It made a racket. I said to Bill, 'Did you put the fiddle in the back?' He said, 'No, didn't you put it in?' I said, 'Ah, you gotta be kidding' (we was always ribbing one another and hiding instruments). He said, 'No, I swear, I didn't put it in.' So I told him we better look to see what I run over back there. So, sure enough, when I started moving the bus, it just pushed Bill's fiddle off the bumper, and I ran right over the middle of it. It ground that fiddle up. As luck would have it, Birch Monroe was traveling with us, and he had a case that had two fiddles in it, so I finished out the week with one of his. This old fiddle maker in Nashville put [Bill's] fiddle back together and, man, you couldn't even tell it. It didn't hurt the tone a bit."

During this period of the early '40s, Bill Monroe and His Blue Grass Boys were playing the Opry on Saturday nights. During the week there were appearances at schoolhouses, theaters, clubs, and radio stations. In the summer, Monroe put on tent shows in little towns all over the South.

"There was a tent crew that went along ahead of us," Shumate said. "When we got there, everything was ready to go. We had a big tent that held about three or four thousand people plus bleachers and chairs. They'd put the chairs down out front. They were reserved, and the bleachers were different prices. It was like a carnival, so to speak, except it was under one big roof, one tent. They had a popcorn machine and all that stuff. Lester Flatt's wife [Gladys] operated the popcorn machine. She was one of the Stacey sisters that used to be with Charlie Monroe years ago."

As many a former Blue Grass Boy can testify, working with Monroe meant a lot more than making music. In the forties, the Blue Grass Boys were both a band and a baseball team. Shumate explained how this worked.

"We had quite a ball team back then. We'd get to town early, usually around three or four o'clock. I'd go to the pool hall or somewhere where I could find some young guys and ask them if they had a ball team there in town. Most of them did, and I'd tell 'em who we was and that we had a Blue Grass team and we'd like to challenge 'em. Oh man! They'd get busy and get their gang together and meet us at the field. Sometimes they'd meet us in an hour. We did that all over the country. Sometimes we had good crowds just for a ball game. We had a lot of fun. We played for keeps and had a good team. We had uniforms and everything."

"I played shortstop and was a pretty good hitter too. I could lay the timber to that ball. String pitched; he was a good pitcher. I believe Lester played third base. We had two or three of the tent crew boys that were good ball players. Bill played pitcher, but he was a better hitter than anything else. I've seen him just bust bats and break 'em wide open. They'd just splinter when he'd hit 'em."

What with working tent shows, keeping a band and a baseball team together, plus doing his own booking, Monroe didn't make any recordings in the period between

October 1941 and February 1945. That was also the time when the American Federation of Musicians banned commercial recordings, from August 1942 until—for Bill's label, Columbia—November 1944. Unfortunately, this was when Shumate was working with the Blue Grass Boys.

"We did cut a lot of transcriptions that we used when we'd go out in the towns to ballyhoo the shows. He wrote a lot of stuff and I guess he was just getting it all together. We had our session up to be cut when I left, but it never came through."

By 1945 the members of the Blue Grass Boys had been working together steadily for more than two years. Changes in the band's personnel that fall resulted in a dramatic evolution in Monroe's sound. Many people argue that this event would mark a major turning point in the history of bluegrass. Shumate became a central figure in this episode by suggesting that Bill Monroe audition Earl Scruggs to replace Stringbean [see "Earl Scruggs"].

When Earl Scruggs joined Bill Monroe, Jim Shumate was no longer playing fiddle with the Blue Grass Boys. Shumate had originally been hired to replace Howdy Forrester, who had been drafted into the navy. According to the rules established during the war, a returning veteran can have the job back that he gave up to join the service.

"I found out that Howdy was back and wanted his job, so I turned in my notice. I knew it wouldn't have been fair for me to have stayed. When Howdy joined up, that left Bill with three fiddlers: Howdy, Birch Monroe, and myself. Birch had been singing bass on the gospel songs and fiddling old-time hoedown numbers. I had a job waiting for me in North Carolina, working in the furniture business, and had been wanting to quit anyway. I could have kept on working if I'd've wanted to, but I was glad and it worked out fine. I wanted to come back to North Carolina anyhow; I'd had my 'nuff of it."

"I believe I only stayed a week after Howdy came back. During that week, we all played together on stage. If there was a song, sometimes Howdy would break it and sometimes I would. And sometimes both of us would play it together. We twin fiddled some, but not much. I never was too good at twin fiddling.' Now Howdy was, so I'd take the lead and he would second it."

Even though Jim Shumate had left the Blue Grass Boys and returned to North Carolina, he was still very much active in country music. It wasn't long after returning to Hickory that he joined up with Dwight Barker and the Melody Boys, who had a regular television program on WSJS. Barker also managed a country music park and had his own bluegrass show on radio WHKY.

By early 1948 both Lester Flatt and Earl Scruggs had left Bill Monroe and were putting together their own band. Their first choice for a fiddle player was Jim Shumate, who later recalled how it happened.

"Lester, Earl, and Cedric Rainwater [real name Howard Stanton Watts] came over to the house and said they'd pulled out from Bill and were organizing their own show and were going to call it the Foggy Mountain Boys. They said they were going to use 'Foggy Mountain Top' as the theme song and they needed me to play the fiddle. I debated around a while because I really didn't want to, but I thought, since they went to all this trouble, I may as well. So we decided to just split down the board."

"Lester said they were going to need one more man, so they were going to hire Mac Wiseman. I'd never met Mac. So we got set up and did our first program over WHKY in Hickory. I think we worked a week there. We went from there to WCYB in Bristol, Virginia, and there we set the woods on fire."

"Everywhere we went we turned them away. We played everywhere—at schoolhouses, ballparks, auditoriums, and airports. Wiseman kind of acted as our agent. He could type and was a pretty good bookkeeper. The letters would come in from people wanting us to come to so and so, and Mac would answer back and give them the terms and open dates, and there'd come back a contract, and we would sign it. That's all there was to it in those days. We had no trouble at all getting work. Goodness gracious! If we did anything, we turned 'em down."

Before long, Lester and Earl were signing their first contract to record for Mercury Records. In their first recording session, held in a radio station in Knoxville, Tennessee, they recorded "Cabin in Caroline," "We'll Meet Again Sweetheart," "God Loves His Children," and "I'm Going to Make Heaven My Home." Shumate fiddled on the first two cuts. He tried singing baritone on "God Loves His Children" but, as he admits, "my baritone was so weak, it wouldn't come out. Earl did it on that one. It sounded good; they got a good cut on it. Earl picked the guitar Merle Travis style."

"Everybody was very calm [at that first session]; we knew what we were doing. We'd done it time and time again on the radio, and we knew how we were going to do it. Some people come to a session not knowing what they're going to do. It's not a good idea to practice on a record. You should know what you're going to do. I don't mean you should try to play the same break over and over every time. Every time I'd take a break, I'd try to play it a little bit different. I never did try to play it the same way over and over. I like to try to add a little something to it, or take something away, to give it a little contrast."

"When we went to record, we did have a problem with 'Cabin in Caroline.' My fiddle is so loud. The boy at the controls stopped us a couple of times after we'd got started.

Jim Shumate (left) and Earl Scruggs, MerleFest, Wilkesboro, North Carolina, ca. 2000 (photograph by and courtesy Daniel Coston).

He came in there and said there's something making a noise. They had me on a microphone all by myself with the fiddle. I was kicking it off. Directly, he came steaming out of the control room and said, 'I know what it is.' He said, 'Shumate, hold your fingers off the strings, you're touching them.' I was a little nervous, you know, watching the cue card and the clock on the wall. They said it sounded like horses walking. They had the thing [the microphone volume] set high. They had to have the masters set high. He said, 'Hold your fingers off of that fiddle. That's the loudest fiddle I ever heard.'"

"So, I thought, 'Uh, oh, I'm in trouble, 'cause I've got to have my position on the fiddle.' But I'd played it so much, naturally, I dropped right in. I just held my fingers up 'til he gave me the cue. When I was playing that song when we were on stage, I'd pull the bow on the kickoff. But on the record, I pushed the bow, because I couldn't take a chance of squeaking the bow. You are subject to screech on the fiddle when you're going both ways. If you go the same way all the time, you ain't going to screech. It'll come out smooth."

Leslie Keith had played fiddle with the Stanleys at the beginning of their career, and the two fiddlers met while Shumate was with Flatt and Scruggs.

"That Keith was some fiddler. But the worst I ever saw Keith hurt was when I beat him in a fiddlers convention. He'd take that 'Black Mountain Blues' and win every convention in the country. He could do that thing. When a man writes a song, it's his, you know, and he could handle it like nobody else."

"We did a show at the National Fiddlers Convention at Richlands, Virginia, in 1948. There was a huge crowd—about 9,000, best I can remember. We had Buck Ryan, who was playing fiddle for Jimmie Dean at that time; Leslie Keith, who was doing a show out of Bristol; Chubby Wise, who was working with Hank Snow in Nashville; and myself—I was fiddling with Lester and Earl."

"They run a fiddlers convention sort of like a beauty contest. They started off and matched to see who was going to go first, and I came out last. I usually like to get in the middle or pretty close to the first. That gives you a chance to pick your tune. I would have picked 'Orange Blossom' if I could have got on first. But Chubby Wise got to play first, so he played 'Orange Blossom.'"

"Keith came up next and he did the 'Black Mountain Blues.' Then Buck Ryan came up and did 'Listen to the Mockingbird.' He really laid the timber to that thing. He could really play it. So, I said, 'Cedric, what in the dickens am I going to play? They've done played everything.' He said, 'Play the "Lee Highway Blues," and them fellows can't touch you with a ten-foot pole.' That made me feel more confident because those boys were good fiddlers—they were the best."

"Mac Wiseman backed up all of us on guitar. That way, they'd be no feudin'. Nobody could say, 'If I just had so and so behind me, I could have won.' The only disadvantage I could see to those guys was that Mac was working with us at that time, and he knew that 'Lee Highway' up one side and down the other. Every time I'd turn, he'd be right there. So that was a lick in my favor too."

"So I played 'Lee Highway' and just laid them boys in the shade. After the first round the judges dropped off Keith. The next round they dropped off Chubby. The next one they dropped off Ryan and that left me standing there. That made me feel good. I'd taken that thing by a landslide."

"I've taught a lot of young guys over the years. One I remember was Lester Woodie. I sort of started him off. He used to come to my radio show when he was just a kid and hang around with me. I [took] him to get his fiddle and helped him. He'd just play along with me and, first thing I knew, he was just a splendid fiddler."

"The Stanley Brothers came down to Hickory and wanted me to play the fiddle for them. I told them I wasn't interested in playing the fiddle at that time and they asked me if I knew anyone that might be interested. I told them, 'I know a fella that could cut the mustard with you boys if he's interested.' I told them he lived in Valdese, North Carolina, at that time. They got hold of Lester [Woodie] and he just fell right in there with them. He fiddled with them a long time; he made a good fiddler."

As a veteran player, Jim Shumate had the opportunity to influence many young musicians he came in contact with. He is without question one of the finest bluegrass fiddlers to ever draw a bow and long overdue to receive credit for the changes he helped to create in bluegrass music.

The above is largely based on numerous personal interviews I conducted with Jim Shumate at my home in Hickory, North Carolina, in 1976–77. It originally appeared in Bluegrass Unlimited *in April 1979.*

Lester Woodie—Coming Up the Hard Road

In the summer of 1949, a shy boy of eighteen rode up to Bristol, Virginia, for his first professional job as a fiddle player. Behind the steering wheel was a man in his early twenties who had encouraged the boy's music from the start. The older man's name was George Shuffler.

In a March 1980 interview with the author, George told the younger man riding beside him, "This is a good break for you. The Stanleys are tough, and what with making a guaranteed $50 a week, why, you could send some home to the folks and still have more money than you would have ever made working in that bakery. And besides that, it's time you got out of Valdese [North Carolina] and see a bit of the world," he kidded. "Yeah, boy, those Stanley Brothers are tough."

In the early evening they arrived in front of radio station WCYB, where the young fiddler was to meet the Stanley Brothers. George helped get his heavy suitcase out of the trunk and patted him on the back to say goodbye. "Don't forget the hometown boys," George shouted out of the window as his car accelerated past the fiddler standing there on the sidewalk.

With his fiddle under his arm and tugging at his suitcase with the other hand, Lester made his way down the stairs to the basement where the radio station had its office. By the time he got to the bottom, Ralph and Carter Stanley were waiting for him. He shook hands with Ralph, and Carter reintroduced him to the Stanleys' mandolin player and high tenor singer, Pee Wee Lambert.

Though it's only about seventy-five crooked miles from Valdese to Bristol, the young fiddler had come up a hard road to get there. Leaning over a cup of coffee, an older Les Woodie remembered some of the bumps.

"When I was about eight years old, we moved out in the country near Valdese. Not more than a few steps away lived the Shuffler family. They raised more kids than I can remember the names of. There was the oldest girl, Lena, then came George, then Betty, John, Dude, Sue, then the one we called Gus, and the one we called Joe. They were a big, very closely-knit family, and all the kids could play some instrument or another. Only the mom and dad didn't play, though they did sing in church. John, George, and I became like brothers, and I was always over at their house eating supper, or they over at mine. John is just my age, but George was about three years older. George, being the oldest boy, was the most advanced musically, and even when he was ten years old, knew what a guitar was for."

With Christmas 1939 approaching, both Lester and his older brother Lloyd hoped for bicycles. Their father was on the conservative side and didn't want to lose either of his boys to the cars that hot-rodded past their house. Instead of bicycles, he bought his sons musical instruments. To Lloyd he gave a brand-new Harmony f-hole, archtop guitar, and to Lester he gave a brand-new Harmony mandolin. The boys were disappointed at first but soon hid their sorrow with the sounds of their new duet.

Lester Woodie from Valdese, North Carolina, ca. 1949 (courtesy Lester Woodie).

"Lloyd and myself were so different. He always loved to display his talent. Whenever anybody mentioned music, he was ready to perform. I was on the shy side and very reluctant to perform in front of people, though I loved to play by myself. Of course, Mom and Dad had to show off the family talent, so when company came, we always had to play for them. I hated to play for people so much that several times, in order to avoid performing, I would wind up one of the strings of my mandolin so tight 'til it broke. Then I'd have an excuse for not playing. Lloyd, he didn't care. He went on with the show anyway. He was a one-man band, just him and his guitar."

"There was an old man in Valdese by the name of Zenie Page who worked on fiddles. He was an old-time fiddler and I guess my first exposure to the fiddle. He was kind of a handyman, and when something would break around the house, we'd call Zenie, and he'd come and fix it. He generally brought his fiddle with him and, if we coaxed him enough, he'd drag out that old fiddle and play for hours. The old man had asthma so bad that he'd built himself a little one-room workshop, just behind the house, so he wouldn't bother his wife with his asthma attacks. He had a bed rigged up in there. He was out there to himself, and I used to go by there and get him to play the fiddle for me. He played the old hoedown fiddle. He'd play 'Bill Cheatham,' 'Ida Red,' 'Turkey in the Straw,' the old standards. He only played the fiddle with two fingers, and by then I guess his playing was a little scratchy, but to me it was beautiful."

"Old man Page used to tinker with fiddles and always had several that he'd promised people he would work on stuffed under his bed. By today's standards I guess he wouldn't be much of a repairman, but he did the best he could. I remember he used to take combs and make bridges out of them. He'd inlay the combs with stars and dots carved out of old toothbrushes. They'd look beautiful and sound terrible. He taught me how I could use a comb, with some of the teeth removed, for a mute. Old Zenie taught me to cut corners and improvise any way I could, because I didn't have any money."

"It was my brother Lloyd who bought me my first fiddle from Zenie. He did a few odd jobs to collect a dollar here and there. He paid Zenie around $20 for that fiddle. He went to all that trouble to get me that fiddle just so he'd have someone to play with. He didn't wait for Christmas or a birthday but gave it to me as soon as he had arrived at the figure of $20."

"Since George, John, and I were spending so much time together, it was natural that we should start playing music together. Somehow or another, my brother Lloyd got left out of it, but he apparently didn't care, because he liked to play by himself. Before long, me and the Shufflers started working on our singing. We had heard records of the Sons of the Pioneers, and we copied their singing style. I used to sing lead, George the baritone, and John, he had a great tenor. We did stuff like 'Tumbling Tumbleweeds' and 'Cool Water.'"

"Occasionally we'd try a Monroe Brothers song, me and John. I had been listening to Bill and Charlie Monroe over the radio since I was in the first grade of school. They were on a noontime show on WPTF in Raleigh, North Carolina. I used to listen to them while I came home from school to eat lunch. There was a lot of good music on that station. Johnnie and Jack used to play there. Most of the music we heard was on record, though we did catch some stuff on the radio. John had dropped out of school and took a job in a cotton mill, so he had plenty of money, compared to us. So we used to gang around John's record player and listen to the records he bought every Saturday when he went to the record store in Hickory."

"Now and then a good group would come by and play at the ballpark in Valdese. Promoters would sometimes book entertainment as a draw to the ball games. Sometimes a group would be booked at the ballpark even when there was no game. Groups like the Louvin Brothers would play. We learned a lot about harmony singing by listening to the Louvins. They really sang it right and had the feeling in it. Ira was a real genius with music. I got to know them pretty well, and I never missed one of their shows around Valdese."

"It seemed sometimes like we learned as much by listening to those 78 records as we did by watching the local musicians around Valdese. You know, there weren't all that many musicians that played around Valdese then. Of course, there were old fiddlers here and there, and there were some homes that had a banjo hanging on the wall that was played for sheer enjoyment once in a while. But good musicians were really rare. There must have been more music played when my daddy was growing up than when I was. As time goes on, there seems to be more things to do for entertainment, and it wasn't as necessary to entertain yourself. When I was growing up, the old music was kind of on its way out."

"After I got that fiddle, George, John, and myself organized ourselves into a band. We called ourselves the Melody Mountain Boys. Soon we picked up a guy from Drexel named Curly Williams, who played steel guitar. It was like an electric Dobro. We did country stuff with western harmonies. George played guitar, John the bass, me on the fiddle, and Curly on the lap steel. While we were playing together, I remember that things got so tight once that when all the hair of my bow fell out, I was reduced to playing the fiddle with a wire coat hanger. You can imagine what it sounded like."

"Just about the time we started getting our sound the way we wanted it, George got a call from the Bailey Brothers, who wanted George to come play with them in Nashville. It was a chance to play on the Opry, so George left. The last thing George said when he left, though, was for me to keep practicing on that fiddle, because when he came back, we'd do something with the band. George worked for about a year with the Baileys and did a short stint with the York Brothers."

"When George came back, we really got serious, and started playing radio shows. Up until that time, we had contented ourselves with playing neighborhood functions, like cornshuckings. I had a favorite uncle who lived on a farm. He raised a lot of corn, and at harvest time, he'd bring in his corn by the wagonload and pile it real high. Then he'd have a big party and invite the neighbors and anyone who could play."

"It was the radio shows that really made us tighten up our show. I remember we did a live program in North Wilkesboro, did one in Lenoir, and played over radio WHKY and WIRC in Hickory. George had been to Nashville, so he did the MC work. He could really be funny. I think what makes George so funny is that he reduces things to its lowest terms and brings it right down home. If he is out slopping the pigs, he won't tell you he's a nutritional engineer for the pork market."

"Besides the country stuff and the western harmonies, we also did a lot of songs we learned off of records of the Blue Sky Boys, Bill and Earl Bolick. I worshiped their music. The first time I met them was when I was working with Carter and Ralph on the *Farm and Fun Time* in Bristol. They came there and worked a stint for a number of months. Both the Stanleys and Blue Sky Boys were about equal in popularity in those days. George, John, and I used to love to do the Blue Sky Boys' songs. We used to do 'Why Not Confess,' and 'The Sweetest Gift, a Mother's Smile,' among others."

"John and I featured a duet and, if the song was adaptable, George would come in on the baritone part. In the Melody Mountain Boys, we used different kinds of harmonies, depending on the song. Often, we'd use a harmony with the lead in the middle, with the baritone below, and the tenor above. On other songs, we'd use a tenor and a high tenor or high baritone, both above the lead. You had to work the harmonies according to the song."

It was during this period, when the Melody Mountain Boys were working on radio, that they got Perry Duncan, who went by the name of "Carolina Slim," to play second fiddle.

"Slim was my greatest influence on the fiddle. His touch on the fiddle was simply fantastic. He was from Cagers Mountain, which is across the Catawba River at Rutherford College, near Valdese. He lived up there in a log cabin with his mother and dad. In fact, before joining us, he had a group called the Log Cabin Boys. Slim and I played twin fiddles. I usually played lead, and Slim would second me. I learned more through playing with him than anything else. We had heard groups that had two fiddles, like the Skillet Lickers, but that wasn't the sound we were looking for. We were trying for a little more modern sound than they had. Slim and I used to get note for note harmonies. We'd slow down a tune to make sure we were getting it right. After we had played together for a while, it was like I could read his mind; I knew exactly what he was going to do even before he did it. I guess we played together off and on for four or five years."

"During those years we played about all the time. We played just about every day and all Sunday afternoon, after church. That's the secret of being a musician, playing every day. You about have to learn when you spend eight hours a day doing something. We lived with the music, and we understood what it was supposed to sound like."

"Brothers always have an advantage when they're entertaining together because they understand each other so well. That was kind of our situation. George, John, and I were just like three brothers. If you could say we ever had a leader, I guess it was George, because he was older, and he was the only one who knew how to get out of Valdese. When it came to a decision, we all would have to agree. But you didn't need too much of a leader, because there was no money being passed."

"In June of 1949 I graduated from high school and went to work in a bakery. I was working the night shift there one night when about ten o'clock they called me up front. Somebody was there to see me. I came out and introduced myself to the two strangers standing there in the front of the bakery. It was Ralph Stanley and Pee Wee Lambert. They had been to see Jim Shumate in Hickory about him playing fiddle with the Stanley Brothers. He wasn't able to join them, but he recommended me. So, there they were, asking me to join them. I didn't debate about it too long, because I wanted to get out of that bakery. I was to meet Carter Stanley the next day. They had reserved a room in the Hickory Hotel for me to get together with them to try me out."

"I had heard the name, the Stanley Brothers, but that's about all. I hadn't heard any of their records. The Stanleys had been playing in Bristol since '46. They did a few shows back then and bought themselves a brand-new Cadillac. That was really the big time for them. They had just signed a recording contract with Columbia Records before I joined them."

"When I found the hotel and walked up the stairs to their room, we got out the instruments and played two or three tunes. I believe I played 'Fire on the Mountain' and 'Sally Goodin.' I think they sang one song to see what I could do as far as backup. It was 'Little Glass of Wine.' Back in those days, they played and sang most everything high and fast. If Pee Wee couldn't get up high enough, Carter would get on him. 'Oh, you can do it,' Carter would say. 'Get on up there!'"

"The only thing that really bothered me about playing with the Stanley Brothers at first was their speed. They played everything so fast. But when you're eighteen years old, it's not too hard to get your speed up. It wasn't long before I fell in with them."

"It did take me a while, though, to learn their songs. When I played with the Melody Mountain Boys, I often sang bass on the quartet numbers. As it turned out, the Stanleys needed a bass singer for their quartet, but I didn't know their songs. I remember one night we were playing out at a ballpark when I first joined them. They were going to do 'Over in the Glory Land.' I told Carter I didn't know the words, so Carter told me to just fake it. So, I jumped in there and sang, even though I didn't know the words. If I was lucky, I'd hit a word right here and there. But since they were going so fast, it really didn't make much difference."

"In those days Pee Wee did more singing on the show than Ralph. Ralph was on the shy side and was content to sit back and play the banjo and let Pee Wee do all the singing if he wanted to. It was only after Carter died that Ralph's music really came out. With Carter gone, it had to come out."

"We used to ride all night in an automobile to get to a show. There it was, two o'clock in the morning and everyone trying to sleep, with Ralph at the wheel keeping himself awake by singing the old Primitive Baptist hymns. He really used to sing some weird songs. To me, the lonesome sound of those Baptist hymns is what gave the Stanleys their identity."

"Of course, there were other influences in the Stanleys' music as well. They all worshiped Monroe and his music. Pee Wee, especially, just idolized Monroe. In fact, to me Pee Wee even looked a little like Monroe. When he put his hat on it was uncanny. He even did a lot of Monroe's stuff on the shows, songs like 'The Prisoner's Song' and 'Molly and Tenbrooks.'"

"Monroe didn't take kindly to other groups using his material and copying his style. Since the Stanleys were Bill's biggest challenge, there grew up quite an animosity between them. Later on, Carter worked with Monroe, and Bill got over his jealous feeling. At the time, however, it was quite intense. About that time, the Stanleys signed a recording contract with Columbia Records, Bill's label. Columbia also signed Wilma Lee and Stoney Cooper and their group, the Clinch Mountain Boys. Columbia made them change it to the Clinch Mountain Clan. Monroe was incensed that Columbia would sign another group with his sound, so he left and went to Decca."

"At the time the Stanleys were in Bristol, we had a new record out. There arose pretty stiff competition between several ratio stations there. Station WFHG was jealous of WCYB because of the success of their live shows. This disk jockey was doing a show on WFHG, and he played the Stanley Brothers' new record. He followed it with Bill Monroe saying, 'Now this is what it is supposed to sound like.' Carter got so mad that he went down there and got that disk jockey by the collar and pulled him out of that studio and had his words. And that just fueled the flame between the two stations. They never came to actual blows, but there were some pretty strong words. Of course, all of this was just coming up the hard road. Today, everyone's just friends. But back then, it's understandable that if you are doing a thing, anybody that's similar threatens you."

"About that time, we also had Leslie Keith working with us. Leslie had worked with them before. He and I had an act together on stage. About halfway through the show Ralph and Carter would do some duets, and I would go back and get on a Raggedy Ann outfit, with old clothes and wide tie. I played the comedian. Leslie was a real hand with a black snake or bull snake whip. I would come out in my comedy outfit and would hold papers for Leslie between my legs and light [them] on fire. I'd even put cigarettes in my mouth, and Leslie would cut the fire out of [the lighted papers and cigarettes]. We had a real circus act. Leslie was really good with that whip. Otherwise, I wouldn't have done it. I must admit, I was pretty scared the first few times. But Leslie talked to me and told me that he could touch me and never hurt me or he could cut my nose off if he wanted to. That was supposed to make me feel better."

"While Leslie was working with us, we used to promote fiddle contests to promote our show. It was always a contest between Leslie and myself; it wasn't just open to anybody. We'd get on the air about a month before a certain show date. We'd talk to each other and boast about how we were going to beat the other. I'd ask him what he was going to play, and he'd tell me that he wouldn't say but that I'd better watch out, because he was going to get his revenge for the last time I beat him. Leslie was better known than I was, because he had been around a lot longer than I had, so he had quite a following. In those days, people would really follow a fiddler."

"These contests were a great draw for the Stanleys. It was sort of like advertising for a wrestling match. By the time of the show, everyone was in a real fighting mood to see who was going to win the match. There was a real contrast in styles between Leslie and myself. Leslie played the old-time, single-string style. I played using more double stops, double notes, than he did. In the contests, he used to play 'Black Mountain Blues,' 'Cacklin' Hen,' and 'Listen to the Mockingbird.' I played 'Cotton Eyed Joe,' 'Orange Blossom Special' and 'Lee Highway Blues.'"

"I guess I learned 'Lee Highway Blues' from Jim Shumate over in Hickory. I'd listened to the Opry and heard Curly Fox play it too. Fox was one of my big favorites then. I also loved to listen to Fiddlin' Arthur Smith play his long-bow notes. I learned what I could from Shumate, Fox, and Arthur Smith, but when I really got to playing the fiddle, I was really trying for Benny Martin. The best fiddling that I ever heard Benny do was when he first came to Nashville with Big Jeff. It was on WLAC in Nashville, before Benny went with Flatt and Scruggs. Big Jeff was married to Tootsie, who had Tootsie's Lounge, the infamous bar and grill next to the Opry where all the performers hung out. Big Jeff had a six o'clock program then. Benny really was relaxed and laid back then. He could play anything he wanted to play and really got some fantastic stuff."

"I guess the thing I learned most from Benny was about tone. He got better tone out of a fiddle than anybody I ever heard. Benny did a lot of double-string harmonies, while people like Chubby Wise were known more for their sweet single notes. Benny would take a chance on hitting anything, and he'd usually hit it. He'd do pretty up-the-staff harmony parts, and he always did it with a beautiful tone. He did a lot of stuff on the bottom two strings. The hardest thing I ever tried to learn on a fiddle was Benny's way of playing that real slow vibrato. That's what really set him apart in my book. It took me years to get that. I've always hated to hear a scratch on a fiddle. I hate a sound that sounds like it's coming off of a washboard. I like a full, resonant tone. I used to call Benny Martin the bravest fiddler, because he would always try some difficult position. I think that's what makes a musician great."

"I believe you can learn licks from just about any fiddler, no matter how much he knows. There's usually something good he does that you can pick up, or something wrong he does that you may be doing too and make an effort to correct it. Some of the better-known fiddlers that I've learned from include Dale Potter; Chubby Wise; Kenny Baker; and even Sonny Loden, now Sonny James."

"When you're playing every day, you more or less work out a break, or a certain lick, and you play it pretty much that way every time. Especially when you're in a studio recording a record, you tend to rely on your memory and play it the way you worked it out. You play it safe. But when you really feel the music and really feel like you're creating, that's when you feel inspired to play something you never dreamed of playing. And that's something you just can't do every day. You can't just walk out and say, 'Let's play,' and really fall into it. If you've memorized a break, you can do it anytime, but if you're really feeling the music, and feel like you're creating, you'll probably play it different every time you play it."

"I recorded most of the Columbia stuff with the Stanleys. We did 'Drunkard's

Hell'; 'The Fields Have Turned Brown'; 'I Love No One but You'; 'Hey, Hey, Hey'; 'The Old Home'; 'We'll Be Sweethearts in Heaven'; 'Too Late to Cry'; 'The Lonesome River'; 'Pretty Polly'; and 'Man of Constant Sorrow.' I've gotten more comments on the breaks I took on 'Man of Constant Sorrow' than anything I recorded with them. I never really felt satisfied with what I did, and for years afterwards I thought it was just another break. I remember how we recorded 'Hey, Hey, Hey.' I was doing a crazy thing on the fiddle. I was doing a shake on the bow like they do to the train sound on 'Orange Blossom Special.' Carter just loved it, and he made me put it on that record. Carter wrote that song. I didn't think that much of it at the time."

"Carter wrote a lot of his songs while we were riding along in the car. I remember we were staying at a hotel in Huntington, West Virginia, while we were doing a TV show up there. That was one of the first live TV shows that there were. He was working on that song 'Let Me Love You One More Time.' I think I helped him with a word or two on that one. Carter seemed to write on impulse. A lot of times riding along in the car, he'd get a line or two and maybe by the next morning he'd have the rest of it. He may be riding along and just start singing. He'd sing two or three lines, or maybe a whole verse. Then that night when we were warming up for the show, he'd get his guitar and run over it again. Maybe by the next day, he'd have the rest of it."

"We left Huntington and went to the *Louisiana Hayride*. It wasn't too long after we got to the *Hayride* that Ralph got homesick, so we came back to Bristol. Ralph thought the world of his mother and couldn't be that far away from her, so we came back to the *Farm and Fun Time*."

"From there I was drafted into the Korean War. The whole time I was in the service, I was lucky enough to keep playing. Everywhere they sent me, I ran up on a band. When I got out of the service, I headed back to Valdese, North Carolina. John Shuffler had been fighting in Korea, and he had just gotten out too. There we were, back in Valdese, the end of the line. I told John I was thinking of re-upping and going back into the service. He was sure that he had had enough of the service. John talked me into going up north to Ohio to look for a job, but we never did find one and came back home."

"Just as I was ready to re-enlist, George had just come back from Charlottesville, Virginia, where he had recorded with Bill Clifton. On the way through Lynchburg, he met up with Curly Lambert, who was playing with Bill and Mary Reid. George found out they needed a fiddle player and encouraged me to join them. I went up to Lynchburg and decided to take a job with them. Not long after I joined them, we cut two sessions for Columbia Records. We had three TV shows a week, radio every day, and our personal appearances."

"I was getting a little dissatisfied and felt like I wasn't accomplishing anything, so I enrolled in a business college. It happened that the college was right across the street from the radio station. I got up every morning and went to school, and at lunchtime I'd go across the street and play on the radio. It was a hectic schedule, but I stayed with it for a year or so. About this time, I got married, just at the time the group was getting ready for a move to Nashville. Troy Martin, a promoter, was getting [everything] all lined up in Nashville. Before we made the move, my wife and I were expecting our first child so, instead of going to Nashville, I decided to get off the road and we moved back to Hickory."

"I went to work for a dime store in Hickory and stayed there about four years. Then I got transferred to Roanoke and I got in with Bill Jefferson's band up there. We did TV, dances, and I started helping him with the MC work on the TV shows. Bill kept encouraging me to get into radio and told me he could use me. I was about to be transferred again, so I quit the dime store business and went into radio, where I've been ever since. I'm now the manager of station WKDE in Altavista, Virginia."

"I guess you could say I'm still quite active in music. After a few years of semi-retirement from pickin,' I became interested in bluegrass all over again. I started playing at bluegrass festivals, and in the last two years with Stan Dudley and Bluegrass I, and an album with Roby Huffman, a fine bluegrass singer from North Carolina. Recently I went into the studio with my friend Charlie Moore. That album hasn't been released yet, but I thoroughly enjoyed pickin' with Charlie. He's one of the finest bluegrass songwriters today. Just a couple of weeks ago Stan and I did another album, to be released soon."

"But my biggest accomplishment is an album of my own, *More Pickin'—Les Singing! Les Woodie and Friends*. It's been out about a month. It's a vocal and instrumental album. It's not quite solo because I had a gang of my friends playing on there too: James Bailey on banjo and mandolin, Stan Dudley and Carl Clark on guitars, Spider Gilliam on bass, Steve Wilson on Dobro, and Greg Woodie on a couple of drum licks. Carl Clark and Ken Bentley of the Tunstall Trio helped on the vocals. The Trio is a bluegrass gospel group from the Danville area. They are a very talented and dedicated group who sing some of the finest harmony you'll hear today. I work with them mostly these days."

"Most of the songs and tunes on the album are my own. They're a little different from most bluegrass material. I don't really consider myself a writer. I write only when I feel like it. Sometimes it hits me when I'm driving alone, say, from Danville to Lynchburg. It usually happens as fast as I can write it down. I don't understand it, but it's almost as if someone else is doing the writing, not me. I sure wish I could find out who it is!"

The above is the result of a personal interview I conducted with Lester Woodie at a restaurant in Hickory, North Carolina, in 1979. It originally appeared in Bluegrass Unlimited *in March 1980.*

Aynsley Porchak, Fiddler

Any dyed-in-the wool fan of bluegrass fiddling will instantly recognize the names of such legendary fiddlers as Chubby Wise, Jim Shumate, Fiddlin' Arthur Smith, Kenny Baker, and Bobby Hicks. The list goes "On and On," as Bill Monroe would say.

One name you might not yet be familiar with is Aynsley Porchak. This young Canadian fiddler is setting the woods on fire with her amazing bluegrass fiddling. She not only won the U.S. grand master fiddle championship (2015) but also the Canadian grand master fiddle championship (2017). No other fiddler has ever clinched both of these prestigious competitions. Before that, she also beat all her rivals at the Tennessee state fiddle championship (2014).

In December of 2017 I found out that Aynsley was in the bluegrass program at East Tennessee State University in Johnson City, just up the road from my home in Asheville, North Carolina. The next thing I knew was that she had joined Carolina Blue, an up-and-coming bluegrass band based in nearby Brevard, North Carolina. I already knew the band, because a few years earlier they picked live on my *Country Roots* radio show on WCQS, an NPR station in Asheville. I immediately got in touch with the band and invited them to play live on the air. They accepted. When the band walked into the studio, I was delighted to meet Aynsley for the first time.

The band was so good that I gave them all the airtime they wanted that night, nearly two hours. I didn't want them to stop. When the band paused to take a break, I asked Aynsley if she would play Kenny Baker's "Roxanne's Waltz." She said she would be delighted to play it, but the band didn't know it. But with her coaching, they learned it on the spot and expertly backed her up when we resumed broadcasting a few minutes later. It turned out that Carolina Blue liked the tune so well that they soon incorporated it in their sets.

Recently, I sat down with Aynsley to learn what sparked her interest in wanting to play the fiddle. She explained that when she was a young child, her mother used to put her in the car seat and drive around the countryside near Ontario, Canada, with the radio on to help her fall asleep. What parent hasn't done that?! Her folks weren't fans of traditional music, so it came as a surprise when her mother was turning the dial on family car's radio when little Aynsley cried out from the backseat, "Stop it, Mommy, stop it right there!" It was a country music station that her parents never listened to. However, her mom kept the radio on that channel until Aynsley fell asleep. The next time they went for a drive, the exact same thing happened. "Stop it right there!" It was that country channel again. After Aynsley was able to articulate a little better, her mom figured out that it was the fiddle that her daughter liked so much. Knowing that, her mom soon took her to a local fiddle contest not far from their house. Aynsley had fallen in love with the fiddle and firmly told her mom that someday she wanted to play that instrument.

Aynsley Porchak, ca. 2020 (photograph by Bailey Robinson).

That time came when Aynsley was nine when her parents arranged for her to take fiddle lessons from Gerald Hamilton, a well-known fiddle instructor in the area. Gerry had taught a number of fiddle champions over the years including super fiddle star Shane Cook. Gerald instantly realized that this little girl was serious about learning to fiddle. Even in their first lesson, Gerald could easily detect Aynsley's fierce determination, laser focus and drive.

Aynsley started on the Ontario fiddle contest circuit when she was 11 years old. "I started fiddle lessons at age nine, which was much later than most of the kids I was competing against. I soon realized I had some catching up to do. Most of my competitors were classically trained, and while I was brought up reading sheet music, I never took lessons from a classical instructor. It took me a few years to get the hang of competing and get my nerves under control. The Canadian competitions were honestly even more competitive than I expected going into it, and while everyone was very kind and supportive behind the scenes, there was definitely a very serious undertone to the whole thing."

Over the eight years that Gerald Hamilton worked with her, he not only exposed her to Canadian reels, jigs, hornpipes, and waltzes but also to all the great bluegrass fiddlers, who she was especially drawn to. One time while traveling out west, Gerald brought her back Craig Duncan's book, *Blues Fiddling Classics*. He invited her to learn a certain tune, but when she came back for her lesson the following week, Aynsley had mastered all 25 tunes in that book. Before this, she didn't even know that blues fiddling existed.

After working with Gerald for eight years, Aynsley moved on to her second fiddle mentor, Doug McNaughton, who helped her place in the top 10 at Weiser, Idaho, when she was just a teenager. In particular, Doug explained that Aynsley had the "fire in her eyes," meaning she would never quit perfecting a tune until she had mastered it completely and beyond. Both of her fiddle mentors frequently extended her one-hour lesson to up to five or six hours at a time. In these extended sessions both of her teachers exposed her to Stéphane Grappelli jazz tunes, Québécois reels, Randy Howard double stop waltzes, and blues fiddle. Aynsley has said, "I always thought that I didn't want to be just a bluegrass fiddler or just a contest-style fiddler, but I wanted to be a fiddler who could play bluegrass, contest-style, and so much more. I didn't want to be pigeonholed into just one style growing up, because I felt like I could learn something important from each style that I tried. I still believe that helped me greatly."

She went on to say, "When I started contest fiddling, I was almost obsessively playing the tunes

Aynsley Porchak, ca. 2020 (photograph by Laura Tate Ridge).

exactly as I had practiced them for months before. However, as I got gradually more confident, I saw that there was value in controlled on-stage improvisation, and I used it to some degree. Do I know how I'm going to execute the tunes when I go on-stage now? Pretty much. But do I know the exact route I'm going to take to get there? Not entirely. Sometimes, if you pick tunes that you have fun with, you can find some improvisational gems that you just feel spur of the moment, and now, as a judge, I definitely look for that."

When I probed further about how to prepare to compete in a high-level fiddle contest, she explained, "The biggest secret to me about contest-style fiddle, which, frankly, I didn't learn until later, is that over-preparedness can get the best of you. I had fiddle teachers who very firmly emphasized that you don't want to be under-practiced, so I went to the extreme and would pick my set of three tunes in some cases four or five months before and practice each day for about five or six hours. Sometimes my daily practice sessions would go even longer than that! By the time the contest season rolled around, I definitely knew my tunes, but my brain had been working on them for so long that the performance itself sometimes felt stale to me."

"Around the time I was about starting bluegrass fiddling I started messing with my contest routine and paired a reduced routine of physical practicing with mental practicing (something that I experimented with after bouts of tendinitis that cut my practice time down). I found that bluegrass helped my contest-style improvisation skills, helped me be more comfortable on stage, and helped me listen more closely to the accompaniment on stage to get more out of the groove. In short, the best way for me to be calm about contests was to be prepared, but to always have one other thing in the back of my mind to avoid over-concentrating on my own playing. The more I had fun with my contest sets, the more contests I won."

Then I asked Aynsley what she meant by "mental practicing." "For as long as I could remember, I heard 'practice makes perfect.' Then I heard 'PERFECT practice makes perfect' and that got me thinking … how does one practice perfectly? Being an analytical sort, I decided to get to the bottom of that when I had to take weeks off playing due to an injury. What I found out is that if you really take the time to learn your instrument, you can visualize exactly where your fingers need to hit and where your bow needs to be to play what you want. Sometimes, you can even hear the pitches in your head and mentally 'think' through a tune. I use this a lot, as sometimes I'll be riding in a car, or doing some mundane tasks, a song will pop up in my head and I'll think something like 'wait—what if you added the Jim Shumate "Cabin in Caroline" second break starting bar' or 'that Dale Potter double stop sliding lick fits perfectly in your new song.' A lot of times, I'll have put in hours of mental practice time before I even try to play a lick on stage, and then when my fingers finally try it, it's quite gratifying—and often stops me from messing up! A lot of people don't really teach that—I had to figure it out on my own, sort of. Now, as a teacher, I occasionally have lessons where we don't even pick up a bow, instead thinking critically."

By the time Aynsley finished high school, she decided that she wanted to go to a university and major in music, but her options in Canada were limited. Her two major stylistic passions were American contest-style fiddling and bluegrass, but neither were available at Canadian universities. As luck would have it, Aynsley traveled to Asheville, North Carolina, to study with bluegrass fiddle legend Bobby Hicks and then went on to Nashville to take a few lessons from famed fiddler Buddy Spicher. As Aynsley explained,

"Both Buddy Spicher and Bobby Hicks got me thinking creatively about fiddle playing in their own unique ways. Obviously, both are tremendous technicians, but with Buddy, I got to think outside the box more when it came to a swing feel and chordal structure as it relates to double stops. Bobby definitely was influential to my double stops but was rooted more firmly in bluegrass."

After one of her lessons with Buddy Spicher, they went out to lunch and there they ran into Dan Boner, the director of East Tennessee State University's Bluegrass, Old-Time, and Country Music Studies. After Dan told her about the university, she quickly realized that ETSU was exactly what she was looking for, so she enrolled the very next semester, in the fall of 2013. During her studies, Aynsley took fiddle lessons from Dan as well as from Hunter Berry, the fiddler for Rhonda Vincent and the Rage. She also played in the ETSU Bluegrass Pride Band. When she graduated, she received two bachelor's degrees—one in bluegrass, old-time, and country music studies, and a second one in English, plus a master's degree in Appalachian studies.

Once she delved deeply into bluegrass fiddling, Aynsley realized that this style of fiddling came to her easily from a technical standpoint but thinking like a bluegrass fiddler took more time. She explained that "anyone can play a bunch of technically impressive notes and make the crowd sit up and pay attention, but to play what fits in well with everyone else and supports the singer is a whole different ballgame. In fact, to that point, bluegrass fiddling to me is really about being a good team player."

In December of 2018, while getting her master's at ETSU, she was hired by Carolina Blue, an up-and-coming bluegrass band from Brevard, North Carolina, about a two-hour drive from the campus in Johnson City, Tennessee. While touring with the band, she not only learned a lot about music but also about the music business itself. When the band stopped touring, she was suddenly without a band but was determined not to let this slow her down. Out of this situation the Tennessee Bluegrass Band was formed, drawing upon the singing and playing of talented industry sidemen who truly appreciated the same sort of music that she did. Their shared goal was to continue playing traditional bluegrass but with an updated image and sound—showing audiences the "future of the past," if you will. In fact, that is the title of their debut album with Billy Blue Records.

The Tennessee Bluegrass Band consists of Ainsley on fiddle, Lincoln Hensley on banjo, Tim Laughlin on mandolin and vocals, Annissa Burnett on bass and vocals, and Geary Allen on guitar and vocals. While she had never been in a leadership role in a band before, she has found it both rewarding and challenging. It forced her to grow in many industry-related ways, caused her fiddling to become more informed, and it helped her to grow in her faith. On May 13, 2022, the band released its first single of Tim Rayborn's "I'm Warming Up to an Old Flame" through a world premiere on SiriusXM. Given the enormous talent in the band, it's no wonder they have received overwhelmingly positive support from their growing legion of fans. The Tennessee Bluegrass Band released their first album July 22, 2022. It's packed with the band's unique take on traditional bluegrass infused with joy, energy, and true passion for the music.

Before we wrapped up our interview, I asked Ansley her philosophy about teaching fiddle.

"When you learn fiddle, it's very easy to get caught up in the big picture goal, whether it's playing three tunes in a contest or trying to get through back-up and a break in a bluegrass song. After my students get to a certain level of playing, I ask them not to only concentrate on the minutia (bow speed/pressure, double stops or not, gritty/

smooth sound, etc.). Instead, I like teaching students to not just rely on patterns and musical formulas to make music, but also to think about the song's past (e.g., are you going for an 'impression' of a particular fiddler to lend a feeling of history to this break), and to listen carefully what the singer is singing about and what feeling you are going to evoke through your backup."

With so many talented musicians such as Aynsley Porchak coming along, us old geezers can now relax and lay back and know that bluegrass music will be in capable hands.

The above is the result of interviews I conducted with Aynsley in May 2022.

Fiddles, Fangs, and Folklore

People have always had a strange fascination with rattlesnakes. As one of North America's most poisonous snakes, they are both feared and hated, and yet their rattles are prized for their mythical and magical properties.

While doing research for this section, I ran across an amazing number of stories, some true, some pure myth, about rattlesnakes or "rattlers," as they are sometimes

Crockett Ward, leader of Ballard Branch Bogtrotters, at his home on Ballard Branch Lane, Galax, Virginia, ca. 1938 (Library of Congress).

called. One old timer personally told me the following story as the gospel truth, but I have since found versions of it that were collected both in the Southern Appalachians and in Western Europe.

It seemed that a Civil War soldier's boots were jinxed. He died not in battle but contracted a mysterious disease and quickly passed away. When his son got old enough, he proudly wore his father's old boots, and he too contracted a strange illness and died. In fact, anyone who ever wore those boots soon came down with a mysterious illness and soon passed away. Finally, a mortician closely inspected the boots and found out why they were jinxed. Protruding up through the sole of one of the boots was the fang of a large rattlesnake, which had died many years before, but his venom was still lethal.

As I perused the literature of rattlesnakes, I found that rattlesnakes are thought to be a sure cure for a variety of ailments and conditions, including hysteria, mental illness, tremors, phobias, delusions of grandeur, feelings of worthlessness, fantasies of persecution, and diabolical possession. In Kentucky, a belt made of rattlesnake skin was said to cure rheumatism. If you were unlucky enough to have tuberculosis, a common cure was to cut the head off a rattlesnake, put it in a bottle of rum, and drink the rum two or three times a day.

Not only have rattlesnakes been considered good for what ails you but in Texas they've been used to foretell the weather. If a dead snake is tossed in the air and lands on the ground with its back up, rain is on the way. On the other hand, if it lands with its belly up, dry weather will continue. If you're being chased by witches, be sure to sew pieces of rattlesnake skin to your clothing; that is guaranteed to drive them away.

Rattlesnakes were an important part of Native American mythology and were commonly used for healing. In addition to the idea that the rattles would facilitate childbirth, there was the common belief that rattles would pacify teething children. They were placed in a bag and hung around the neck or worn as a necklace. Sometimes a child was allowed to chew on them. One story claimed that for this to work there must be at least three rattles, and the cord around the child's neck must be red. Rattles were also used to prevent fits and convulsions. One Native American legend tells of an Indian who trained a band of rattlers to join him in song. By using their rattles, the snakes were able to carry four harmony parts: soprano, alto, tenor, and bass.

Strong beliefs about the magical powers of rattlesnakes were widespread in nineteenth- and early twentieth-century America.

- If you receive rattles from someone, no harm will come to you while that person is near you.
- If you kill a rattler, keep the rattles for a good luck charm.
- If you kill a rattler and rub the rattles on your eyes, you will always see a rattler before he sees you.
- Satan will come to your aid if you get a rattle off a graveyard rattlesnake and sew it with a piece of silver into a red flannel bag that you wear over your heart.
- If you display the rattle of a dead snake, it will keep other rattlers away and act as a charm against a rattlesnake bite.

Stories and songs of snakes and children have always made the heart throb and the eyes moisten. An example of this is the fiddle tune "Rattlesnake Bit the Baby." And let's not forget Bill Monroe's composition "The Little Girl and the Dreadful Snake." Here's a particularly heart-wrenching variation of an ancient story of a little girl and a snake.

There was once a little girl who befriended a snake. Every day she carried her lunch out to the yard. Finally, the curiosity of her parents was aroused, and they followed her and watched her sit down to enjoy her bowl of bread and milk. Suddenly, a huge rattlesnake slithered out from the grass and coiled beside her, to be fed bread and milk from her spoon. The horrified parents killed the snake with the result that the heartbroken child, pining for her dead playmate, became disconsolate and soon died.

Rattlesnakes made great fodder for other tall tales. One is of a miner who kept a large rattler as a pet. One night a burglar snuck into the miner's cabin to steal his gold. Wanting to protect his master's booty, the rattler bound the burglar to a bedpost with its coils and hung its tail out the window to rattle for the police. Then there was a hunter who saved the life of a large rattler, which then became his constant companion. When the hunter accidentally fell on a train track just as the locomotive was about to run over him, the snake pulled the hunter's red bandana out of his pocket and waved down the train.

One farmer built a fence consisting of five hundred posts that he drove into the ground with a sledgehammer. When it warmed up, the posts proved to be rattlers who crawled off, dragging two miles of barbed wire behind them. And then there was the family in Texas with nine children. Only one of the nine had never been bitten by a rattler, and that child developed an inferiority complex.

Even though rattlesnakes and fiddles make strange bedfellows, there exists a great deal of lore and superstition about their sometimes bumpy relationship. Many Appalachian fiddlers have long believed that it was good luck to put a rattlesnake rattle inside their fiddle, the bigger the better. Perhaps it had to do with the fiddle long being known as the devil's instrument. Many fiddlers would have agreed with an old timer from Missouri who said that the rattles "keep the devil out."

Even for the superstitious-minded, not even the presence of a rattlesnake rattle was strong enough medicine to keep old Satan at bay. One Florida fiddler's wife stubbornly refused to allow the fiddle inside the house, because it would be like inviting the devil for supper. Instead, he had to hang his fiddle on a wall of the barn, where mud daubers, wasps and mice would build their nests inside his fiddle. But if the farmer kept a rattlesnake rattle inside his fiddle, the scent would scare away all but the most persistent pests.

Besides driving off pests, vermin, and the devil himself, fiddlers have had far less sinister reasons for keeping a rattlesnake rattle inside their instruments. Many have suggested it gives the fiddle a sweeter tone or that it gives them good luck. Bill Monroe, the legendary mandolin player, kept a large rattle inside his precious Lloyd Loar mandolin. In California, it was thought that a rattle tied to a banjo head would help preserve the skin. I've also heard of a Brazilian guitarist who strongly believed that a rattle inside his guitar not only made it sound better but also improved his singing.

In the early '80s I asked legendary fiddler Tommy Jarrell why he put a rattlesnake rattle in his fiddle. He explained that when he was growing up in North Carolina nobody had a case for their fiddle. Instead, they carried their instruments around in an old flour sack. At home they usually hung their fiddle on the wall, where spiders liked to build their webs inside, hoping to trap a tasty treat. It was said that a rattle inside the fiddle would scare away spiders because of the snake scent of the rattle. Also, when the fiddler would play his fiddle, the rattle would move around and tear up the web.

Some old fiddlers claimed that, when they played their fiddles, the rattles "sang along" with the tune, giving it sweeter tone. A North Carolina fiddler claimed that his grandfather told him that the fiddle used to be a woman's instrument and that adding a rattle to the instrument made it more masculine.

One of the more practical reasons some fiddlers carry a rattle inside their instrument is to help keep the moisture out of their fiddles. I read one myth that said a swimming rattler always held its rattle high to keep it dry, so that's why some fiddlers thought it would keep their fiddles dry.

Many Southern fiddlers strongly believe that a rattle in their fiddles gives them more mojo when they compete at a fiddlers convention. Fiddler Martin Fox has said that he always shakes his fiddle before getting onstage at a fiddle contest to wake up the rattle so it will release its magic. Some years ago, in a recording session, the engineer complained about a strange sound coming out of my fiddle. We had to put the session on hold while we investigated. It turned out that the rattle inside my fiddle was "singing along" as I played. After I removed the rattle, the rest of the session went smoothly, but who knows how much mojo was lost when the rattle was removed?

The Hanging of Fiddlin' Joe Coleman

The story of the hanging of Fiddlin' Joe Coleman is enough to send chills up and down your spine. In 1847, near the town of Slate Fork in Adair County, Kentucky, a shoemaker and fiddler named Joe Coleman was living with his wife and his wife's mother and sister. According to some accounts, Joe had been acting erratically and, not long after that, someone smothered his mother-in-law to death with a pillow.

A few days later, Joe's wife went into the woods to gather bark and never came back. Joe went searching for his wife in the woods. When he returned, he was carrying her dead body. Some claimed that

Unknown fiddler, ca. 1861. Attached to his pegbox is possibly a ribbon from his sweetheart's hair which he used to hang up his fiddle in the days when fiddle cases were rare.

Joe killed his wife because he knew she suspected him in the death of her mother. His bloodstained shoemaker's knife was later found at the scene of the crime.

From the start of the trial, the evidence against Joe Coleman was circumstantial at best. The case was based solely on the testimony of Coleman's sister-in-law. Apparently, there was bad blood between Coleman and his wife's sister. The jury found him guilty in the first degree and sentenced him to die by hanging.

On the way to his hanging, Coleman reportedly sat on his empty coffin and played his fiddle, as a two-wheeled ox cart slowly carried him to the site where a hastily built wooden gallows had been erected. The slow, dirge-like tune that he played has since been known as "Coleman's March."

Even as the noose was being tightened around his neck, Joe Coleman maintained his innocence. Before his sentence was carried out, one legend tells how Joe promised to give his fiddle to anyone in the crowd who could play the tune better than he could. A fiddler named Franz Prewitt stepped forward and took Coleman up on his offer. Before he started fiddling, Prewitt tuned the instrument into what is called "dead man's tuning" and managed to out-fiddle Joe Coleman. Minutes before the trap door opened under Joe's feet, the condemned man handed over his fiddle to its new owner, as the assembled crowd held their breath and waited for justice to be served.

Immediately after the execution, several of Coleman's relatives secretly spirited his body away and somehow managed to bring him back from death's door. After he regained his health, Coleman supposedly boarded a steamboat that took him down the Cumberland River toward Nashville, Tennessee. From there, Coleman headed out west, and from there the trail grew cold. Coleman's claim of innocence was supported many years later by the deathbed confession of an old lady who admitted to the killing of Joe Coleman's wife.

Even though Joe Coleman himself was never again seen in eastern Kentucky, the tune named after him lived on and is commonly played today as "Coleman's March" or "Joe Coleman's March." After all these years, the tune still retains its dirge-like rhythm and feel, which is rare in old-time and bluegrass music. Most instrumental tunes are either fast breakdowns, danceable reels, or waltzes. "Coleman's March" is unique in that respect.

As it turns out, Joe Coleman did not compose the tune that now bears his name. Instead, he reworked an old Celtic tune known as "The Irish Jaunting Car." No doubt inspired by his own looming execution he changed the rhythm of the tune from a sprightly dance into a mournful dirge.

A few years later, at the start of the Civil War, an Englishman named Harry McCarthy was in Jackson, Mississippi, at the signing of Mississippi's Ordinance of Secession. McCarthy took the very same Irish tune that Joe Coleman had played and used it as the melody for a new set of lyrics he had recently composed to honor the Confederacy. The result was "The Bonnie Blue Flag." Next to "Dixie," it was the most popular tune of the Confederacy. But unlike Joe Coleman's mournful melody, Harry McCarthy kept the lively and jaunty flavor of the original Celtic tune, accurately reflecting the early and naïve optimism of the Southern cause.

As for McCarthy himself, he didn't stick around long enough to find out whether his newly composed song would help inspire the South to victory. Instead, he hightailed it to Pennsylvania and then California, where he spent the rest of the war far from the fields of battle that he helped to inspire with his song of Southern patriotism.

Banjo Picking

Walter Davis—Fist and Skull Banjo

One of the most fascinating of all the two-finger pickers was a gentleman by the name of Walter Davis. Residing in Black Mountain, North Carolina, Walter came to know most of the western Carolina banjo players such as Clarence Ashley, Samantha Bumgarner, Mack Crow, and Dock Walsh. He was also acquainted with Jimmie Rodgers—who once lived in Old Fort, North Carolina—and Blind Lemon Jefferson, who played on the streets of nearby Johnson City, Tennessee. He also knew Jimmie Davis, who came to visit his mother in a hospital in Morganton, North Carolina, and was friendly with Fiddlin' Arthur Smith.

I first met Walter Davis after a concert of banjo styles held at Warren Wilson College in Swannanoa, North Carolina. His stunning two-finger renditions of some of the old tunes like "Little Old Log Cabin in the Lane" had me mystified. How could anyone get that many notes and sound so full and right using only his thumb and index finger? I had to find out. I approached him after the show and introduced myself.

I found Mr. Davis to be an extremely witty and friendly gentleman and was promptly invited to his house for coffee and, of course, music. That evening and the many more that followed were rare treats. Here was a man of seventy-five years of age who still played much as he did thirty and forty years earlier. His music remained full of life and musical creativity.

Just like Walter Davis himself, his banjo was usually pulling musical jokes on you, tugging your ear sometimes this way and sometimes that. Much of his music was "traditional" in the sense that he often played the old tunes. But each tune bore his personal signature, almost as if he wrote it himself. Unlike most old-time musicians, he was not bashful about composing tunes, including some delightful marches, hoedowns, rags, and blues.

After the coffee had settled a few inches lower in our cups, Walter went into the bedroom and returned with his arms full of musical instruments: a guitar, a banjo, and a fiddle. As he tuned his imported Japanese banjo, he recalled the expensive Gibson Mastertone that he used to own.

"I used to have a Master Gibson banjo that the music store had to order special. I give about $500 for it back then; I bought it on the installment plan. It took me a year or two to pay it off! One time the Stanley Brothers, Ralph and Carter, were playing nearby, and someone told them about me and about how I had this Gibson banjo. They come over to the house and wanted to see that banjo. Ralph, the one who picks the banjo, had a good banjo, but it wasn't as good as the one I had. He wanted to buy it, but I guess it was a little too high priced for him."

"You know a lot of people are hot for the old instruments. I like them, but to get out there and play them in public's a different story. I wouldn't think about taking most of them out on stage, because they'll give way on you, they'll blow up on you. I know enough about them to know that. You take any kind of old instrument and they're likely to give out on you. Pick them up and they'll note perfect from one end to the other. But once you get them out on stage, they're gone. It's kindly embarrassing."

"You always have to be careful about playing another man's instrument. There was a feller who was playing with us one time. He played left-handed. We was putting on a program and I decided to fill in, so I grabbed his guitar and went out there and found out that the thing was strung left handed! That boy just lay down and hollered. I said, 'You dirty rascal, you knew that. Why didn't you stop me?' He said he wanted me to go out there, the smart aleck."

After playing several tunes together in Walter's living room, I managed to turn our conversation toward Walter's past.

"I started playing the banjo in about 1914, when I was nine years old. I reckon that makes me an antique. My dad and I were living in Newport, Tennessee, at the time. He had an old fiddle that he gave me, but I insisted that I wanted to play the banjo, not the fiddle. Although I can start a tune or two on the fiddle, I never could do much with one. My dad said I could play any kind of musical instrument that I wanted, so I traded that fiddle for a banjo. I believe that banjo I traded for was a Maybelle; I played that instrument for several years."

It was his father who first taught the young Walter Davis how to play the banjo. The elder Mr. Davis was originally from Madison County, North Carolina, where he learned the two-finger style of picking. Walter recalls that his father didn't care for the clawhammer style, which he referred to as "boom-a-loom, boom-a-loom." They had another name for the clawhammer lick: "fist and skull." Walter explained that many of the dances in Madison County ended up in a fight, hence the name "fist and skull." His

Walter Davis at his home at 102 Center Street, Black Mountain, North Carolina, ca. 1982 (photograph by the author).

music buddies would later kid Walter and call his two-finger style "fist and skull," but Walter didn't care. He always enjoyed a good joke, even if it was on him.

Not long after his father had taught him the rudiments of two-finger banjo playing, the young Mr. Davis was ready to ply his newfound trade on the world. At his urging, his father deposited him at the busiest corner of downtown Newport, Tennessee (population then 250, now 7,000). There he entertained the passing shoppers and pedestrians with his banjo. After a day of street playing, the young Mr. Davis had amassed $4 or $5 in his hat. He was rich.

When Walter played on the streets of Newport, it was by himself. Several years later, however, Walter's family moved to Old Fort, North Carolina, and Walter found plenty of companions to play with him on the street. A favorite gathering place for musicians in western North Carolina was in front of Lackey's Hardware Store in Old Fort. On any Saturday, you could find gathered in front of the store a whole assortment of local musicians. It was there that Walter Davis really learned to play.

His mentors were the best musicians in the area. On guitar and French harp (harmonica) was Gwen Foster. Other regulars at Lackey's were Clarence Greene on fiddle and Roy Neal playing banjo in a three-finger style. Occasionally, musicians from out of town, like Will Abernathy, who played the autoharp, would join the mob assembled on the front porch of the store. None of the musicians ever made much money from the hat that was left out front for bystanders to pitch a penny, but Lackey's Hardware was an important meeting place for musicians, nonetheless.

It was at Lackey's that Walter Davis first met Gwen Foster. Foster was a good guitar player and an outstanding French harp player. With dark skin and an oriental look, Gwen quickly acquired the nickname "China." The two musicians became fast friends and could frequently be found playing on street corners across North Carolina. Walter remembers one time when they were together.

"Me and Gwen were in Morganton one time, broke and looking for some way to make a little money. Gwen said he knew of a way to make some

Blind Lemon Jefferson, ca. 1926 (John Edwards Memorial Foundation Records [20001], Southern Folklife Collection at Wilson Special Collections Library, University of North Carolina at Chapel Hill).

fast. He was going to pretend that he was blind while we played on the street corner in front of the courthouse. He put on some sunglasses and told me to pass the hat around. I told him, 'No, you attach the tin cup to your guitar strap and people will sympathize with you more. I don't want any part of this deal.' So he played for a while and some lady came up and tried to put a fifty-cent piece in his cup. But she missed the cup, and the coin went rolling down the street. Gwen went right after that coin like a man who could see. That lady said something like 'That boy don't look so blind to me.' At that point me and Gwen took off running, and I believe that was our last engagement in Morganton. Playing on the street for a handout now ain't what it used to be. The cops almost never bothered us then, but now they got laws again[st] it."

Walter remembers that the best musician he ever saw play on a street corner was a blind blues singer and guitarist by the name of Blind Lemon Jefferson. Walter spent many hours listening in rapt attention to every note the street singer played. "That's where I learned to play the blues, by listening to that old colored gentleman play. He could really play the blues, I want you to know. The musicians who played on the street were called 'back lot musicians' then. That's because the musicians would sometimes play on the back lots where farmers would set up and sell their produce. People would come to get their vegetables, hear the music, and throw a penny or two into the hat. That's the only way some of us had to make a living back then."

"We also used to gather and play in barbershops. I remember we used to go up to Elizabethton, Tennessee, and play in a barbershop there. They'd let a gang of us play and pass the hat. There was a feller who used to shine shoes there by the name of DeFord Bailey. He could really play the harmonica. He later became quite popular on the Grand Ole Opry."

"I guess I really got my start in the music business when I played one time with Riley Puckett, Clayton McMichen, and the Skillet Lickers. One day a bunch of musicians came by my house and asked me to go with them to play up in Cranberry, North Carolina. Among the group was Earl Johnson on fiddle, a banjo player by the name of Backston, Riley Puckett on guitar, and Gid Tanner and Clayton McMichen on fiddles. There was also Clarence Greene, Bert Layne, and Arthur Tanner, Gid's son. Anyway, they came over and asked me to play guitar with them on this show they had lined up. I remember that when we reached Spruce Pine, North Carolina, Riley Puckett got mad at something and started walking off down the road by himself. He was blind, you know. We had to catch him and bring him back to the car. He was awful hard to get along with. When I saw him play, he played with a thumb pick and a forefinger pick."

"People didn't start playing with what I call a 'fan pick' [flat pick] 'til way after I took up the guitar. And I never saw any grand bar chords [barre chords] when I first started playing the guitar either. I never did see that 'til some of them fellers from the North came down here."

"Anyway, we put on that show in Cranberry with that bunch. I never will forget the drive over there. There was a feller mowing hay down there beside the road where we were driving along. A bumblebee flew into the car and stung McMichen, who was driving. Suddenly, he jerked the car to a stop and started to holler that something was eating him up. We about died laughing."

"It was after playing with the assortment of musicians who went by the name of the Skillet Lickers that Walter Davis and Clarence Greene decided to strike out by themselves. We figured that they had enough musicians without me and Clarence, so we decided to try to make it on our own. I was still pretty young, so Clarence had to ask permission from my dad to let me travel with him. After promising that he'd bring me back safe and sound, me and Clarence started playing all over the country."

Before long, Walter Davis and Clarence Greene had added several members to their growing band.

"We picked up Gwen Foster to play the guitar and French harp and Will Abernathy to play the autoharp. We traveled around the country playing anywhere we could find. We often played at filling stations. We'd pull up and take out our instruments and play right there near the pumps. It wouldn't be long 'til we gathered fifty or seventy-five people there, and we'd really put on a show. Then we'd pass the hat and usually did pretty good. Most of the time the gas station attendant would set up and sell candy and gas to the crowd that had gathered, and sometimes he'd show his gratitude and fill up our tanks, and off we went."

"One time we teamed up with Mack Crow, who billed himself as the 'King of the Five-String Banjo Players.' We did several shows over in his territory near Hickory, North Carolina. We heard there was going to be a banjo contest down there, so we went down to see if we could maybe take home a little prize money. Mack, he usually won every contest that he entered. I'd played the banjo since I was nine years old, only not many people knew I played the banjo, 'cause I usually followed the guitar. So I decided to enter that contest and, wouldn't you know, I won first place. Mack Crow couldn't believe I beat him, 'cause he didn't know I even played the banjo. I played 'Little Old Log Cabin in the Lane.' I really believe it was the novelty of the way I played it, and the fact that the judges were surprised that I played the banjo at all, that caused me to win that thing."

"We used to go to all the fiddlers conventions in our part of the country. I went to one near Bristol, Virginia, back in the twenties, where I met Charlie Poole. I never did play too much with him, but I heard him play. We entered the contest, but Charlie was hired to play so he didn't compete. Dock Walsh was there too. He played in a two-finger style. I guess you could say he played a little like Charlie Poole, but people didn't pattern after each other like they do now. You've got to have your own style. Let them pattern after you."

"I remember one fiddlers convention that they had in Asheville, North Carolina. We went down there, and so did Jimmie Rodgers, who was living in Old Fort, North Carolina, at the time. He worked for the railroad out of Old Fort and used to play music in a restaurant there. We'd get together and play together some. So Jimmie went down to this fiddlers convention and played. Clarence Greene, who was a fiddler, went and he played guitar in that contest and won first place over Jimmie Rodgers. Clarence played 'The Chattanooga Blues.' I never will forget that."

"Speaking about the blues, there was a fiddler who came through town one time that kind of had a blues lick on the fiddle. That was Fiddlin' Arthur Smith. I'm all the time kidding musicians and I remember, when I saw Smith, I went up to him and handed him a nickel. He asked me what that was for, and I told him that if ever I saw a man uglier than I was, I'd give him a nickel. He said, 'Wait a minute, I think I'll give it back.'"

"We used to have some times back then. I remember that George Morris and I used to buddy around together quite a bit. George is Zeke and Wiley's older brother. George more or less learned off of me, and his brothers Wiley and Zeke more or less learned off of him. They were the ones that came up with that song 'Salty Dog.'" [The

Morris Brothers updated "Salty Dog Blues," first recorded by Charlie Jackson, an African American.]

"I made some records but never made much money off of them. I did some recording with Gwen Foster as the Carolina Twins. We recorded several numbers for Columbia, including a song we called 'This Morning, This Evening, Right Now.' Art Satherley was the man in charge up there. I also recorded with Gwen, Dock Walsh, and Bill Short for Romeo. We called that group the Blue Ridge Entertainers. I can't remember the names of all the songs we recorded, but I do remember recording 'Bring Me a Leaf from the Sea' and 'Corrina.' I also recorded two guitar solos. One number I wrote was called the 'Crooked Creek Blues' and the other was called 'Going Back to Coney Isle.'"

"The last record we made was recorded in New York. We had Clarence Greene, Tom Ashley, and Will Abernathy along with us. We acted like we were going to put on a fiddlers convention in Tom's house. We had a little skit worked up where Tom had some whiskey and I said something like 'Give me a drink of that whiskey.' Then Tom barked like a dog and asked his wife to put the dog out. I played the guitar on that record. I believe that our skit about drinking whiskey came out way before the Skillet Lickers started doing theirs."

"After I got married, I settled down and never really wanted to try to make it as a musician. Carpentering's my trade. I did organize me a band and had regular square dances for about a year. We had a dance team, cloggers, and a stage show booked into the Carolina Theater in Spruce Pine. I used different fiddlers, because no one fiddler would want to stay put that long. J.C. McCool played the guitar for me. We still play together occasionally."

It wasn't long before our conversation drifted back to the instruments sitting idle on our laps. They'd grown cold sitting quietly there, but now were warming up as we began playing some good old tunes.

The above is based on numerous personal interviews I had with Walter Davis at his home in Black Mountain, North Carolina, in 1980. It originally appeared in Bluegrass Unlimited *in March 1981.*

Snuffy Jenkins

When looking into the roots of three-finger banjo playing in bluegrass music, fingers often seem to point toward one man: Snuffy Jenkins. I was lucky enough to meet this legendary banjo player at several festivals and shows in the mid–1970s and early 1980s. Like the humble man that he was, he was slow to take credit for the important role he played in the development of the bluegrass banjo style.

Born DeWitt Jenkins on October 27, 1908, in Harris, North Carolina, Jenkins never took himself too seriously. Even his nickname, "Snuffy," was kind of a joke. During one of the hilarious skits with his band, Jenkins was dressed as a woman from head to toe. For laughs he kept wiping his nose with the sleeve of his dress, and the band's leader, Byron Parker, nicknamed him "Snuffy." The name stuck and Jenkins later reported, "My wife even calls me Snuffy." Jenkins was once asked why he eventually gave up playing music professionally. With characteristic wit he answered, "I quit on account of my health. I was starving to death!"

Snuffy Jenkins, ca. 1998 (photograph by Jim Carr).

Snuffy's relaxed attitude and ready laugh made him one of the best-loved performers in the Carolinas. It didn't hurt, of course, that he was also a master of the three-finger banjo style.

Like thousands of other North Carolina youngsters, Jenkins grew up around old-time banjo and fiddle music. He and his brother Verl built their first homemade banjos using a wagon hub and then an old automobile brake drum. In 1927 Jenkins graduated to a mail-order banjo from Sears Roebuck.

While developing his style, Jenkins came under the spell of two banjo players of some local renown, Smith Hammett and Rex Brooks. Little is known about these shadowy figures, but it is clear that Jenkins learned three-finger banjo from them, and they went on to perform together throughout the Carolinas. By 1934 Snuffy had formed the Jenkins String Band, which was soon hired by the *Crazy Water Barn Dance*, broadcasting over WBT in Charlotte, North Carolina.

With these early performances, Snuffy Jenkins became the first three-finger banjo player to broadcast over the radio. Because of the importance that early radio had on people's lives, Snuffy's influence on other banjo players was immense. Before long, many banjo players within earshot of WBT were trading in their clawhammer and two-finger licks for the new way of picking the banjo using three fingers.

"I've never called my music anything other than country. We were playing bluegrass years before it received the name," according to Jenkins.

From WBT, Snuffy moved to WSPA in Spartanburg, South Carolina, and then to WIS in Columbia, South Carolina. While at WIS, Snuffy met Byron Parker, who had been promoting the Monroe Brothers. Parker was a natural-born salesman who could sell ice to Eskimos.

Besides being a popular announcer on WIS, Parker formed Byron Parker's Hillbillies in 1937, with George Morris and Leonard Stokes on guitars, J.E. Mainer on fiddle, and Snuffy on banjo. This band recorded for RCA Victor's Bluebird subsidiary as J.E. Mainer's Mountaineers in August of 1937. Jenkins's work on three of those tracks—"Floating Down the Stream of Time," "Don't Get Trouble in Your Mind," and "Kiss Me Cindy"—marked one of the earliest times that this type of three-finger banjo playing was heard on record. The band itself had a sound that was eerily close to what we now call "bluegrass."

In addition to his banjo playing, Snuffy helped keep alive performing traditions of the previous century. Comedy skits and outlandish costumes were always used on the "kerosene circuit," as it was called. Snuffy frequently wore baggy clown pants and a slouch hat. Some of his skits included "Snuffy Cures a Snakebite," "Hookeyville School," and "Dead or Alive," where Snuffy played the part of an undertaker.

Taking the lead in many of these skits, after the group morphed into the Hired Hands, was Julian "Greasy" Medlin. A veteran of the vaudeville stage, Greasy had worked for eleven years in a medicine show, selling tonics, herbs, and remedies that claimed to make the lame walk and the blind see. When he joined the band, he brought a wealth of both minstrel and medicine show songs, gags, and skits.

Snuffy's powerful banjo style made a strong impact on two young musicians who would later play a key role in the development of bluegrass: Earl Scruggs and Don Reno. Both have acknowledged learning a great deal from Snuffy. Scruggs, in particular, remembered hearing Snuffy with Byron Parker's Hillbillies over WIS radio in 1937–38. In 1971 Don Reno told interviewer Bill Vernon, "Snuffy taught me the basic three-finger roll on the five-string banjo when I was just a little boy … that's what turned me on to banjo. Before Snuffy's style, banjo sounded harsh and crude to me."

The funniest tale I've heard about Snuffy was the time he was interviewed by Charles K. Wolfe, who solemnly asked him, "What is the first thing you remember hearing on the radio?" Snuffy's answer was simple: "Static!"

The above is partially based on a personal interview I had with Snuffy Jenkins at a TV studio in Hickory, North Carolina, in 1977.

Earl Scruggs

Earl. To bluegrass people that one word says it all. For those of you who are new to this music, "Earl" is the Earl in Earl Scruggs. Without him, bluegrass just would not have been bluegrass. To give you some idea of how important I think Earl is to the roots of bluegrass, I'll tell you how I indoctrinated my banjo students at Warren Wilson College in Swannanoa, North Carolina. On the first day of class, after I took the roll, I always asked them to turn around toward the east-facing windows. I then told them that exactly sixty-eight and a half miles southeast of the campus is the wide spot in the road known as Boiling Springs, North Carolina. That is where Earl was born—ground zero for the birth of bluegrass banjo.

To get a handle on exactly what Earl did that affected bluegrass so much, you must look at Bill Monroe's band in 1945. At that time, the Blue Grass Boys consisted of Bill Monroe on mandolin, Lester Flatt on guitar, Sally Ann Forrester on accordion, Jim Shumate on fiddle, Andy Boyette on bass and comedy, and David Akeman (better known as "Stringbean") on banjo and comedy.

That summer Monroe hired dancer, musician, and comedian Lew Childre to work the

Earl Scruggs, ca. 1960 (John Edwards Memorial Foundation Records [20001], Southern Folklife Collection at Wilson Special Collections Library, University of North Carolina at Chapel Hill).

tent show circuit with him. When the band wasn't working, Stringbean and Childre would go off fishing. By September they had decided to form a duo and Stringbean gave two weeks' notice to Monroe. As Jim Shumate later remarked, "We hated to see ole String go. When he quit, it left a big hole."

Monroe asked Shumate if he knew of any banjo players in North Carolina and Shumate immediately thought of Earl Scruggs, whose home in Boiling Springs was not more than fifty miles from where Shumate lived in Hickory. "I know a fellow," said Shumate, "but he don't play Stringbean style." Monroe was now curious and asked, "Who is it?" Shumate smiled and said, "Earl Scruggs."

As a shy boy growing up in Cleveland County, Earl Scruggs had heard his father and his older brother Junie play banjo. By the time he was no bigger than a banjo, Earl started picking out tunes himself. Besides his brother and father, he also came under the spell of local banjo players Smith Hammett, Rex Brooks, and Snuffy Jenkins.

He later recalled that because of a quarrel he had with Junie, his mother separated the boys and Earl spent several hours confined to the living room with nothing to amuse himself with except his banjo. He began playing "Reuben," and while daydreaming about something else, he started using a flowing series of notes that we now call "rolls." As Earl tells the story, that's where his style began.

Fiddler Jim Shumate recalls meeting the young Scruggs. "We used to have a thing in the city auditorium in Hickory called the Carolina Jamboree. Earl came up there one night with a bunch of boys from Shelby and Earl was back in the dressing room picking banjo with a fella named Grady Wilkie, who was singing and picking the guitar. And that's where I met him. I liked his banjo pickin' and I [didn't forget it]."

By the time he was a teenager, Earl got his first professional job playing with Wiley and Zeke, the Morris Brothers. After about eight months, Earl went to Knoxville, Tennessee, to audition with a band that played on radio WNOX. Although they didn't hire him, Earl did get the attention of Lost John Miller, who asked Earl to join his band, the Allied Kentuckians. In addition to playing on WNOX, the band traveled once a week to Nashville to do a 9:00 a.m. radio show on WSM.

One morning as Earl was leaving the WSM radio studio, he was surprised to see Jim Shumate waiting for him. Earl remembered meeting Jim in Hickory, North Carolina,

Flatt & Scruggs on the stage of Grand Ole Opry, ca. 1958. From left: unknown bass player, Paul Warren, Earl Scruggs, Curly Seckler, and Lester Flatt (courtesy Ken Landreth).

several years earlier. Shumate explained that Bill Monroe had recently asked him if he knew of any banjo players in North Carolina to replace Stringbean. He immediately thought of Earl Scruggs and had called Earl's mother to find him. She told Shumate that Earl was in Nashville doing a radio show with Lost John Miller.

Shumate told Earl that Monroe was looking for a banjo player and asked if he was interested. Although apprehensive about leaving Lost John, Scruggs said he would like to try out with Bill Monroe.

At the time Shumate was living at the Tulane Hotel in Nashville, so an audition was arranged. Shumate recalled, "We took the mandolin, fiddle, and banjo there in my room. Earl was as nervous as all get out. Boy, he really laid the timber to that banjo! Bill had never heard anything like that. I asked Bill, 'What do you think?' Bill said, 'Gosh, that's good; I'm going to hire him.'"

Shumate had already turned in his notice to leave the Blue Grass Boys. Returning home to North Carolina, he tuned in the Grand Ole Opry that Saturday night, heard Earl, and knew that Monroe had hired him. Shumate recalls with pride, "When Earl hit the stage, he really tore that place up."

Shumate hit the nail on the head. Earl's hard-driving banjo playing fit in perfectly with Monroe's style. For many people, Earl's jaw-dropping banjo playing was the final ingredient that jump-started Monroe's band and helped to jell the style which would soon be called bluegrass music.

Raymond Fairchild—Making His Own Way

They call him "The Old Man of the Mountains." At the spry age of forty-two [when this was written in 1981], that makes Raymond Fairchild a rather youthful "old man." No matter. The mountains can age you before your time, and Raymond has lived far enough back in the Smoky Mountains to be several generations old by now. This man, who some consider to be the fastest and the best banjo player alive, lays a genuine claim to playing mountain music. He's lived it.

Born near Cherokee, North Carolina, to a Cherokee Indian mother and a father whose duties in the military kept him gone most of the time, Raymond Fairchild grew up in the hard times. Raymond spent most of his early years working the family farm, doing odd jobs, and walking the trails in the woods alone. Long back roads and winter snows kept Raymond from the one-room schoolhouse for most of the year. He did manage to finish the fourth grade but never completely mastered reading and writing. There were other teachers for Raymond.

His mother's people taught him the ways of the woods. Completely at home deep in the forest, Raymond knows his way around, a true mountain man. In the fall of the year, he still hunts ginseng, which has a root highly valued for its legendary curing properties. Although some ginseng hunters in the mountains take their sack of "sang" to nearby Asheville, North Carolina, or Knoxville, Tennessee, to sell for more than $200 a pound, Raymond keeps all that he digs.

Raymond Fairchild at his home near Maggie Valley, North Carolina, ca. 1981 (photograph by the author).

Drawing upon lore learned from his mother's

people, he combines ginseng with eighteen other roots and herbs to produce a medicine which he takes daily as a tonic. Going far into the woods in search of ginseng and other roots, Raymond has been known to stay gone for nearly a month. After one such trip he told of killing more than a dozen deadly rattlesnakes. Besides bringing home a poke full of wild roots, he often returns from the mountains with a fat groundhog in his sack. Claiming that groundhog is the finest wild meat in the world, Raymond also renders grease from the woodchuck to make a tonic for the croup. "Just a spoonful or two," he cautions.

Occasionally, on a Saturday night, he would go over to his aunt's house to listen to a little old-time music. Being left-handed, Aunt Ballew played the five-string banjo upside down in a three-finger style. Sometimes she would be joined on guitar by Uncle France or Raymond's mother on the mouth harp. This was the first music Raymond heard, and he never forgot the sounds of his aunt's cabin.

Banjos, Raymond remembers, were scarce back in those Smoky Mountains. Religious people thought the banjo was the work of the devil and would have nothing to do with it. Guitars, fiddles, and harmonicas were fine, but the banjo had a mark on it. "You were hell-bound if you picked a banjo."

Raymond was just ornery enough to want to play the banjo. Although he listened to Aunt Bellew for years, it wasn't until he was eighteen years old and nearly grown that he could afford one. His first banjo was fretless with a squirrel hide tacked over the hoop. He next ordered a Silvertone model from Sears Roebuck. The banjo came with an instruction booklet, but Raymond had always shied away from book learning. He was learning to play it his own way.

His dad noticed his progress on the instrument and finally took the young man to Dunham's Music House in Asheville and bought him a Gibson RB-150 model. Along with the banjo, his dad bought him some picks, but it was some time before he realized that Raymond was playing with the picks on backward!

On one of those rare trips to Asheville, Raymond discovered jukeboxes. There's no telling how many hard-won quarters Raymond dropped in the slot to listen to Earl Scruggs play "Flint Hill Special," "Earl's Breakdown," or "Randy Lynn Rag." Like many struggling banjo players in the early 1950s, Scruggs's playing set Raymond on fire.

Unlike many who bought Scruggs's records and studied them at home, Raymond did not have the luxury of electricity. To this day he does not own a record player. By the time he was nearly fully grown, his family had purchased a battery-powered radio. Then Raymond was able to tune in the Grand Ole Opry on Saturday night, broadcasting from Nashville, or listen to the Stanley Brothers on *Farm and Fun Time* out of Bristol, Virginia. He also heard pioneer banjo player Snuffy Jenkins, with Pappy Sherrill and the Hired Hands, over a station near Statesville, North Carolina.

Except for this limited exposure to professional banjo players heard on radio, Raymond had to make his own way with his music. He had to "hold it in his head," as he has said. Besides his Aunt Ballew, there were scarcely any other banjo players around who could show Raymond how to play. But there were plenty of good fiddlers to learn from. Raymond fondly remembers the fiddling of oldsters Carrol Massey and Robert Richards. These and other fiddlers gave Raymond contact with a large store of traditional mountain tunes from which he would later draw.

Raymond has always had a deep feeling for the blues. To some, the banjo might seem unsuited to playing the blues, but that's before they've heard Raymond. As a boy of ten he would often see Black convicts in stripes, working on the road crews under the watchful eye of an armed guard. Raymond would creep up to where they were having their dinner break and listen while they sang the blues. That lonesome singing made a strong impression and would weave a deep thread in his music.

He also sat in rapt attention to the music of Bill Monroe, who he often heard on the radio. It wasn't until sometime later that he realized that the banjo player he was listening to in Monroe's band was actually a string of different players. He does recall that Rudy Lyle was one of his favorites.

Occasionally Raymond would get to see professional banjo players in person, on their show dates in schoolhouses and tiny auditoriums in western North Carolina. He was especially impressed with Wade Mainer from nearby Weaverville, who he called "the real McCoy."

Even though Raymond did get to hear banjo players in person and on the "piccolos"—the name he calls jukeboxes—he stubbornly refused to copy anybody else's playing. Even as a beginner he was determined to go his own way. He does admit, "You'd hear parts of a tune and that's as much of it as you'd get. You'd have to pick out the rest of it in your mind. My style is just something I came up with, something I had to do. If I had a record player and had people to show me, I'd probably have done just like anybody else. I always listen to all kinds of music: Chet Atkins, the Delmore Brothers…. I do yet. You don't know where you'll get it from. If you see a young kid who only knows two tunes on the banjer, don't ever walk by him, because you're liable to pick up something that nobody else can show you."

It was during the middle 1960s that Raymond first attempted to take his music to the public. Moving from Cherokee to Maggie Valley, North Carolina, he found a receptive audience at the Hillbilly Campground. Seven days a week for more than twelve years, Raymond played for tips next to the road in front of the campground, from eight in the morning until midnight. He was often joined by Roy Mull on guitar, Frank Buchanan (who had earlier recorded with Bill Monroe) on guitar and mandolin, the late Wilford Messer on fiddle, and Buck Duncan on bass. According to Raymond, they'd really pull the cars in.

Raising a family with three kids, Raymond supplemented the money he made playing for tips by working as a stonemason. He hired on as a helper but soon became partners with James Worley, doing contract work around Maggie Valley. Worley was somewhat of a musician himself; a harmonica rack bolted to his autoharp enabled him to blow the French harp and strum the autoharp at the same time. By 1972 Fairchild had totally and forever quit the bottle which once had quite a hold on him.

During this period Raymond was approached by Uncle Jim O'Neal to record for Rural Rhythm Records. A string of albums produced over the next several years included *Mama Likes Bluegrass Music*, *Smoky Mountain Banjo*, *Raymond Fairchild and the Maggie Valley Boys*, and *Honky Tonkin' Country Blues*. Raymond seemed willing to experiment with sounds and styles that few others had ever attempted on the banjo. Included on several of these recordings were drums, saxophone, and steel guitar.

As Raymond's style on the banjo became more inventive, his reputation as a unique individual and musician started to spread. In early 1970 Nat Winston hired Raymond and the Maggie Valley Boys to play for a party at his cabin on Grandfather Mountain. A struggling banjo player himself, Winston recognized Raymond's genius and set up an informal audition in Roy Acuff's dressing room at the Grand Ole Opry. While Loretta

Lynn and Ernest Tubb were entertaining the Opry audience with "Sweet Thang," Raymond was playing the daylights out of "Whoa Mule" and "Orange Blossom Special," to the slack jaws of the crowd that gathered backstage.

The assembled group included such dignitaries as Roy Acuff, Archie Campbell, Bill Carlisle, Billy Grammer, and Bill Monroe. Campbell approached Raymond about appearing on *Hee Haw*. Hal Durham, manager of the Opry, was also listening in and asked Raymond to appear as a guest. For Raymond, playing the Opry was the break he needed. As he put it, "When you step in front of those WSM microphones on the Grand Ole Opry, that's the highest you're going in this type of music, buddy."

Raymond's first appearance at the Opry literally drove the audience wild. Even though he stands motionless when he plays and never smiles, sings, or talks on stage, his playing makes him, in the words of Roy Acuff, "the best showman I've seen." In addition to being the first banjo player since Earl Scruggs to bring down the house at the Grand Ole Opry, he is also the first musician known to walk in front of the WSM microphones with a loaded .38 revolver in his pocket. Raymond explained, "There's a lot of meanness in this world."

Although playing the Opry symbolizes success to country and bluegrass musicians, the real success—or failure—happens at the end of long drives, when the artist stands in front of his audience. Here is where the real stuff of country music lives. Raymond can tell you that things haven't always come easy for the musicians who face the crowds night after night. "If you're out there playing a show, you've got to play from the heart. You've got to feel it; you've got to live it. A lot of people sing, but they have their mind on something else while they're singing."

"The people who've made bluegrass music what it is today, buddy, they've lived it. Back when bluegrass first started, you know they couldn't have been making much money doin' it. But they wouldn't change, they wouldn't quit."

"Just the other night I done a show with Don Reno in Blue Ridge, Georgia. Man, he was so sick. Most of these young musicians would have been at home in bed, with somebody rubbing their chest with Vicks salve. But Don Reno was up there doing his show. Any minute it looked like it was going to be his last breath. Now, I ain't kidding. He told me he had something like bronchitis and felt like he was smothering. He'd talk a while and then take a deep breath. That's love. That's what's helped bluegrass music out, people like that."

"Bill Monroe's traveled the roads many, many times and didn't always make money. So did Ralph and Carter Stanley. Ralph has told me many times they'd have to play a show before they could eat. I've seen Ralph and Carter come into Spruce Pine, North Carolina, back in the '50s and play for eight or ten people. They were playing on a percentage basis and people were paying thirty or forty cents to get in, so you can figure out how much they made. It was the love of it that kept 'em going."

"There are some great young musicians, but they don't understand what the hard life is. If it boiled down to the hard times again, they'd be quittin'. They wouldn't have the backbone to stand up. They don't love it well enough where they'd hang with it and play for nothing. Them fellers played for years and years and never made nothing—Bill Monroe, Reno and Smiley, Mac Wiseman, Ralph and Carter, the Goins Brothers. That's who we can thank now. They're the ones who handed it down on a silver platter. It was fellers back then that held 'er together."

For Raymond, one of the hardest things has been finding musicians with the sound he was looking for. "A lot of people will tell you the woods is full of guitar pickers. The woods is full of frammers, not guitar players. You can name [great] rhythm guitar players on your right hand. What I like to hear is straight, solid pickin'. I've been into it for twenty-five years and, with all honesty, I'll have to say the one I've got now, Josh Crowe, is the best rhythm picker I've ever heard in my life. The bass player too, Wayne Crowe, he's the best bass man I've ever heard. I've always known in my mind what I wanted, but I never found it until I run up on the Crowe brothers. That was in 1975. When I met them, I knew I'd found what I'd been looking for."

"It don't take a stageful to play music. You take three men and all of them pushing time, and it sounds right … a lot of people tell me to pick one with drive. They think you have to be playing fast to have drive. But the 'Tennessee Waltz' has drive if the timing's right. Time is drive. Drive is time. You can drive a waltz just the same as when you're burning one up if everybody's there. Listen to Bill Monroe's 'Kentucky Waltz' or Jimmy Martin's 'Widow Maker' and you'll hear drive. That's one thing a lot of 'em's got to learn. I've played with a lot of fellers who had time but didn't know the melody. And I've played with fellers who knew the melody but didn't have time."

"I never did try to get hired by any of the professional bands. I knew if I did try to play with any of those guys, I'd have to change my style. When you go to pick with a man like Bill Monroe, you've got to pick the Monroe sound. I could have changed, but I didn't want to leave my work behind. I never did want to change what I started; I knew someday I'd put it out, my way. You can't do that working as a sideman for somebody else."

"You know, I've played for years with these fellers and they wanted to do all Bill Monroe, or all Jimmy Martin, or all somebody else. You can't get nothin' going doin' that, it ain't going to do you no good. Them fellers are great, they're the ones who made it, but you can't get on stage in front of them at a festival and do their stuff. That's what's the matter with bluegrass. They claim they love it, but they don't love it enough to sit down and learn some new songs or new chords. Bluegrass musicians are the laziest people on earth. They want to play something they can use one chord, or something somebody else already has out. You've got to take the old stuff and make it your own way."

Making his own way for Raymond meant breaking new ground on the banjo. He made banjo showcases out of tunes that have seldom been featured on the banjo, such as "Yakety Sax" and "Steel Guitar Rag." When Raymond plays his version of "Orange Blossom Special," you can see the steam rise off the engine, smell the smoke pour out of the stack, and feel the ground shake as the train pulls out of sight. And, like that train, Raymond Fairchild is going places. His new record on Marc Pruett's Skyline label is getting the exposure it deserves. Named after his youngest boy, "Little Zane," the record features Raymond's unique banjo style, along with Wallace and Wayne Crowe, plus Mike Hunter on mandolin, Steve Sutton on lead guitar, and Tim Galyean on drums.

Although the summer festivals take Raymond far from his home in the Smoky Mountains, in the winter he stays close to Maggie Valley, where he plays at the Stompin' Ground. If you don't find him there, you can guess that Raymond's gone off in the woods hunting ginseng, groundhog, or solitude.

The above is based on an interview I did with Raymond Fairchild at his home in Maggie Valley, North Carolina, in 1981. It originally appeared in Bluegrass Unlimited *in March 1982.*

Why Are There So Many Banjo Jokes?

Maybe you've heard the one about the banjo player who always sits in a level spot so the tobacco juice will run out of both sides of his mouth.

Or the guy who made a perfect score by throwing a banjo in a Dumpster without hitting the sides. He earned extra points for landing on top of an accordion.

Or why did the banjo player cross the road? It was the chicken's day off.

Or what do you call a banjo player in a three-piece suit? A defendant.

The fact is, people love making jokes about banjos and the people who play them. These banjo jokes have taken over where the moron, blonde, lawyer, and Polack jokes left off. For the heck of it, let's try to figure out why people get such a kick out of picking on banjo players and what is it about the banjo that makes it the brunt of so many jokes.

To answer this question, we need to take a little trip back to 1843. At that time minstrel music was just taking root, and it soon surged in popularity to become America's first national musical obsession. The minstrels were part of an entire stage show, consisting of rowdy dancing, boisterous singing and playing, biting humor, and outrageous skits. Of course, minstrel shows were done in blackface, with the performers wearing loosely fitting ragamuffin garments, oversized shoes, and slouch hats.

Minstrel bands performed everywhere, from concert stages in the North to the goldfields of California, on the decks of Mississippi River boats, and in the camps of Civil War soldiers. At the core of minstrel music was the five-string banjo. In time, the instrument itself came to symbolize an entire era of minstrel music, and it's no wonder that the banjo was forever linked to the comic characters depicted in the minstrel show.

When the movie *Deliverance* hit the big screen in 1972, it became an instant classic. Almost overnight, the faded image of the blackface minstrel banjo player was replaced by the stereotype of the banjo as the favorite instrument of low-intellect hillbillies.

With its sordid past, the poor banjo continues to be America's whipping boy. Banjo jokes, although told in the spirit of fun, do reveal remnants of America's ambivalent attitudes toward the banjo and those who play it.

For example, many banjo jokes paint the banjo player as stupid, or worse.

How do you get a banjo player's eyes to sparkle? Shine a light in his ears.
What has sixteen legs and three teeth? The front row of a banjo concert.
There's not much difference between you and a fool, is there? Just this here banjo.
What did the banjo player get on his IQ test? Drool.
What is this: X X X ? Three banjo players cosigning a loan.
Why was the banjo player staring at the bottle of orange juice? Because it said "Concentrate."
A man went to a brain store to get some brain for dinner. He asked the butcher, "How much for fiddle player brain?" "Two dollars an ounce." "How much for guitar player brain?" "Four dollars an ounce." "What about banjo player brain?" "One hundred dollars an ounce." "Why are the banjo player brains so high?" "Do you know how many banjo players it takes to get one ounce of brain?"

Attributes of the banjo itself have helped to make it the brunt of jokes. For example, the banjo is a rather loud instrument, especially when played with the picks most bluegrass players use.

What's the difference between a banjo and a chain saw? You can turn a chain saw off.

Because the banjo is a loud instrument, and bluegrass music demands a certain aggressiveness or attack, banjos players have been seen as showoffs.

Banjo players are like sharks. They think they must keep playing or they'll sink.
How is playing the banjo a lot like throwing a javelin blindfolded? You don't have to be very good to get people's attention.

Multiple banjos are discouraged in a band or jam session.

How do you get two banjo players to play in unison? Shoot one.

Bluegrass banjo music is thought by many people to be highly repetitious.

What's the difference between a banjo and an Uzi? An Uzi only repeats forty times.

Bluegrass is typically rather sentimental and resistant to change.

How many banjo players does it take to screw in a light bulb? Five: one to screw it in and four to lament about how much they miss the old one.
How many banjo players does it take to screw in a light bulb? Five: one to screw it in and four to complain that it's electric.

Bluegrass banjo traces its existence to one man, Earl Scruggs.

How many banjo players does it take to screw in a light bulb? Five: one to screw it in and four to complain that Earl wouldn't have done it that way.

Banjo players are often lambasted because they don't earn much money.

What's the difference between a run-over skunk and a run-over banjo player? The skunk was on his way to a gig.
What will you never say about a banjo player? That's a nice Porsche.
What's the difference between a banjo and a pizza? A pizza can feed a family of four.
How do you get a banjo player off your porch? By paying for the pizza.
How can you make a million dollars as a banjo player? Start with two million.
What's the difference between a certificate of deposit and a banjo player? The CD eventually matures and earns some money.

Many people think that all banjo tunes sound the same.

How can you tell the difference between all the different banjo songs? By their names.

Banjo players have frequently been accused of being less than stellar musicians.

How can you tell if there's a banjo player at your door? They can't find the key, the knocking speeds up, and they don't know when to come in.

By their nature, banjos easily get out of tune, so there's lots of banjo tuning jokes.

What's the best way to tune a banjo? With wire cutters.

Most banjo players learn either by ear or by tab, which is a shortcut way of writing down banjo music. Very few banjo players use standard musical notation.

Can you read music? Not enough to hurt my playing.
How do you get a banjo player to slow down? Put some music in front of him.

The banjo has been perceived by some as a difficult instrument to play well.

What's the difference between a good banjo player and Bigfoot? There have been sightings of Bigfoot.

Although banjos can be quite expensive, some people don't value them.

Yesterday my car was broken into, and I had my banjo in the back. Did they take it? No, but they left me two more banjos.

In some banjo jokes, players are depicted as lacking taste.

How do you tell where the pink flamingos live? There's a banjo player on the front lawn!

After all this research I have firmly decided that there is really only one banjo joke. The rest are true stories.

More Bluegrass Pioneers

Cleo Davis—The Original Blue Grass Boy

On March 9, 1919, a doctor rode in his horse-drawn buggy through the hills of northwest Georgia to the home of Ben and Effie Davis. He was summoned because Effie was about to have a child. By the time the doc had left, Effie and John were the proud parents of a healthy baby boy. As yet, they had no name for him. By and by they gave him the name Cleo.

As young Cleo grew up, he was surrounded by music. His mama played the pump organ and sang the old hymns along with her brothers and sisters, who practically filled

Bill Monroe and the Blue Grass Boys, ca. 1940. From left: Art Wooten, Bill Monroe, Cleo Davis, and Amos Garren (courtesy Mary Johnson).

up the church where they worshipped. His dad picked a five-string banjo in the old clawhammer style. Cleo remembers his father taking the banjo off the wall and holding it next to the fireplace or woodburning oven to warm the coonskin stretched over the banjo. This, his dad told him, would tighten the head and give it the proper "thump." Cleo couldn't get near enough to that banjo. Sometimes on a Saturday night, his uncle Jim Davis would come over to the house with a mouth harp. They were often joined by his mama's cousin, Efrid McDowell, who always brought a shiny black Stella guitar.

In the summer months the men gathered on the porch to play. With the older folks looking on, the children would join hands and dance in the light of an oil-burning lamp or the nuts that were set ablaze in the yard. When Cleo wasn't dancing, he'd often wrestle the lard bucket from his brothers Dale or Bob and beat rhythm on it like a drum. After his mama died, Cleo went to live with his uncle Marcus, who kept the boy entertained with a five-string banjo. Marcus and another uncle who played the fiddle made Cleo more determined than ever to learn to play string music.

When he was about ten years old, Cleo heard that there was going to be a music program at the schoolhouse just down the road. He had never heard of Gid Tanner and Riley Puckett, but he knew if they were coming all the way from Atlanta to play they must be good. On the night of the concert, Cleo walked barefoot to the schoolhouse. There he found that admission was fifteen cents more than he had, which was nothing. Not to be turned away, he slipped around the side of the building where he could listen through the window. Since it was summertime, the windows to the auditorium were open, so young Cleo could hear everything that went on in the hall. He remembers hearing them play "Down Yonder" and "Back Up and Push," tunes Gid Tanner and Riley Puckett had made famous with the Skillet Lickers on Bluebird Records.

Inspired by what he had heard, Cleo walked home determined to make himself a guitar. He searched until he found an old oilcan, to which he attached a sawmill strip for a neck. After punching a hole in the top of the can, he stretched a single strand of screen wire over the top and his one-string guitar was complete. "I sang and yodeled and strummed that guitar until my sister chased me out of the house. There wasn't a barn, so I had to go out into the woods to play. I kept on singing and carrying on 'til I drove all the wild animals back into the river swamp."

Then the resourceful Cleo Davis caught some rabbits and traded the skins to a peddler he met on the road for a harmonica. After growing weary of blowing on the harmonica, he swapped it and a Barlow pocketknife for an old beat-up Stella guitar. Even though the guitar had edges that had come unglued, a warped neck, and no strings, Cleo marveled at his prize. With the help of some shoe tacks, he managed to attach the top back to the guitar. He then took a worn out set of his uncle's banjo strings and before long his guitar was strung up and ready to play. His sister took a dim view of this, however, and Cleo soon found himself back in the woods, happily singing and playing to himself.

When Cleo got a little older, he started working as a farm hand in Collard Valley, near Rome, Georgia. He'd plow cotton and corn and perform other farm duties for thirty-five cents a day plus room and board. After several months he was able to save enough to order a guitar out of the Sears Roebuck catalog for the sum of $2.40. This guitar was to replace the old Stella, which one of his brothers had sat on and broken. Cleo's new guitar finally arrived, along with an instruction book and a pick. He learned how to tune it and could soon play G, C, and D. The first tune he attempted was "It Ain't Gonna Rain No More."

Although phonograph records were rare and treasured commodities in the north Georgia mountains where Cleo was living, he managed to get a copy of the Carter Family's 1928 release of "Wildwood Flower." Like many a country guitar player, Cleo soon mastered the guitar part to "Wildwood Flower," and he also learned guitar runs and songs from Blue Yodeler Jimmie Rodgers. He remembers plowing a mule while singing and yodeling his way through many of Rodgers's songs. "It got so that the mule couldn't work unless I was singing and yodeling. I did notice that the old mule would shake his head when I'd hit a high note. I thought at first he was just flipping off the horseflies, but I later realized he was trying to tell me I was giving him a headache."

Cleo and the mule parted company when he moved in with another uncle in Cedartown, Georgia, near where he was born. "I had a cousin there named Georgia McDowell, who did a better job than I did on her Kalamazoo guitar. In the evening we would sit on the porch, strum guitars, and sing 'My Old Pal of Yesterday.' That's where I learned to harmonize. It wasn't long before I could sing most any part. We'd just switch the harmony around and play guitars right on. My uncle played the five-string banjo and the harmonica, so we were in pretty fair demand to play for parties. I still didn't know any more than G, C, and D, so if we couldn't play a song in G, we didn't play it."

The year was 1938 and Cleo found himself again on the move, looking for work. This time he crossed over into Alabama and landed a job as a farmhand for an old gentleman named Hans Graves, a tenant farmer. By the time Cleo laid that crop by, he had made up his mind that there must be more to life than plowing a mule. He collected his $18 for a month's work and told his buddies he was going to look for something better. Dressed in his Sunday clothes, he caught a ride on a truck headed for Atlanta. There he met a cousin who invited him to stay with him while he looked for a job. As luck would have it, the next day he was hired to work on an ice truck for the sum of $1 a day, the best wage he'd ever earned.

"One night in late August 1938, a friend, who was a policeman named Ed Daniels, came running over to the house waving a copy of the *Atlanta Journal* in his hand. He spread open the paper and pointed to a small ad wanting someone who

Bill Monroe (left) and Cleo Davis, ca. 1938 (courtesy Cleo Davis).

could play guitar and sing old-time songs. I tried to convince Ed that I barely knew how to hold the thing and that I didn't even know an entire old-time song, but he wouldn't listen. He and my cousin fairly insisted that I check out the ad and promised a little violence if I didn't. Since I didn't even own a guitar at that time, my cousin went down to the hockshop and bought me one for about $2.40. So, dressed in my Sunday best, I picked up that guitar and a copy of that newspaper clipping and went across Atlanta to check out the ad. My cousin went with me to make sure I didn't lose my nerve."

"We got to the location in the ad and found it to be a small trailer sitting next to a service station. When we approached the trailer, we heard country music coming out of that thing. I was a little hesitant to knock on the door, so I waited until the music stopped. Two or three guys came pouring out, and the man inside told them if he'd decided he'd give them a call. We were then invited in, and I trailed in last. Introductions were passed around, but I never did get his name. He said, 'Well, who plays the guitar?' I eventually pulled it out from behind me where I had it hid and said, 'I do, sir.' He asked, 'Well, what can you play?' 'Oh, maybe a verse or two of 'This World Is Not My Home' or 'What Would You Give in Exchange for Your Soul?' not knowing at that moment who I was talking to."

"My mind then flashed back, and I remembered how I had learned those two songs. Several years before, I had picked up the Grand Ole Opry over radio WSM. There I heard people like Arthur Smith and the Dixieliners, Clayton McMichen, and the Delmore Brothers. I thought the Delmore Brothers were out of this world. A little later some other brother acts came on the scene, such as the Callahan Brothers and the Shelton Brothers. Then I heard two brothers who had exactly what I thought I'd been looking for: the Monroe Brothers. I had no idea where they were located and had never seen them, but I had picked up one of their records of 'This World Is Not My Home' and 'What Would You Give in Exchange for Your Soul?' and that's how I learned those songs."

"I was awakened out of my thoughts when the man standing before me asked, 'You can sing "What Would You Give in Exchange for Your Soul?"' "I said, 'Yes, sir, I think I can sing that.' So, we proceeded to tune up together, but I soon found out that my $2.40 guitar would not tune up to that beautiful mandolin he had. So, he tuned down to my guitar and we hit out."

"We had done about a verse and a chorus of 'What Would You Give in Exchange for Your Soul?' when I recognized the voice. I didn't recognize the name, but I recognized the voice. This had to be one of the Monroe Brothers. I got so scared that I lost my voice and had to quit playing. He asked me what was the matter and I told him I had forgot the song. So, we talked for a moment, and I tried to calm down. I think he knew what had really happened to me. I had realized that I was standing there singing with Bill Monroe and I was shocked beyond reason."

"So, I finally recovered, and he said, 'Let's try "This World Is Not My Home,"' so we tried that. I was beginning to get brave and sang nearly two verses until I got scared to death and lost my voice again. He had to laugh a little about that and kidded me and said, 'You'll get over that.' We did a better job of it the next time. His wife, Carolyn, was sitting at the end of the trailer, listening. He said, 'Carolyn, what do you think?' She said that I sounded more like Charlie than any man she ever heard not to be Charlie Monroe. I seen a grin come over Bill's face and he said, 'Let's try that number again.' I think we did it still a little better that time, and he turned around and told Carolyn, 'I think I found what I've been looking for.'"

"I figured he couldn't have been looking for very much to have found it in me. To my amazement, I found out that he was satisfied with our sound and that he and Charlie had split up in Raleigh, North Carolina, some time before and that Bill had stopped in Little Rock, Arkansas, and formed a group there called The Kentuckians. He stayed there a few months and either they didn't go over too well or he was unhappy with their sound. So, he headed back to Atlanta, Georgia, where he and Charlie had worked a guest spot a few years before."

"Bill asked me if I could come back to the trailer the next morning about 8:30. I told him I would, not knowing what was in store for me. So, I caught a streetcar and was right back there the next morning. We drank some coffee, and Bill asked me if I knew of any music shops downtown where we could go look at some instruments. I told him I did, so we went downtown and looked at the guitars hanging in pawnshop windows."

"We finally found a big orchestra-type guitar that Bill strummed approvingly. He handed it to me and asked me how I liked it. I'd never played a guitar that cost more than $2.40, so this $37.50 guitar was the most beautiful thing I'd ever seen. I nodded furiously. Bill told the man we'd take it, and at that moment I hit the door hard and fast. This old country boy only had about a dollar in my pocket and there was no way I could buy that guitar. Bill paid the man and walked out with that guitar."

"Bill then asked me if I knew of any good men's shops. I told him there was a couple of nice ones just down the street. We went into one and Bill told the man to fix me up with a new suit of clothes. Bill said to 'fix him up from the floor up.' So, the man brought out shoes, pants, shirt, tie, and socks, and I tried 'em on. Bill told the salesman he wasn't finished yet. 'Do you have any John B. Stetsons?' So, the man brought me out a John B. Stetson [hat] with a wide brim and, when I got through dressing, James Cagney or George Raft had nothing on me, so long as I kept that Stetson pulled down over my eyes."

"Then Bill told the man to fix him up in the same style. So, Bill paid the man, and we walked out of there looking nearly alike, except that Bill outweighed me by about forty pounds. When we got back to his trailer, I started to carry the guitar inside, but he told me to take it home with me. I still didn't know what the score was, and I didn't dare ask. Bill Monroe is a man you don't get a lot out of, and sometimes it's better not to ask. He didn't talk a lot, but when he did talk, he made it count. I thought to myself that I'd play the guitar for a couple of days and then Bill would come and pick it up, so I took it home with me."

"The next day I got a call from Bill, and he wanted to know if he could come out. I said 'Sure,' so he came out and told me then what he had in mind. He wanted to come out to my house, where there was plenty of room and no one to run off and rehearse. So, we rehearsed every afternoon for about two and a half hours 'til way up about Christmas time, when we knocked off for the holidays."

"He said that he wanted to teach me all the songs that he knew, all the guitar chords that he knew, and all the runs that he knew. Since Bill knew all the guitar chords and runs that his brother Charlie had played, it wasn't very long until Bill had me sounding just like Charlie Monroe. I truly think that at that moment what Bill was looking for was not a group but the Monroe Brothers' sound. I'm not even sure Bill realized this fact. But whether he knew it or not, Bill was trying to follow the Monroe Brothers' style. And we did sound very much like the Monroe Brothers, with our extreme high harmony and smooth sound."

"I remember that when Bill was helping me with my guitar playing, I always used a flat pick, a Nick Lucas pick. I was never able to use a thumb pick and finger picks like some fellers did. I would get those things tangled in the strings like a bull caught in a barbed wire fence. And I never did use a capo when I was with Monroe, not even in the key of A. I had long fingers, so I could make the long A chord. With my fingers being so long, I could make all my runs without using a capo. In fact, I can't recall seeing any capos in the early days. Charlie Monroe used to have a run that he'd do in the key of G, and Bill taught me how to make it."

"As the weeks went by, it seemed like Bill and I kept picking up speed until we were playing faster and faster. But we were as good on the slow numbers as we were on the fast ones. I found out quick that you don't make mistakes when playing with Bill, so we practiced never making mistakes. In order to stay up with Bill, I used the old Charlie Monroe G run until it got to a point where I could no longer make it and keep up with Bill Monroe. So, I had to find something I could do and keep up with the fast pace that we had set. So, with the help of Bill, I modified the old Charlie Monroe G run. I made it into what is now known as the famous 'Lester Flatt G run.' I not only could make it in G, but also in the keys of C, D, and even in A."

"When the Christmas holidays were over, we went down to WSB in Atlanta for an audition. The *Crossroads Follies* were very popular over WSB at that time but, after we auditioned, the manager told us that they only used groups, not duets. He told Bill to go out and pick up a few other guys and that he'd make a place for him on the *Crossroads Follies*. Bill chose a few choice words and told the manager that that wasn't what he had in mind, and we walked out."

"We then went down to WGST radio in Atlanta and got an audition with them. They told us they liked us very much but that they couldn't use us because they already had a fine duet team working with them at that time by the name of The Blue Sky Boys, which was Bill and Earl Bolick. Bill was rather disgusted, so we went back home. He then asked me if I could be gone for a few days, and I told him that I could. He told me to pack a few things and tell my people I'd be gone for two or three days and to be at his trailer in the morning."

"When I got there, Bill had his 1938 Hudson Terraplane loaded up and ready to go. So, we got in and headed out, although I had no idea where we were going. After we got out on the open road, I asked Bill where we were going. He said we were headed for Asheville, North Carolina. I thought, 'Where in the world is Asheville, North Carolina?' This country boy had never been anywhere, so Asheville could have been in Europe as far as I was concerned. He said it's up in the Blue Ridge Mountains, but I didn't know where that was at either. I had heard of the Blue Ridge Mountains, but I sure didn't know where they were."

"We rolled on to Greenville, South Carolina, where we spent the night. In the morning we checked with WFBC radio in Greenville, but the Delmore Brothers had just started at that station, so they didn't need another duet. We rolled on to Asheville, where the Delmores had just left. In Asheville we auditioned at a small station named WWNC. They asked us if we could come back and take over a fifteen-minute program called *Mountain Music Time*, which was broadcast at 1:30 in the afternoon. Bill answered that we could, so we piled into Bill's Hudson and headed back to Greenville to pick up the trailer. At last, we had found a home base from which to start building our reputation."

"On the way back to Asheville, with Bill's trailer in tow behind, I had a need to know what Bill was going to call us. I really didn't know his intentions about a band because Bill doesn't talk much. Bill said, 'Bill Monroe and the Blue Grass Boys.' I questioned 'Blue Grass Boys,' being from the hills of Georgia and not knowing anything about bluegrass. So, I asked him about it, and he said, 'I'm from Kentucky, you know, where the bluegrass grows, and it's just got a good ring to it. I like that.' We used to get a lot of kidding about that name in the early days. You could hear all sorts of little remarks when we'd play schoolhouses like 'Bill Monroe and the Glue Brass Boys.' As the years pass by, of course, I'm real proud that I was an original member of the Blue Grass Boys."

"When we got to Asheville, Bill parked his trailer next to an old service station and I got a room across the street for a dollar and a half a week, plus a meal ticket to the Asheville lunchroom, and boy, we were set! I thought Asheville was the coldest place on the face of the earth. It froze your thoughts before you could think 'em. We walked up to the radio station each day and played our fifteen-minute program. I believe the announcer referred to us as Bill Monroe and Cleo Davis, although quite often our mail was addressed to the Monroe Brothers. Apparently, that's who many people thought they were listening to. Of course, we did sound very much like the Monroe Brothers and featured many of the songs that Bill and Charlie had made popular. I think that Bill was trying to stay close to the Monroe Brothers' style. He was back in the area where the Monroe Brothers had once worked, so he was trying to stay with that sound to regain his popularity over the airwaves as he was building his own group."

"As the days went by, Bill and I spent a lot of time rehearsing. We had to get each note exactly right before it went on the air. It was almost as if you don't make a mistake on one of Bill Monroe's shows, especially on the road. That's bending the truth a little, but that's about how Bill was and probably still is. You must be nearly perfect. We weren't, but we thought we were."

As Bill Monroe and Cleo Davis kept rehearsing, they continuously added new songs to their repertoire. "We picked up numbers that other people were using. We learned the Delmore Brothers' old tunes like 'Southern Moon,' 'The Nashville Blues,' 'Gonna Lay Down My Old Guitar,' and 'When It's Time for the Whippoorwill to Sing.' We also learned some of the Callahan Brothers' songs. They were very popular and had a beautiful sound. They sang the blues type of songs, the tearjerkers. The Callahans were especially known for their duet yodeling. The Monroe Brothers also featured the duet yodel, but we turned the blue yodel, with the duet yodel, into our theme song on the air. That's what we always came on the air with and what we'd use to sign off. As we went off the air it sounded like two fog horns moving out into a deep fog."

It wasn't long after Bill Monroe and Cleo Davis started their radio program over WWNC in Asheville that Bill started advertising over the air for other musicians to join their band. As the hopeful musicians would show up for an audition, Bill and Cleo usually auditioned them together, with guitar and mandolin. Among the first musicians to show up was Fiddling Art Wooten, from nearby Marion, North Carolina. In addition to his fiddle, Wooten brought with him a contraption he called a "one-man band." Cleo remembers, "It was like half an organ, with Art sitting with his knees under the thing. He also had a five-string banjo and a guitar built into it. He picked it with one foot and chorded it with the other while at the same time playing the fiddle. He also had a harmonica rack around his neck and played the fiddle and the harmonica at the same time. We used that act on stage with the Blue Grass Boys many times."

Although Art Wooten had a smooth fiddle style and was known to have played some beautiful harmony on the fiddle, his style was not quite what Bill Monroe was looking for. But Monroe took his mandolin and worked with Wooten until he had the fiddler playing in the style that he wanted.

Another hopeful musician showed up at radio station WWNC, Tommy Millard, from Canton, North Carolina. Cleo fondly remembers him being extremely good at playing the role of the blackface rube comedian. "He would always break me up with his act when he'd go out on stage. As a matter of fact, I couldn't even play straight with him 'cause I'd get so tickled. Bill would have to take my part and play straight with him while I stood off in the wings and laughed. He didn't sing or play an instrument, though he did have two big tablespoons that he'd play back to back. He would beat those spoons on his knees, between his hands, on his shoulders, under his arms, and up and down his legs. He was real good at it. I also believe he had a couple of bones in his suitcase that he'd use from time to time on our shows."

In addition to calling for other musicians, Bill Monroe used the fifteen-minute radio program to advertise shows they were playing in the area. People would write to the station to arrange for the Blue Grass Boys to play a show, and Bill's wife, Carolyn, took care of most of the correspondence at that time. Bill made sure the handbills were printed to promote the shows in little schoolhouses around Asheville. Many times, Cleo Davis and Carolyn would make the rounds of the schoolhouses, making arrangements for the shows. After the handbills were printed, they'd go back and distribute them and maybe play that night or possibly the next night.

Cleo remembers, "We charged fifteen and twenty-five cents admission and would often play to fifty or seventy people. One of our earliest shows was held at the Franklin County courthouse. We played right in the courtroom. Those kind of shows were sponsored by the PTA or some church. Sometimes, we'd have to play two shows. We generally played an hour and a half program."

"At that courthouse, I remember we opened with a fast fiddle tune like 'Fire on the Mountain,' had two or three fast duets like 'Roll in My Sweet Baby's Arms,' maybe an old blues number, a duet yodel, and a skit of ten or fifteen minutes. We had a skit that was very popular called 'The Pickpocket Game.' I always came up short on that deal."

"I recall one show we played at the city auditorium in Knoxville, Tennessee. I rolled my trousers up to my knees and put on a long dress, so I looked like a young girl. Bill was supposed to be my sister and had herself a hot date, which was Art Wooten. I got jealous and was on the stage fussing real big about how she was able to get a date and I wasn't. Tommy Millard was supposed to come out on stage to quiet me down. He had a *True Story* magazine that he was going to show me to quiet me down, but I wouldn't pipe down, so he hauls off and whops me upside the head with it. That old floor had just been oiled and was slippery, so I slipped, and both feet went straight up in the air. The audience went wild, thinking it was part of the act, but I can assure you it wasn't!"

"The very first schoolhouse I played was at the Cashiers Valley School auditorium, near Brevard, North Carolina. We started with 'Katy Hill,' and then hit 'em with 'Foggy Mountain Top' with a fast duet yodel, and then some of the old blues numbers similar to the Callahans. We came back with the Delmore Brothers' 'Southern Moon,' and then did one of our skits. For a gospel song we did 'What Would You Give in Exchange for Your Soul?'; that always brought the house down."

"That night we were going to do this gospel number, 'When the World's on Fire.' We sang a verse and a chorus and Bill played the chorus on the mandolin. When he finished, I could not for the life of me think of the first words of the next verse. It just simply wouldn't come to me. Bill quickly picked it up and played it through again. By this time, I'd turned every color of the rainbow, and he saw that I was scared to death. He looked over at me and grinned and I came up with something, some verse. Possibly the people didn't even notice what was going on. That song was the last number before Tommy did a comedy skit."

"I was off in the wings, and I told Bill I didn't think I could go back out there and face those people again. At that point Bill made one of the greatest moves that he ever made for me. He assured me that I had to go back out there. He said that not because of him, but because of me. He said you must go back out. He said if I'd let that stop me, I'd never be able to go back out again. He said I had to go back out there to prove to myself I could do it. He assured me that I could do the job and said I was going to do just fine. He said I just got scared and that it wouldn't happen again. So, I went back out there like a veteran, and I never did forget my lines from that time on."

While in Greenville, South Carolina, Monroe, as usual, kept his trailer parked next to a service station. They needed a place to rehearse, and the owner of the station, Gene Rampy, suggested they were free to use an old grease house behind the station if they cleaned it up. So, Monroe and the Blue Grass Boys pitched in and cleaned up that old grease house and even added a few seats. Their practice room was complete. Cleo Davis remembers that during the practice sessions they'd hold every afternoon, sometimes they'd draw bigger crowds than at some of their shows.

"Out of that grease house came the now famous 'Mule Skinner Blues,' 'Footprints in the Snow' and 'No Letter in the Mail.' Songs that are now considered American standards like 'Roll in My Sweet Baby's Arms' and 'Foggy Mountain Top' had their birth in bluegrass style in that old grease house. It really takes me back to think of the practice sessions we held there. We had so many good times, so many laughs in there. Bill started working on 'Footprints in the Snow,' a song I'd heard my mother singing when I was a little boy. Bill started singing it, and I didn't think he was singing it the way it was supposed to go. He changed it around to suit himself, and it worked. People really loved it."

"Also in the grease house, Bill started working on 'Mule Skinner Blues.' I thought he had written it. I'd never heard Jimmie Rodgers do it until later. So, Bill worked it out with that yodel and almost brought the house down with it. I remember how we worked up 'No Letter in the Mail.' The writer of that song was Bill Carlisle. The Carlisle Brothers had recorded it pretty fast. I copied the words off the record and tried to remember the tune. I worked it out at my house with the guitar, with the help of Art Wooten on the fiddle. I slowed it way down, as it's sung today. After I got so I could sing it pretty good, I sang it for Bill, and we made a powerful duet out of it. Later on, it went over good on the Opry."

The Blue Grass Boys stayed in Greenville, South Carolina, for about six months. Though the band maintained a busy schedule of rehearsals and performing, pickings were rather slim. But even though the band was not financially rewarded during its stay in Greenville, they could plainly see that this period was a valuable one for honing their music to polished perfection. It was in Greenville that Monroe established the basic sound that would soon carry the Blue Grass Boys to the Grand Ole Opry.

While in Greenville, the first Blue Grass Boys quartet was formed. Cleo Davis remembers how this happened. "People don't realize it now, but I sometimes harmonized with Bill. In the early years I was very capable of harmonizing with him. I had a real high-pitched voice, so I would harmonize with him in many instances. It may seem strange to say, but Bill Monroe and I used to do 'He Will Set Your Fields on Fire' as a duet. I would lead it and Bill would sing the tenor, and then Bill would pick up the bass lead, and I would follow him with the second part. On the tail end of the bass, I would come in and Bill would jump up to the tenor. Later, when the Blue Grass Boys came into being, I sang bass all the way through. My good friend Amos Garren did the lead, Bill sang tenor, and Fiddling Art Wooten did the baritone. On 'Life's Railway to Heaven,' Bill would lead it and we all came in on the chorus. I always sang bass on the quartets and lead on the trios."

In addition to the trios, duets, and quartets, Monroe often sang solos. Cleo Davis remembers one of the first solos he heard Bill do was "I'm Thinking Tonight of My Blue Eyes." "We used it in a comedy skit. Tommy Millard came out in blackface while Bill was singing that song. Millard would be crying as Bill was singing 'Blue Eyes' so sad and lonesome. Millard would lean on Bill's shoulder, almost going into convulsions. Not only did Bill sing 'Blue Eyes' as a solo but also numbers like 'Mule Skinner Blues,' 'Footprints in the Snow, and 'Blue Yodel Number 9.' Bill did them as specials and put them over with such style that he was continuously searching for new ones."

When Monroe finally recorded with the Blue Grass Boys for Victor on October 7, 1940, he chose "Mule Skinner Blues" for his first recording. Much importance has been placed on the fact that Monroe himself played guitar on that first recording. Some writers have explained it by saying that Monroe played the guitar to give that special "bluegrass time" that only he could give. It is more probable that Monroe simply felt more comfortable playing the guitar rather than the mandolin when he went to the microphone to sing solos. After all, when playing with what must be considered the original Blue Grass Boys, composed of Cleo Davis, Art Wooten, and Amos Garren, Monroe nearly always accompanied himself on guitar when he sang solos. When Davis was in the band, Monroe would trade his mandolin for Cleo's guitar and sing solos like "Mule Skinner Blues," "Blue Eyes," or "Footprints in the Snow." Later, apparently, Monroe grew more accustomed to singing solos while playing the mandolin and never again recorded playing the guitar.

After working out of Greenville for about six months, Bill Monroe was growing restless. As Cleo Davis explained, "It was a struggle to get the group up and off the ground. It took a lot of patience and determination, and I think Bill was loaded with that. In the six months we were in Greenville, we had done about all we could do. Things just weren't that good. We were making progress, but not as fast as Bill wanted."

"One day Bill called me up to the house and asked me what I thought about going to the Grand Ole Opry. I foolishly said, 'Do you think we're good enough?' He laughed and said, 'We're as good as the best over there, and right now, we're better than most of the rest.' I thought that, if Bill Monroe thought we were good enough, we were good enough. I said, 'Man. I'm for it.' 'Course the Grand Ole Opry is, in my estimation, the ultimate dream a country musician can have. He told me to go back and tell the other boys to get their toothbrushes ready; we're going to Nashville."

"We arrived in Nashville and got an audition, and it was with none other than the Solemn Old Judge—George D. Hay—and David Stone, who listened in. They put us in one of the studios and we really put on the dog. We started out with 'Foggy Mountain Top,' then Bill and I did a duet tune with a duet yodel, fast as white lightning. We came back with the 'Mule Skinner Blues' and 'Fire on the Mountain,' and I think that really sewed it up. George Hay and David Stone came walking in and asked Bill if he could be here to take over the first spot on the Grand Ole Opry on Saturday night. Bill said, 'Yes, sir.'"

"As we left the studio, Bill told us we had a job to do. We had to travel back to Greenville and get that trailer and be back in Nashville in time to open the curtain Saturday night. We were for it. You ought to have seen those country boys move. We moved across those mountains like they weren't there. We were back in Nashville way ahead of time. We were wild and rough and ready."

"That first Saturday night we pulled off a few firsts. We were the first to ever walk out on the stage of the Grand Ole Opry dressed in white shirts with neckties on. I also think we were the first country music quartet to ever hit the Grand Ole Opry. When we hit the stage, such performers as Roy Acuff, Pee Wee King, Uncle Dave Macon, and Sam and Kirk McGee were standing in the wings watching the Blue Grass Boys. When they pulled the curtain on us, they could not believe when we took off so fast and furious. Those people couldn't even think as fast as we played, I believe. In fact, there was absolutely nobody living who had ever played with the speed that we had."

"I believe we opened up with 'Foggy Mountain Top,' with that wild duet yodel that we had, and came right back with 'Mule Skinner Blues,' some fast tune like 'Fire on the Mountain' or 'Katy Hill' and 'Roll in My Sweet Baby's Arms.' Those people liked to have played us to death that night. I don't think there was any other act that got to play more than one tune that night. To say the least, the show was really on the road. We had done exactly what we started out to do."

After Bill Monroe and His Blue Grass Boys joined the Grand Ole Opry, requests to play came flooding in. One tour took the band to Virginia. Cleo Davis remembers, "We were in Staunton, with a great fiddler friend of mine, Tommy Magness, who was fiddling with us at that time. He came up with a fiddle tune called the 'Orange Blossom Special.' We were doing a two-day stand at the Twilight Theater, and Tommy and me were rooming together. I had my guitar in the room, and he had his fiddle, and he played me the 'Orange Blossom Special,' and man, I thought I'd never heard such a train tune. 'Train 45' wasn't that good, and neither was the 'Lee Highway Blues.' The 'Orange Blossom Special' took it all, and Tommy knew the words. We went over the words and learned the song."

"We went downstairs and got a portable recorder at a music shop and tried to record it in the lobby. We couldn't get a true sound in the lobby, so the man took us in the public restroom and locked the door. We set the recorder on the john, and me and Tommy Magness recorded the 'Orange Blossom Special.' I sang tenor in the duet. While in the bathroom, we also recorded 'Peach Picking Time in Georgia' and 'The Hills of Roane County.' When we got back to Nashville, we called Bill over to listen to it. He liked it. Tommy had picked up an old record by the Rouse Brothers. They copyrighted it and recorded it, but Tommy Magness and me took it to Nashville. Bill, he let Tommy Magness and me do the 'Orange Blossom Special' on the Grand Ole Opry the next Saturday night. The following Saturday night and from then on, me and Bill did it."

"I stayed at the Grand Ole Opry until late 1940, when I left the Blue Grass Boys and came to Lakeland, Florida, and took on a brand-new show of my own over radio WLAK. I formed a group there and worked at this station for about a year. At that point the service separated me from the radio station."

"But, while in the service, my music caught up with me. While in the reception center in Atlanta, Georgia, there was a big country music show being held that night. It just so happened that some longtime friends of mine were appearing on the show. It was Hank Penny's Radio Cowboys, with James and Martha Carson and Leon Payne. I naturally got as close to the stage as I could get, along with the thousands of other men in khaki uniforms. And lo and behold, Hank Penny spotted me. He pulled me out of the crowd and pulled me backstage and insisted that I had to be on the show that night. Me, being a new recruit, I thought you couldn't do anything without permission, so he got permission right quick from the colonel and I appeared in the entire show that evening. They had a contest as part of the show and, needless to say, there wasn't much contest to it that night, 'cause I won. I sang an old song called 'What Is Home Without Love.' Of course, I won the hearts of all of those GIs by being in uniform, just like them."

"When I got out of the service, I went back to Florida and back into radio. I formed my own group and played on radio WLAK with a longtime friend of mine, Floyd Lewis, for about fourteen years. In my years in Florida, I went by the name of J.C. Davis, so our band was called the J.C. Davis/Floyd Lewis Show. We were widely received over the local station. Finally, some new owners bought the station, and it went to rock, and they naturally turned me out to pasture. So, I disbanded and became rather inactive, though I did work with a gospel group throughout central Florida for a couple of years and made several albums with them."

"In the first part of 1980, a man by the name of Jack Henderson out of Nashville, Tennessee, came down here and opened what he called the Sunshine Opry House. He bought property and built a thousand-seat auditorium in the style of WSM's Grand Ole Opry. After six months, he was unhappy and sold out. In the meantime, he asked me to come over and join him. Two weeks later I had my own show on Saturday night. It was very popular, no longer than it had run."

"When the Sunshine Opry House closed, some of us musicians formed a corporation and bought what is about seventeen acres of land, and we're building us an opry house. In fact, we'll be opening very soon. What we're opening is a family theater, and we feel we have some of the finest musicians here in central Florida, and I've traveled this country far and wide. So, I'm back playing music again. The new opry house, called the Florida Opry House, is located between Auburndale and Lakeland on Highway 92, three miles east of Lakeland. It's beautiful inside, I assure you, and the whole world is invited."

"I am thankful to have been a part of the history of bluegrass music. I am also thankful for all the things that my bluegrass followers have contributed to make bluegrass what it is today. We worked hard to make it what it is. We struggled to get it off the ground, and I'm proud of it."

The above is largely based on a series of interviews I conducted with Cleo Davis in 1980–81. It originally appeared in Bluegrass Unlimited *in February 1982.*

Tommy Millard—Blackface Comedian and Blue Grass Boy

When the full story of country music is told, the name Tommy Millard will not be forgotten. Dubbed "Snowball" by Bill Monroe, Tommy was a legendary performer who made important contributions to country music. Working with numerous medicine

Carl Sauceman and His Green Valley Boys, ca. 1944. Back row, from left: unknown fiddler, unknown announcer, Tommy Millard, and Red Rector; front row, from left: J.P. Sauceman and Carl Sauceman (courtesy Tommy Millard).

shows up and down the East Coast, Tommy was one of a small number of comedians who made the transition from the racially insensitive blackface act to the more acceptable role of the rube comic. In addition to a freckled face, tattered baggy pants, oversized shoes, and a slouch hat, his constant companion was an old leather satchel containing an inventory of countless props and "instruments" like bones and spoons.

Rube comics inherited much of their material and style from the era of the minstrel show. Such shows flourished from the 1840s until well past the Civil War and introduced professional comedy to the American public. Once minstrelsy went out of style, some of its traditions passed on to variety shows, then to vaudeville, and later to medicine shows. Country music eventually inherited these hand-me-downs and has kept them going in modern times with shows such as *Hee Haw*. But let us not forget that it was performers like Tommy Millard who saved from oblivion much of the humor and drama of the earlier minstrel era.

It all started in Chattanooga, Tennessee, in 1930, when a nineteen-year-old Thomas Millard joined his first medicine show, working in blackface. As a kid he'd always played the fool, told stories and jokes, and kept his pals in stitches. By hanging around Lee Holden, an experienced comedian, Tommy perfected his jokes and stories. Lee hired Tommy to work with him and an Indian named Big Chief Tonic in starting their own medicine show. They played their first show in Caryville, Tennessee, to a packed house.

Tommy explains, "Without really rehearsing our skits much, we went over like we'd been doing it for years. It just came natural to me."

After working with Lee and Big Chief Tonic for some time, Tommy joined Mitzie Shelton and Her All-Girl Band. Performing with an entourage of fifteen young women and three men, Tommy acted as emcee and comic when they toured through Georgia, South Carolina, Alabama, and Tennessee. During his travels Tommy even made several appearances on the Grand Ole Opry, telling jokes and doing monologues. Occasionally he beat spoons with the other Opry acts. Wages being what they were on the Opry in those days, Tommy drifted out of Nashville and back to the medicine shows.

Tommy then joined up with Indian Chief Kadat and worked everywhere from the Deep South to Pennsylvania. They performed mainly in the small towns and in coal mining areas where they were often paid in scrip or "dugalo," as they called it. Their basic method was simple. They came into town, set up a canvas-covered platform to act as a stage, and the five or six performers and musicians would entice the crowds to get close enough to hear the "pitch," delivered by Chief Kadat or Tommy. They would sell shampoo, soap, and snake oil to the crowd.

On one trip through West Virginia, Tommy explains, "I stopped at a snake farm and bought a rattlesnake and a black snake to use as an attraction in the show. That was a foolish thing to do, because the two don't get along. Anyway, we go to Atlanta and set up our stage to do a show. I hit the guitar a time or two to attract attention, then started hollering and ballyhooing to get the crowd in there so I could start my pitch."

"When I took the black snake out, it curled around my neck and boy, the crowds really came out! They swarmed in there. While I was holding the black snake, the rattler was in the box next to the stage. A black snake can smell a rattler a mile away, so when the black snake smelled the rattler, it started squirming and pulling and tightening up and then it whooped around and bit me right on the hand. I let go but I didn't want to lose it, so I picked it up again and it bit me again. Before I got it back in its box, it bit me four or five times. At the time the snake bit me, I was lecturing the crowd on the snake oil, the liniment. Well, my hand started bleeding and the people's eyes were bugged wide open, just looking for me to drop dead at any moment."

"I assured the crowd that there was nothing to worry about and got a bottle of that liniment and poured it on there and pretty soon it stopped the bleeding. I finished my pitch on the liniment, but I never did one time say it was good for snakebite. But from what they saw, they figured it was the best snakebite remedy in the world. Man, did we sell that stuff! They bought it by the half dozen bottles. We sold plum out of it at fifty cents a bottle. Nearly everyone standing out there bought some."

"Then the chief got out there to make his pitch. He was an intelligent man and had even graduated from college but, when he lectured the crowd, he talked nonsense and in circles that you couldn't understand. But the fact that he was an Indian and wore a headdress and all, the people just bought that medicine as fast as we could hand it to them. He never made claims or promises about the medicine. People got fired up about it just because he was an Indian. Anyway, after that snake-bite incident, we sold all we had bottled. After the chief got out there, the people wanted to buy more."

"We had more bottles in the trailer, but without labels. Our wives got in there and started labeling them and passing them out the door as fast as they could. We sold all that, but we had a barrel of tonic in there which wasn't bottled or labeled. They started bottling and labeling it and passing it out the door. I mean to tell you, we sold that stuff!"

"I don't remember many of my exact pitches I made in those days, but they usually went something like this: 'Now, ladies and gentlemen, I'd like to call your attention to a product here tonight. It's Big Chief's Tonic. It's good for stomach troubles, it's good for indigestion, and we highly recommend it for elderly adults and the young. It will bring out your vim, vigor, and vitality. When you and your wife are sleeping in different rooms, after you take this medicine, you'll find yourself going up the steps to meet your wife and you'll find her coming down the steps to meet you.'"

"We didn't stress too much about it being a cure. It's really not a cure; it's a laxative. It was pretty good stuff to clean your system up. You know, the Chief was very secretive about what went into the tonic, so we never knew what was in there. But the fact that he was an Indian really helped sell it. Sometimes, he'd put a small headdress on me and called me 'Chief One Feather.' I do have dark skin and some of my people were Indian, so I could play the part."

"After we were ready to leave a town where we sold a lot of tonic, the demand would sometimes be so great that we'd make arrangements with a drug store to sell it. We'd set up on the sidewalk in front of a drugstore, do our pitch, and let the people buy from the druggist. We'd sell the store about four gross of it and let him make about 10 percent. He'd sell it for a dollar a bottle."

While traveling with the medicine show, Tommy often met other medicine show musicians. One he remembers was Roy Acuff. Although working with different shows, they often camped near each other. Tommy remembers that they often used to make coffee in half-gallon buckets. He fondly recalls, "Me and Roy shared many a half-gallon bucket of coffee together."

"In those days, the Depression, times were plenty hard. We always lived in tents, which we pitched right behind the stage. We'd pool our money and get twenty-five or thirty cents out of the whole bunch. Then we'd go and buy bologna and a loaf of bread. You could get a loaf of bread for five cents. If we'd get a little bit rich and get a dollar or two, we'd buy hot dogs. That was like steak to us. Me and Roy's broke many a hot dog in two and divided it. But we didn't often go hungry. There was a place in Knoxville where you could go in and eat all you want for fifteen cents. That's right. We visited those places a lot."

Besides performing for medicine shows, Tommy also had a band (the Blue Ridge Hillbillies) that started doing a regular show on the *Mid-Day Merry-Go-Round* plus performing locally at schoolhouses in the Knoxville area. This band included, at various times, such legendary performers as Carl Sauceman, Jack and Curly Shelton, fiddler Shorty Barton, and Wade and J.E. Mainer. In addition to doing the emcee work and being the booking agent for the group, Tommy also played the role of comedian.

It was during his stay in Knoxville that Tommy made the switch from blackface to country rube. After hearing his regular blackface skit on the *Mid-Day Merry-Go-Round*, a black preacher called up and complained about the racial overtones. Realizing that times had changed, Tommy gave up blackface. According to Tommy, back when he did blackface, it was really accepted by both blacks and whites and there were no hard feelings. In fact, Tommy explains, "I've had colored people come around and talk to me, shake hands and they had no hard feelings, or anything like that."

After playing out the Knoxville area, Tommy moved his base of operations to Asheville, North Carolina. It was there that Tommy met up with Bill Monroe. Monroe had recently parted company with brother Charlie and had just formed a band in Asheville which included Cleo Davis on guitar and Art Wooten, the one-man-band, on fiddle. Tommy was hired to do the emcee work and play comedian.

Cleo Davis fondly remembers Tommy as one of the greatest of the country rube comedians. In fact, Cleo had so much trouble controlling his laughter while working straight man with Tommy that Monroe himself often acted as the straight man. It was during this period that Bill dubbed Tommy "Snowball." Even after all these years, the name has stuck, and Tommy is still often called Snowball.

From Asheville, Bill Monroe and His Blue Grass Boys, as they were now called, moved to Greenville, South Carolina, and stayed there for six or eight months. During this time, Monroe was corresponding with the Grand Ole Opry and, in October of 1939, he managed to secure an audition there. At this same time, however, Tommy and his wife were expecting their first child, so they decided it would be best to move back home to Asheville to have the baby. Tommy was tired of the road anyway, so he gave his notice to Monroe. Some months after the baby was born, Tommy moved his expanded family to Winston-Salem, North Carolina, where he played with such musicians as fiddler Tommy Hunter and the three Morris brothers: Wiley, Zeke, and George.

For many musicians, the end of World War II marked a turning point in their professional careers. Tommy explains, "At the same time the boys were returning from the service, a lot of little radio stations began to pop up all over the area we were broadcasting in, in such places as Waynesville, Black Mountain, and Marshall. Everybody and his brother grabbed a guitar and a fiddle and whatever and started playing on those little stations. They also started playing personal appearances around the country. I got wind of a lot of them that put on rotten shows, or even dirty shows, and along about that time I decided to get out of it. I left the *Farm Hour* and also left WLOS where I was also working at the time."

"Shortly after that I gave my heart to the Lord and knew I had to quit show business. The very night I was saved, I was supposed to do a show in Haw Creek, North Carolina, with Carl Story. I went to the stage door and motioned for Carl to come to me. I told Carl I was sorry and that I didn't mean to stand him up but explained that I was saved and couldn't make this appearance with him. He said, 'Yes, you can,' and dragged me out on the stage and told the people, 'Friends, this is Tommy Millard, comedian and musician. He said he couldn't make this appearance tonight because he surrendered his life to the Lord. It's not that he thinks there's anything wrong with it, it's just that his life has changed, and he's going into a different profession.'"

"Do you know what the crowd done? They stood up and applauded. I thought they was never gonna stop. When they finally stopped, I thanked them, but I just couldn't talk much. I did manage to say that if I don't see them in this world again, I'd see them up yonder. They stood up again and just kept applauding as I went out the back door. And that was the last time I was ever onstage. After that I went into the ministry and have been a preacher all these years."

The above was based on several personal interviews I had with Tommy Millard at his home in Asheville, North Carolina, in 1985. It originally appeared in Bluegrass Unlimited *in May 1986.*

Clarence White and the Roots of Bluegrass Guitar

In the early 1960s I lived practically within earshot of the Ash Grove, a legendary folk club on Melrose Avenue in West Hollywood. Monday night was called "hoot night" and the house band was The Country Boys. When I first heard the band in mid-1962, it consisted of Clarence White on guitar, Billy Ray Lathum on banjo, LeRoy Mack on Dobro, and Roger Bush on bass. I had no idea that in years to come this band would become legendary.

In the fall of 1962, the band got the opportunity to record their first album for Briar International. At that time the founder of the band, Roland White, was in the army, so he did not appear. The producers of the record were none other than Merle Travis and Joe Maphis, two legendary guitarists and leaders of the West Coast country music scene. Merle suggested that the name of the band was too generic, and someone pointed out that Mac Wiseman was also calling his band The Country Boys. Since Merle was from Kentucky, he suggested the band change their name to The Kentucky Colonels.

Late that fall I was in the audience at the Ash Grove and could clearly see the band's excitement when they proudly showed off their new record from the stage. It was called *The New Sound of Bluegrass America*, and emblazoned across the front cover was the band's new name. During this period, I was trying to learn the guitar, so it was like a bolt of lightning when I watched Clarence White perform with the band. The syncopated timing of his guitar breaks and his smooth rhythm playing were unlike anything I had ever heard. At the time I had no idea just how unique and innovative he was. I only knew that he knocked my socks off.

The next year I was lucky enough to be at the guitar workshop at the 1963 UCLA Folk Festival. During the workshop, someone raised their hand and asked Clarence where he learned his stuff. He shyly responded that two of his big influences were sitting next to him on stage, Joe Maphis and Doc Watson. Clarence's association with Joe Maphis went back to 1955.

Clarence White, ca. 1962 (courtesy the estate of Mark F. English).

In 1954 the White family had formed a band called The Three Little Country Boys, with Clarence on guitar, Roland on mandolin, and Eric Jr. on tenor banjo. Their sister, Joanne, played the bass and their father, Eric Sr., occasionally joined them on harmonica. By the next year Joanne had dropped out and Eric Jr. took over the bass duties.

Things started to come together for the band when they entered and won a talent contest sponsored by radio KXLA, broadcasting from Pasadena. The event was the brainchild of a country radio personality named Carl Deacon Moore, who called himself "the Squeakin' Deacon." I'll never forget listening to his show as the Deacon told his radio audience that bluegrass music was "as good as home cookin' and short sleeve eatin'." As a prize for winning the contest, The Three Little Country Boys got to appear as guests on a local TV show called *Country Barn Dance Jubilee*, hosted by Ralph T. Hicks.

More than anything else, the performance on the *Jubilee* jump-started the career of The Country Boys, as the band was now calling itself. Appearances on several southern California country radio shows followed, and they were soon noticed by Joe Maphis, who called himself "King of the Strings." Joe later went on to co-write "Dim Lights, Thick Smoke (and Loud, Loud Music)," a song that was covered by Flatt and Scruggs. Joe was a popular country music star who often performed with his wife, Rose Lee, along with Katie Warren, who billed herself as Fiddlin' Kate. Joe's trademark was his double-neck electric guitar. Joe took Clarence under his wing and demonstrated to Clarence how the guitar could be a powerful lead instrument.

In 1963 the recently renamed Kentucky Colonels played in Berkeley, California, at a folk club called the Cabale Creamery on San Pablo Avenue. While in Berkeley the band visited with Sandy Rothman, who had earlier played guitar in Bill Monroe's band, the Blue Grass Boys. Rothman introduced Clarence and Roland White to Campbell Coe, the owner of a music store called Campus Music, situated a block from the UC Berkeley campus. Coe was an outstanding and versatile guitar player who played both country and swing and who led a band called the Country Cousins.

Coe was adept at the music of Django Reinhardt and exposed both Clarence and Roland to Reinhardt's music via his 78 RPM record collection. Coe gave the White brothers a reel-to-reel tape of Django Reinhardt with Stéphane Grappelli and the Hot Club of Paris. When they returned to Southern California, Clarence mentioned to Joe Maphis that he had discovered the music of Django Reinhardt. Joe readily admitted that he had learned many of his hot licks by listening to Reinhardt's 78 records.

Soaking in the influences of Joe Maphis and Django Reinhardt, Clarence White was also profoundly affected by the music of Doc Watson. In 1962 Doc made an appearance at the Ash Grove as part of an old-time band that consisted of Clarence "Tom" Ashley on clawhammer banjo, Clint Howard on rhythm guitar, Fred Price on fiddle, and Doc on lead and rhythm guitar. The band was supposed to come back several months later, but they cancelled that date. It might have had something to do with the fact that Ashley refused to travel by airplane.

Doc reluctantly agreed to do a solo set at the Ash Grove, where he was greeted with unanimous approval. This performance helped launch Doc's solo career. On subsequent visits that Doc made to the Ash Grove, Clarence was able to absorb more of Doc's amazing guitar playing. In particular, he was inspired by Doc's ability to play fiddle tunes like "Black Mountain Rag," "Soldier's Joy," and "Beaumont Rag" on the guitar.

During this time Roland White, the mandolin player, was in the army, so Clarence started to play more lead guitar breaks. In September of 1963 Roland rejoined the Kentucky Colonels after seventeen months in the service, reassuming his leadership role with the band. Roland told me that, during this time, they held rigorous rehearsals late into the night, practicing when they were already bone-tired so that "we could give it all we had." Rehearsing long hours paid off.

Each week, when they performed at the Ash Grove and served as the house band for hoot night, the band seemed to get tighter and tighter. I think that Roland brought some of the "spit and polish" attitude of the army to the band, and it paid off in spades!

Listening to Clarence play with the Colonels each week was like going to guitar college for a lot of us in the audience. There's no telling how many budding guitarists like me were profoundly affected by watching and listening to this band and especially hearing Clarence on guitar. While Joe Maphis, Doc Watson, and Django Reinhardt were Clarence's inspiration, it was Clarence himself who forever changed the role of the guitar in bluegrass music, in California and beyond.

Although I never interviewed Clarence, I did see him perform almost every week at the Ash Grove in 1962–1964 when he played with the Country Boys. The band was later renamed The Kentucky Colonels by Merle Travis. Clarence did borrow my 1947 00021 Martin guitar at a hoot at the Ash Grove on a Monday night in the early 1960s. I was not surprised when he tuned the B and E strings, which it surely needed. I never wanted to tune it again!

Bill Clifton

In 1981 I was working on a book called *Backpocket Bluegrass Songbook*. I have always loved log cabins, so I wanted to include the song "Little Whitewashed Chimney." The only artist that recorded it was Bill Clifton. I managed to get his address, and I wrote to him to ask permission. Months went by without any response, so I used another song instead, "Little Log Cabin in the Lane." In early 2000 I received a letter from Bill Clifton without mentioning that almost twenty years had passed since he received my letter. He recently had been cleaning off his desk to make way for the millennial and found my letter. He then proceeded to give me permission to use that song. Of course, it was far too late by that time.

The first time I met Bill Clifton was in the mid-nineties. I was doing a bluegrass radio called *Country Roots* on Asheville's public station, WCQS. The control room is in the middle of a historic building to shield it from city noises, but I managed to hear a knock on the door, and there before me was Bill Clifton. Surprised, of course I invited him in and ended up interviewing him on the air that night. He said he had just dropped off his daughter at the Asheville School, and while driving through town, he scanned the radio dial for some country music. I had been playing some records by the Carter Family, which Bill was delighted to hear. He decided to see what the show was about, so he found the station, knocked on the door, and that's how we first met.

Recently, I managed to interview Bill. Even at 92, he was still sharp, and I learned a lot about him. One of my first questions was how he first became interested in country music. "When I was a child, I got measles and was stuck in bed for weeks. To keep me occupied my folks gave me a radio, and I listened to all types of music." His sister Ann had discovered WWVA in Wheeling, West Virginia, and she "showed me where to find it on the radio dial. I was especially taken by the Lilly Brothers and Don Stover."

I asked Bill why he took a shine to country music, rather than the other music he was listening to. "What grabbed me was the stories. I fell in love with the stories that were often featured in country music. I could relate to that. When I was starting to recover from the measles, I started buying records by artists like the Morris Brothers, Eddie Arnold, and the Carter family. I particularly liked the song 'Did You See My Daddy Over There?' by Eddie Arnold. It was the story in that song that I liked so well. I also enjoyed listening to *The Old Dominion Barn Dance* on Richmond, Virginia, radio. My favorite show was hosted by 'Sunshine Sue,' Sue Workman, on Saturday evenings."

"When I was fourteen, during World War II, I got my driver's license. I would go with my friend Hap Hapney to see Roy Acuff. The opening act was Uncle Dave Macon with Sam and Kirk McGee. I spotted Uncle Dave and the brothers just outside the door, so I immediately went up and asked them questions while they were signing autographs. Roy saw me talking with them and he grabbed me by the arm. He said he had to change into his street clothes, so he invited me to come in and talk with him. Apparently, Acuff figured that a young boy interested enough to talk with those other performers must really love country music."

Bill Clifton playing banjo on radio WINA, Charlottesville, Virginia, ca. 1953. He recently admitted (in 2022, when I interviewed him the last time) he rarely played banjo (courtesy Bill Clifton).

At one point in my conversation with Bill, I pointed out that I considered him more of a crooner instead of a "belter," like Roy Acuff or Bill Monroe. He replied, "I couldn't sing as high as Bill Monroe or Lester Flatt or as loud as Roy Acuff, and I just wanted to sing what was natural for me. I never considered trying to do it differently."

I then asked him where and when he picked up the guitar. "I was originally an accordion player, but I found it very difficult to sing with that instrument strapped on my chest, so I felt like the guitar would be easy to sing with. I had no idea how I was going to learn. There was a place out in Fullerton, Maryland, that played country music and I would go there on Saturdays to hear the Piece Brothers. One of them had a son named Bill Piece, who was my age, and he played guitar. When I asked him if he would teach me, he readily agreed and introduced me to two different styles—the Merle Travis style and one using a flat pick and playing chords. He was a wonderful help coming over to my parents' house bringing his guitar and showing me everything he could. Soon enough, I realized four chords was all I needed to emulate most of the songs I wanted to play—G, C, A7 and D7. I respected his ability tremendously and was appreciative of him taking the time to teach me. I could never read music and played everything by ear."

Bill Clifton was one of the very first to use the guitar as a lead instrument in bluegrass with his mid-fifties recordings of "All the Good Times Are Past and Gone" and "Blue Ridge Mountain Blues." I took the opportunity during our interview to quiz him about that. "For some reason Bill Monroe would only feature the mandolin, fiddle, and banjo for breaks. I was more interested in the Carter family and wanted to try and get the melody out of the guitar. I guess I was aware that nobody else was doing it at that time. I had a good mandolin player, Curly Lambert, playing with me as well as Johnny Clark on the banjo, and they would take their lead parts and I would start to take a little instrumental guitar break back then."

One of Bill Clifton's many achievements was hosting the first bluegrass festival that was held in Luray, Virginia, at Oak Leaf Park, July 4, 1961. During our conversation, I asked Bill about that. "I had been over to Luray a few times and thought it was a place we could get a lot of people in to come, so I invited Bill Monroe, Flatt and Scruggs, Jim and Jesse McRenolds, Mac Wiseman, the Stanley Brothers, and my band and to try and make a day of it. I had flyers made up and sent them out to radio stations plus took some up to New York to see if musicians would make the trip down to Virginia, and boy, they did! About 3000 people stood and listened. I was not able to book Flatt and Scruggs." During the festival, Bill Monroe and Carter Stanley were on stage and Carter had the mic and said, "We have a lot of good musicians here, but we are missing one band a hell of a lot, don't we?" Most of the audience knew that were talking about Flatt and Scruggs, who refused to come.

Finally, I asked Bill what he wants folks to remember about him. "I want people to know that I treasure the relationships I have had with the musicians all over the world. I've enjoyed getting to meet people like the Japanese and well as the English and Dutch and other cultures. I particularly made friendships with the Japanese, who have had some very good musicians, although sometime the singing is a little difficult to understand, but their instrument abilities have always been way above average. When I first moved to England, I met the man who was responsible for my records being released there. He said because I pronounced the lyrics clearly (whereas others like Bill Monroe would clip words) folks understood me and therefore enjoyed my music. I did not have an accent either."

So, thanks for the music, Bill. It's been a grand ride and it's not over yet!

Songwriters and Songs

The Great American Tearjerker

Fans of traditional country and bluegrass music have always had a soft spot in their hearts for a good ole tearjerker. If you write a song about getting run over by a train while holding a baby on the way to your mother's funeral, you're bound to have a hit. Let's take a little trip back in time to see where the idea of the tearjerker came from.

Mid-nineteenth-century America had a lot to cry about. If the high infant mortality rate didn't kill you, any number of other hazards would. Anyone who lived to be fifty was considered a certified "old timer."

Then came the Civil War, which would claim the lives of nearly a quarter of the young men of the Confederacy and an eighth of their Union counterparts. To comfort soldiers on the battlefield and those that stayed behind, the publishing industry in both the North and South produced and printed songs virtually around the clock. In 1863 alone the North's biggest music publisher, Root and Cady, published 258,000 pieces of sheet music. If these sheets were laid end to end, the publisher claimed it would bridge the entire state of Illinois from Chicago to the Mississippi River.

The most popular songs during the Civil War were clearly nostalgic, like "Home, Sweet Home." These songs reminded soldiers of peaceful, happier times before a war that pitted brother against brother, father against son. Another popular Civil War–era song was "Lorena," about a heartbroken lover. The song was so widely sung, especially by Southern soldiers, that some have blamed it for the Confederacy's loss. Apparently, so many soldiers got lonesome for their wives and sweethearts that they deserted and went home. Several Southern generals forbade their troops to sing "Lorena."

"The Faded Coat of Blue, or, the Nameless Grave," written by J.H. McNaughton near the war's end, is a classic example of a Civil War tearjerker. The first verse will give you the flavor of this song:

> My brave lad he sleeps in his faded coat of blue,
> In a lonely grave unknown lies the heart that beat so true.
> He sank faint and hungry among the famished brave,
> As they laid him sad and lonely within his nameless grave.

Included in a book titled *Heart Songs* (1909), this song was recorded by Owen Mills and Frank Welling, Buell Kazee, and the Carter Family in early country music.

Among the most important early professional songsmiths was Henry Clay Work. His best-known songs included "Kingdom Coming (in the Year of Jubilo)" (1862), "Marching Through Georgia" (1865), "The Ship That Never Returned" (1865), and "My Grandfather's Clock" (1876). But it was Work's song "Come Home, Father" (1864) that clinched the tearjerker as an important American genre. The song tells the sad story of a drunken father who won't come home to see his dying child despite the pleas of his other grief-stricken son. The dying child's last words are that he misses his dear father and wants to see him.

Most authorities point to Charles K. Harris's song "After the Ball" (1892) as the most successful of the early tearjerkers, with total sales approaching five million copies. "After the Ball" has been called the "watershed song" that helped launch the song publishing industry.

It's no secret that bluegrass music is all about lonesome. Songs like "Mother's Not Dead, She's Only Sleeping" are the bread and butter of bluegrass music. As someone recently said, "If she's alive at the end of the song, it ain't bluegrass music." But how did it get to be this way? Why are we so drawn to songs about pain, murder, loneliness, and suffering?

Drawing of a boy in the snow, ca. 1880s, found in an antique shop in Los Angeles, California.

Part of the answer lies in our dark and murky past. The very nature of mankind seems to incorporate a strange fascination with the dead and dying, the forlorn, the lonely and the dark side of life. That's why old, morbid murder ballads from the British Isles remain popular both in England and in Appalachia, long after silly, shallow, and happy songs have been forgotten.

Sad and pitiful songs seem an important way for us to work out deeper and darker emotions. I suppose it's why drivers on the highway slow at the scene of a wreck, hoping to catch a glimpse of the horrific tragedy, even though they strive to avoid such a fate. By singing or listening to heart-pounding songs, we sneak a peek at the darker side of life without having to experience it first-hand. As the Irish poet and playwright Oscar Wilde once wrote, "A sentimentalist is one who desires to have the luxury of an emotion without paying for it."

Mid-nineteenth-century literature, art, and music in America and the British Isles were filled with tragic and emotional scenes of orphan children dying in the snow, mothers waiting at the doorstep for their wayward sons to come home, and bedraggled fathers sent to the poorhouse even though they were blind, deaf, and nearly comatose. The cash registers of the Tin Pan Alley music publishers who sold this type of song were constantly making a loud "ka-ching" as they racked up one hit song after another with themes of despair and hopelessness. Today, we jokingly refer to these songs as "tearjerkers."

Gussie L. Davis—Tin Pan Alley/Bluegrass Songwriter

Some of the greatest traditional bluegrass songs were apparently written by someone named "Public Domain" or "Traditional." What kind of decent mother or father would name their child that? Here I'm going to acquaint you with a songwriter named Gussie Lord Davis, who has seldom been credited as the composer of such well-known folk and bluegrass songs as "Maple on the Hill" (1880), "Make Up and Be Lovers Again" aka "Jack and Mae" (1893), "In the Baggage Coach Ahead" (1896), "Just Set a Light" aka "Red and Green Signal Lights" (1897), "Goodnight Irene" (1899), "One Little Word" (1899), and "He's Coming to Us Dead" (1899).

So, who was Gussie Davis? Have a seat in this comfy chair and I'll tell you about him. Small in size, Gussie Lord Davis (1863–1899) was an African American who grew up in Dayton, Ohio. From an early age he wanted to be a songwriter. He was later quoted as saying, "They tell me that all song writers, as a rule, die in the poorhouse, broken down in health and empty in the pocket." Wanting to avoid the fate of most songwriters, he knew his ticket to success was in receiving a formal musical education. Gussie applied to the Nelson Musical College in Cincinnati. However, he was denied admission because the college did not admit Black students. Not to be deterred, Gussie got a job at the college as a janitor. His wages were $15 a month and he received private musical instruction from several of the instructors.

In 1880, at the tender age of eighteen, Gussie wrote one of his most popular songs, "We Sat Beneath the Maple on the Hill." Because of his race he couldn't find a publisher who would publish it, so Gussie paid out of his own pocket to have

Gussie Davis, ca. 1893.

the song printed and distributed. The phenomenal success of this song opened the doors and before long he was one of the most successful songwriters in New York's Tin Pan Alley. Here is how Gussie himself explained it in the *Cleveland Gazette*, on February 4, 1888.

> I was just eighteen years old, and not caring to enter in the rear, I set to work to study music, and before long I managed to get together a pretty air and had it arranged. It was the "Maple on the Hill," and became quite popular throughout the West. Music publishers are not over generous in taking to publishing or even handling music from an unknown person, and I found a great deal of trouble, but I gave one publisher money to get it out, and he took pity on me. The song proved a great go.

What was Davis's songwriting secret? To quote Tin Pan Alley historian Maxwell F. Marcuse, "Gussie Davis reached for the tender spots that lurk deep within all of us, no matter how thick or tough our outer crusts may be. In an era of 'sing-em-and-weep' melodies, Davis did more than his share to open the tear ducts of America."

When asked by a reporter what it takes to make a successful song, Davis's answer is interesting. "I can best answer you by showing that should a man write a song each day for 365 days and pay $10 for each one to the publisher, he would spend something like $3,650, and if one song was a real go he would be a fortunate fellow."

In 1895 the *New York World* selected the ten most popular songwriters in America to compete for prizes. The contestants were a who's who of popular composers in the 1890s. In addition to Gussie Davis, there was James Thornton, Charles Graham, Felix McGlennon, Charles K. Harris, Harry Dann, Percy Gaunt, Raymond Moore, Joe Flynn, and Charles B. Ward. When the prizes were awarded, Davis won second prize and $500 in gold with his "Send Back the Picture and the Ring."

To give you an idea of Davis's impact on early country and bluegrass music, here is a list of some of the musicians who later recorded Davis's songs: Vernon Dalhart, Ernest V. Stoneman, Bradley Kincaid, Dick Burnett, Al Craver, Posey Rorer and the North Carolina Ramblers, Darby and Tarlton, J.E. Mainer's Mountaineers, Wade Mainer and Zeke Morris, the Callahan Brothers, Ernest Thompson, George Reneau, Fiddlin' John Carson, Lester McFarland and Robert A. Gardner, Andrew Jenkins and Carson Robison, Frank Luther, G.B. Grayson and Henry Whitter, Roy Harvey and Posey Rorer, the Carter Family, the Dixon Brothers, the Morris Brothers, the Monroe Brothers, the Chuck Wagon Gang, Doc Watson, and Ralph Stanley. You may be wondering why Davis's songs struck such a chord with these musicians. The answer is that country and bluegrass musicians have always had a soft spot in their hearts for sentimental songs. Along with other popular songwriters in the late nineteenth and early twentieth century, the sentimental songs of Gussie Davis and the feelings they revealed were woven into the very fabric of bluegrass music, and there they have stayed.

William Shakespeare Who?

His name was William Shakespeare Hays. Even though you've probably never heard of him, he was one of the most prolific composers of bluegrass songs ever. The conundrum is that he was born on July 19, 1837, and died on July 23, 1907. So how can someone so obscure be such a prolific songwriter of bluegrass music, if he died four years before Bill Monroe was born? That, my friend, is what this section is about.

William Hays grew up in Louisville, Kentucky. His name was just William Hays, but his classmates insisted on adding "Shakespeare" to his name because of his penchant for writing poetry and prose. From then on, William Shakespeare Hays was the handle he went by. He did, however, occasionally use the pen name "Syah," which was Hays spelled backward.

Hays went to college in Hanover, Indiana, and Georgetown, Kentucky. While at Georgetown, he became known as the "boy poet." His first published song, "Little Ones at Home," was written while he was at Hanover. This ignited a prolific writing career, which resulted in Hays penning innumerable songs, poems, and newspaper columns. Among his many occupations were steamboat captain, Civil War correspondent, and river editor of the *Louisville Courier-Journal*. He considered songwriting more of a hobby than a profession.

From an early job as a clerk on a riverboat, Hays worked his way up the ranks and eventually became captain of his own riverboat. Despite the rigors of captaining a riverboat, Hays managed to find time to continue writing poems and songs—lots of them. During his lifetime, he churned out at least 350 songs, most with highly nostalgic and sentimental themes. In 1873, it was estimated that his publisher had sold a staggering 2,688,000 sheets of 71 of his songs, no small potatoes in those days.

After the fall of Vicksburg in 1862, Hays navigated the *Grey Eagle* on the Mississippi River between Vicksburg and New Orleans. On one of these trips, he was arrested and locked up in a New Orleans jail for writing the song "My Sunny Southern Home," a tune that angered General Benjamin "Beast" Butler, commander of Union troops in New Orleans. Hays's short imprisonment had less to do with the subject matter of this harmless song and more to do with the fact that Hays was a staunch Democrat, who later supported such Democratic candidates such as George B. McClellan, Samuel Tilden, and Grover Cleveland.

Even though the song "Dixie" or "Dixie's Land" is

William S. Hays, ca. 1872.

generally credited to Daniel D. Emmett, Hays insisted until the day he died that he and Charles Ward composed an early version of "Dixie," which they set to an anonymous Scottish melody. Hays claimed that he sent the song to a local militia group, the Buckner Guards, who took it south in early 1861, after the Civil War began. Since Hays could not offer definitive proof that he wrote it, his claims were dismissed. His wife and daughters tried to pursue it but were unsuccessful.

William Shakespeare Hays was among the most prolific composers of the nineteenth-century songs we now called "tearjerkers." Along with fellow composers Stephen Foster, Charles Harris, and Gussie Davis, Hays made lasting contributions to American music as a composer of some of the most popular sentimental songs. His first successful published song was "The Little Drummer Boy of Shiloh," still sung today around the campfires of soldiers reenacting the Civil War.

What is amazing about Hays's prodigious output of songs is the sheer variety of themes he penned. His compositions included dialect songs (African American, German, Irish, and hayseed or hillbilly), railroad songs, gospel songs, river songs, Civil War songs, love songs, and songs about log cabins. The one thing that most of his songs had in common was more than a pinch of utter sentimentality. In fact, Hays's success at writing songs of sentimentality and nostalgia helped to pave the way for other contemporary songwriters who would copy his popular style.

Hays's songs were not only popular during his own lifetime; many went on to become practically immortal. That's because his sentimental themes of loneliness and despair struck a chord and appealed to the first generation of bluegrass musicians that were drawn to these darker kinds of songs. We're talking about singers like Bill Monroe, the Stanley Brothers, and Lester Flatt. Hays's songs that were later done in bluegrass style included "We Parted by the Riverside" (1866); "Little Old Cabin in the Lane" (1871); "Molly Darling" (1871); "You've Been a Friend to Me" (1879); "I'll Remember You, Love, in My Prayers" (1869); "Nobody's Darling on Earth" (1870); and "Jimmie Brown, the Paper Boy" (1875).

William Shakespeare Hays's songs closely mirrored topics that would later be constants in classic bluegrass music: log cabins, lost love, pine trees, rivers, gravesites, mother, and drinking. It's quite possible that Hays helped set the pattern or blueprint for songs that would later become the core repertoire of bluegrass music. Scan a list of some of Hays's songs and you'll think you're looking at a list of current bluegrass favorites: "Lone Grave by the Sea" (1862); "We May Never Meet Again" (1863); "My Southern Sunny Home" (1864); "Will You Remember Me?" (1864); "Mary's Waiting by the Window" (1866); "Little Old Log Cabin in the Woods" (1866); "Take Me Back Home" (1866); "Down by the Deep Sad Sea" (1868); "Driven from Home" (1868); "Good Bye Old Home" (1868), "The Old Man's Drunk Again" (1870), "My Dear Old Sunny Home" (1871), "You'll Always Find Me True" (1872); "I Have No Home" (1873); "Do Not Turn Me from Your Door" (1873); "My Dear Old Home" (1875); "I Will Be Home Tonight, Love" (1875); "Down Yonder in the Lane" (1875); "Meet Me by the Riverside" (1877); "The Cabin on the Hill" (1878); "Come Back to the Old Home Again" (1880); and "When I'm Gone" (1892).

We all know that the core of the bluegrass repertoire includes many songs about mother. Here again, Hays set the standard. This was probably because his own mother died when he was just ten years old. His mother songs include "Call Me No More, Mother" (1864); "I Am Dying, Mother, Dying" (1865); "What Will I Do, Mother Is Dead" (1869); "Papa, Stay Home" (1872); "Take This Letter to My Mother" (1873); "Kiss Me

Goodnight, Mamma" (1874); "I'm Motherless Now" (1872); "Is Mother There?" (1875); "Mother's Parting at the Gate" (1884); and "The Mothers of the West" (date unknown).

Some of Hays's songs have made an indirect impact on bluegrass music. Take, for example, his poem "The Faithful Engineer" that was first published in 1886 and later reprinted in 1895 as "Old Hayseed's Railroad Train to Heaven." It is interesting to note that Hays's poem was the model for M.E. Abby and Charles Tillman's well-known song "Life's Railway to Heaven" aka "Life Is Like a Mountain Railroad." Of course, they didn't give Hays a lick of credit.

One of Hays's most important works was his "Little Old Cabin in the Lane" (1871). This song was reworked by Fiddlin' John Carson and was on one side of his first recording, which marked the very beginning of country music as we know it today. But it doesn't stop there. This same song was used as the basis of the Western song "Little Old Sod Shanty on the Claim." Hays's melody was also used for the cowboy song "Little Joe the Wrangler" and the railroad song "The Little Red Caboose."

Even though Hays's compositions made a powerful contribution to American music, his name has largely been forgotten. It's no wonder. Many times, when one of Hays's songs was published or recorded, his name was left off. Even when his songs were hits for the artists who recorded them, you can look long and hard and you won't see Hays's name. Examples of this omission include such artists as the Carter Family ("You've Been a Friend to Me"); Fiddlin' John Carson, Ernest V. Stoneman, Uncle Dave Macon, Riley Puckett and Vernon Dalhart ("The Little Old Log Cabin in the Lane"); the Whitstein Brothers, Bill Clifton and Red Rector ("We Parted by the Riverside"); Flatt and Scruggs and Mac Wiseman ("Jimmie Brown, the Newsboy"); and Eddie Arnold ("Molly Darling"). No less an expert historian than Carl Sandburg failed to mention Hays's name as composer of "I'll Remember You Love in My Prayers," which appeared in his well-known book *The American Songbag*. Hays's song "Keep in the Middle of the Road" was printed in a gospel song collection by Homer Rodeheaver and listed as an African American spiritual.

Although William Shakespeare Hays's name has slipped into relative obscurity, many of his songs continue to be sung and recorded by people who relish the sappy and sentimental songs that would bring a tear to a glass eye.

Johnny Bond

"I Wonder Where You Are Tonight" is a proven bluegrass standard that is welcomed in any jam where bluegrass music is played. It was written in the 1940s by Cyrus Whitfield ("Johnny") Bond, a Western singer and songwriter. Several other of Johnny's compositions have been bluegrass favorites for years. These include "Your Old Love Letters," "Tomorrow Never Comes," and "Love Grown Cold."

He grew up on the family farm near Marietta, in rural Oklahoma, and his first instrument was the trumpet. When Johnny's family purchased a Victrola in the early 1920s, he became hooked on the records of Vernon Dalhart and especially Jimmie Rodgers. His older sister, Mary, managed to save enough to buy a radio, on which Johnny was exposed to the Western swing music of Milton Brown, W. Lee O'Daniel, and Carson Robison. In high school Johnny was asked to join the brass band, so he borrowed an E-flat alto brass horn and figured out how to play it. Before long Johnny had amassed the

Johnny Bond in Los Angeles, California, ca. 1951 (John Edwards Memorial Foundation Records [20001], Southern Folklife Collection at Wilson Special Collections Library, University of North Carolina at Chapel Hill).

sum of ninety-eight cents and ordered a ukulele from Montgomery Ward. He then borrowed a guitar and a banjo and became proficient on them. Before long he was playing for dances in rural Oklahoma.

In 1937 Johnny graduated from high school and went to live with his brother, Howard, in Oklahoma City. Wanting to make a career in music, Johnny approached all the local radio stations and was finally given a time slot on KFXR. The main drawback of this job was that there was no pay. But Johnny was happy to just get his foot in the door, on his way to becoming a professional musician. At first broadcasting under the name Cyrus Whitfield, and then Johnny Whitfield, he eventually settled on Johnny Bond.

Before long Johnny was recruited to play with Billy McGinty's Oklahoma Cowboys, which later became Pop Moore and His Oklahomans. Johnny then teamed up with Jimmy Wakely and Scotty Harrel. They called themselves The Singing Cowboy Trio but changed their name to the Bell Boys when they were sponsored by the Bell Clothing Company on KVOO radio in Tulsa. They were dressed head to toe in cowboy outfits, and their repertoire leaned heavily on the Western music of Gene Autry and the Sons of the Pioneers.

Johnny's gamble to play on the radio for no wages paid off in spades when Gene Autry heard one of their radio broadcasts while on tour in rural Oklahoma. Johnny later recalled that Gene invited them to appear on his *Melody Ranch* CBS network radio show. Gene's exact words were "If you boys ever get to California, look me up."

In May of 1940 Johnny took Gene Autry up on his offer. The Jimmy Wakely Trio—Wakely, Johnny, and Dick Reinhard, who had replaced Scotty Harrel—loaded up Wakely's Dodge with instruments, kids, and wives and headed to California. When they arrived in the Golden State, the band had some time to kill while awaiting word on joining Autry's radio show. It was then that Johnny composed "I Wonder Where You Are Tonight."

Here is how Johnny explained it. "Before that, all my songs had been cowboy, but I was convinced we'd have quicker success with a hillbilly love song. In the verse of a song we had sung on the radio in Oklahoma, I found the line, 'I wonder where you are tonight,' and the idea was born. Over the years, many people have come to the conclusion that it is an old Public Domain song, and several newer songs have come to life using the identical melody."

Not only did Johnny make guest appearances on Autry's popular radio show, but he was also a mainstay of that show from 1940 until the show's cancellation in 1956. During these early years, Johnny recorded first for Decca as The Jimmy Wakely Trio and then for Columbia as Johnny Bond and the Cimarron Boys. In 1953 Johnny joined the Los Angeles TV show *Town Hall Party* as a regular performer, lead and rhythm guitarist, and writer. He stayed with the show until its demise in early 1961.

By the end of his career Johnny had written and published hundreds of songs, many of which were major hits for a number of recording artists. These songs included "Cimarron,"

Gene Autry on his horse, Champion, ca. 1939.

"I'll Step Aside," "Tomorrow Never Comes," and "I Wonder Where You Are Tonight." The latter song has been very heavily covered by numerous artists, including Red Allen and the Kentuckians, Bobby Bare, Roy Clark, Flatt and Scruggs, Jerry Lee Lewis, the Louvin Brothers, Bill Monroe, Johnny Rodriguez, Hank Snow, Porter Wagoner, and Hank Williams, Jr.

"Wildwood Flower"

"Wildwood Flower" has been so popular since it was first recorded by the Carter Family in 1928 that many call it "the Hillbilly National Anthem." It was written and published in 1860 as "I'll Twine 'Mid the Ringlets" by Joseph Philbrick Webster (melody) and Maud Irving (lyrics).

One line of the song has confused listeners and singers since the day the Carter

Maybelle Carter, ca. 1930 (John Edwards Memorial Foundation Records [20001], Southern Folklife Collection at Wilson Special Collections Library, University of North Carolina at Chapel Hill).

Family recorded it. Sara Carter sang "the pale and the leader and eyes look like blue." Nobody has known what the heck "the pale and the leader" meant, but they have sung it faithfully that way for nearly one hundred years.

While doing some research at the Library of Congress in the early 1970s, I stumbled on a copy of the original lyrics. That line actually goes "and the pale aronatus with eyes of bright blue." Sometime later, Joe Hickerson, the archivist for the Library of Congress, contacted me because their rare copy of the original lyrics had been lost or stolen. He was disappointed when I told him that I had written down the original lyrics that I found at the Library of Congress but didn't make a photocopy. Pity. Here are those original lyrics:

"I'll Twine 'Mid the Ringlets"

I'll twine 'mid the ringlets
Of my raven black hair,
The lilies so pale
And the roses so fair,
The myrtle so bright
With an emerald hue,
And the pale aronatus
With eyes of bright blue.

> I'll sing and I'll dance,
> My laugh shall be gay;
> I'll cease this wild weeping—
> Drive sorrow away,
> Tho' my heart is now breaking,
> He never shall know
> That his name made me tremble
> And my pale cheeks to glow.
>
> I'll think of him never—
> I'll be wildly gay,
> I'll charm ev'ry heart,
> And the crowd I will sway,
> I'll live yet to see him,
> Regret the dark hour
> When he won, then neglected,
> The frail wildwood flower.
>
> He told me he loved me,
> And promis'd to love,
> Through ill and misfortune,
> All others above,
> Another has won him;
> Ah, misery to tell;
> He left me in silence—
> no word of farewell.
>
> He taught me to love him,
> He call'd me his flower
> That blossom'd for him
> All the brighter each hour;
> But I woke from my dreaming,
> My idol was clay;
> My visions of love
> Have all faded away.

Let's talk about the composers of "Wildwood Flower." The melody was written in 1860 by Henry J.L. Webster, who in 1857 had written "Lorena," reportedly the most popular song of the Civil War on both sides. In 1868 he composed the melody of "In the Sweet By and By." In 1911 Joe Hill, the I.W.W. poet and activist, wrote a parody of "In the Sweet By and By" that he called "The Preacher and the Slave" or "Pie in the Sky."

Maud Irving, who has been credited with composing the lyrics of "Wildwood Flower," has recently been discovered to be a man! His actual name was J. William Van Namee, a poet who professed to be a spiritualist, a channeler of spirits, and a clairvoyant physician. Van Namee wanted to write poems for *Godey's Lady's Book*, an extremely popular woman's magazine from 1830 to 1878. Since the magazine only accepted poems from women, he sent in his works under the alias of Maud Irving. He then used that name when "I'll Twine 'Mid the Ringlets" was published in 1860.

"Jimmie Brown, the Newsboy"

As a young man of sixteen, I was thunderstruck the first time I heard the magic fingers of Earl Scruggs on the five-string banjo. The drive and passion whacked me upside the head with such force that it forever changed the direction of my life. It was 1961, and

Songwriters and Songs

Earl Scruggs (left) and Lester Flatt, ca. 1960 (photograph by Charles Tompkins).

that album was *Country Music* by Lester Flatt, Earl Scruggs, and the Foggy Mountain Boys. At that time, I only had one thing in my sight—the way Earl played the banjo. I was so fixated on his banjo playing that I was completely oblivious to the awesome talent of the rest of the band. To me, they might as well have been chopped liver. It was like they were only there to back up Earl and that fancy banjo.

As soon as I laid my ears on Earl's banjo playing, I knew I had to learn that instrument. That week I headed to McCabe's Guitar Shop in Santa Monica, California, and picked up a second-hand Kay open-back banjo. Where I lived, we didn't have woodsheds, but I spent practically every waking moment practicing the banjo.

When I found out there was an earlier Flatt and Scruggs LP, I dashed off to my local record store with $3 clutched in my hand, itching to take home *Foggy Mountain Jamboree*. This record only added fuel to the fire. I was eating it for breakfast, lunch, and dinner. Nestled among the stunning instrumentals ("Flint Hill Special," "Earl's Breakdown," "Foggy Mountain Special," "Shucking the Corn," "Randy Lynn Rag," and "Foggy Mountain Chimes") was one song with no banjo, "Jimmie Brown, the Newsboy." My first thought was, "Where is the banjo?"

It wasn't until my older sister, Bonnie, mentioned that she loved "Jimmie Brown, the Newsboy" that I gave it a second chance. "Hmmm," I thought. "That guitar playing is pretty good. Danged good, as a matter of fact." I assumed Lester Flatt was doing the fancy guitar picking, because he was holding a guitar on the cover of the LP. It was only later that I learned Earl was a killer guitar player who played not only in the "Carter Scratch" style of Maybelle Carter but also in the fingerpicking style of Merle Travis.

Since I had been learning guitar, I slowed the *Foggy Mountain Jamboree* record to half speed and taught myself a decent version of "Jimmie Brown, the Newsboy." At that time, I had been taking a few guitar lessons, and I proudly showed my teacher the way I played that tune. He was not the least bit delicate on my fragile ego and said it was all wrong. He then proceeded to show me the "right" way to play it. I was seriously confused, because I thought I had faithfully learned it from the record. My teacher and I butted heads because we both insisted that we were right.

Later I realized that, after their initial cut of "Jimmie Brown, the Newsboy" (1951, the one I had practiced), Flatt and Scruggs recorded it again on *Songs of the Famous Carter Family* (1961). This time Earl changed the way he played it. Finally, I realized that we both had been right.

A historian by trade, I recently became interested in the origins of "Jimmie Brown, the Newsboy." Here's what I learned. The year was 1875, and popular music was strongly tilted toward nostalgic and sentimental themes. Songwriters (then called "songsmiths") gloried in creating songs that tugged at the tender heartstrings of a nation that had recently gone through the trauma of the Civil War, and pitiful scenes of dying soldiers and little drummer boys populated the songs of that era.

The songwriting industry was just getting underway, and publishers were vying to see who could make people shed the most tears. Nothing was off limits. Popular songs portrayed impoverished widows and barefooted orphans begging for bread, while others were left to die cold and alone in the ice and snow. Songwriters like Charles K. Harris, Gussie L. Davis, Stephen Foster, and the brilliant young William S. Hays were writing songs that would later be called "tearjerkers."

Although the name William S. Hays may be unknown to modern bluegrass musicians and fans, many of his original compositions have become well-worn evergreens (see "William Shakespeare Who?"). Last but not least among them was "Jimmie Brown, the Paper Boy" (1875).

The Carter Family made the first commercial recording of "Jimmie Brown, the Newsboy" in Atlanta, Georgia, on November 25, 1929, although it wasn't released until June 19, 1931. Below, you'll see the lyrics that were sung by Sara Carter on their only recording of this song. It was only natural that the Carter Family record "Jimmie Brown, the Newsboy." After all, their repertoire was populated by such sentimental and nostalgic songs as "Bury Me Beneath the Willow," "Poor Orphan Child," "The Dying Soldier," "I Have No Loving Mother Now," "Darling Little Joe," "The Dying Mother," "Faded Coat of Blue," "Grave Upon the Green Hillside," "I Have an Aged Mother," and "Poor Little Orphan Boy." "Jimmie Brown, the Newsboy" was also the perfect vehicle to showcase Maybelle's virtuosic guitar skills.

When I went back and compared the Carter Family lyrics with those of the original sheet music by Will S. Hays, I found some important differences.

"Jimmie Brown, the Paper Boy"
original lyrics by William S. Hays, 1875

I'm very cold and hungry, sir, my clothes are worn and thin,
I wander on from place to place, my daily bread to win.
But never mind, sir, how I look, don't sneer at me or frown,
I'm selling papers for I am the newsboy, Jimmie Brown.

Chorus:
I sell the morning papers, sir, my name is Jimmie Brown
Most ev'ry body knows I am the "poor boy of the town."

My father was a drunkard, sir, so I've heard Mother say,
Before he died, how oft for him I've heard her weep and pray.
But I am helping Mother now, I journey up and down,
To sell my morning papers, for I am the newsboy, Jimmie Brown.

My Mother tells me every night to kneel with her and pray,
She says if I've an honest heart, I'll be all right some day.

> And when she's gone to heaven, sir, to wear a starry crown,
> She'll wait up there to welcome home the newsboy of the town.

The Carters separated each couplet (half verse) with a guitar solo. The first three couplets of the original lyrics and those of the Carter Family are almost identical. But on the second line of the second full verse, the Carters' version strays from the original. The Carter Family version also omits Hays's last verse. I think it's fair to assume that they did not have access to the original sheet music when they learned it. Instead, it is more than likely that A.P. Carter collected it from one of his many informants in southwest Virginia or Tennessee. It's also possible he learned it from Lesley Riddle, the African American ace guitar player who traveled the backroads with A.P. collecting songs and who was a major influence on Maybelle Carter's guitar style. Adding further evidence that the Carters didn't learn the song from the original sheet music is the fact that their melody was completely different from that of the original.

Although the Carter Family's recording was far from a big seller for Victor Records, "Jimmie Brown, the Newsboy" was later picked up from that source by Flatt and Scruggs, who recorded it for Columbia on May 9, 1951. With Lester singing lead, it became one of their most requested numbers. Earl's outstanding Maybelle Carter–style guitar playing certainly helped to put the song over the top and helped pave the way for a revival of the music of the Carter Family. Beyond that, Earl's playing was an early example of fancy lead guitar work at a time when most bluegrass guitarists stuck timidly to playing rhythm.

Flatt and Scruggs's lyrics were first published in their 1951 song folio titled *Songs and Picture Album*. In their 1962 songbook, *Folk Music with an Overdrive*, a full page was devoted to "Jimmie Brown, the Newsboy" as published by Peer International, who held the copyrights to many Carter Family songs. By the way, the catchy phrase "folk music with overdrive" was the creation of Alan Lomax, who published it in *Esquire* magazine October 1, 1959. On Peer's sheet music, song credits read, "Words and Music by A.P. Carter."

What really shocked me was that there are two additional couplets in Peer International's sheet music (faithfully rendering Lester and Earl's version) that were in neither the Hays original composition from 1875 nor the Carter Family recording of 1929.

> You can hear me yelling, *Morning Star*, running along the street,
> Got no hat upon my head, no shoes upon my feet.
>
> My mother always tells me, sir, I've nothing in the world to lose,
> I'll get a place in heaven, sir, to sell the *Gospel News*.

These two mystery half verses sparkle with charm. In particular, the *Morning Star* couplet, with a tender message from Mother, is among the best of the entire song. The *Gospel News* couplet was a stroke of genius because it tied the whole song together, creating a unifying and meaningful ending where Jimmie is selling his newspapers in heaven. The big question to ponder is "Where in the heck did those two mystery couplets come from?" The finger points at two likely suspects: A.P. Carter (who is credited in Peer International's sheet music) and Lester Flatt, who recorded the version with the newspaper names. There is evidence for and against both possibilities.

A.P. Carter certainly had the songwriting ability but not the apparent motive to add new lyrics to the song recorded by the Carter Family in 1929. But why bother to rewrite a song that was not an especially good seller when there were no plans afoot to rerecord it? It was not among the songs A.P. and Sara later recorded in the Acme sessions of the 1950s.

It's possible but unlikely that Ralph Peer or Roy Horton, who worked alongside Peer, pressured A.P. to go back and brush up the lyrics by luring him with the promise of future royalties. Perhaps they convinced A.P. that the Carter Family would eventually get the recognition they deserved, so his "investment" in polishing up the song would be rewarded. If this was their vision, it came true in spades because Flatt and Scruggs's success with their own recordings of "Jimmie Brown, the Newsboy" played a part in bringing the music of the Carter Family back into popularity. Remember that Flatt and Scruggs's second version of the song on their 1961 album *Songs of the Famous Carter Family* came out at a time when the folk music revival was taking the country by storm.

A.P. Carter at his home in Maces Springs, Virginia, ca. 1930.

Lester Flatt had every reason to brush up the lyrics of "Jimmie Brown, the Newsboy." During the early 1950s, Flatt and Scruggs were riding high with live radio broadcasts in Lexington, Kentucky, and Bristol, Virginia, and numerous personal appearances. Their records were flying off the shelves, which was a strong incentive to polish their songs to a high gloss. Lester certainly had the songwriting chops to rewrite "Jimmie Brown, the Newsboy," if that's what he did. He had already crafted such songs as "Little Cabin Home on the Hill," "My Little Girl in Tennessee," "I'm Head Over Heels in Love," and countless others.

But the question remains, if Lester added the two additional couplets, why didn't he copyright his arrangement and take credit for it in his and Earl's own 1962 songbook? In the same Flatt and Scruggs songbook, writing credits for "I'm On My Way to Canaan's Land" listed "Words and Music by A.P. Carter, Lester Flatt, and Earl Scruggs." We can speculate that Lester and Earl did not want to upset Maybelle Carter, since they had become close friends and even recorded an album together. Not to throw cold water on this theory, but Earl's wife, Louise, who was Lester and Earl's savvy business manager, was no pushover. I cannot imagine how she would have shied away from claiming copyright credit and royalties if Lester and Earl had, in fact, added two words to the song, not to mention two half verses!

There is a third possibility for the rewriter: Mac Wiseman. Mac had been a member of Flatt and Scruggs's original Foggy Mountain Boys band in 1948. All three were fans of the Carter Family and sentimental songs of the nineteenth century. I have no evidence, but either Lester or Mac may have modified and introduced "Jimmie Brown, the Newsboy" to the live show repertoire three years before the 1951 recording (made after Mac had left the band). In 1959, two years before the second Flatt and Scruggs version, Mac released his own version of the song as "Jimmy Brown, the Newsboy." That single was his lifetime biggest hit, reaching #5 on the country charts. Who got songwriter credit on the record label? "Arr [arranged by]: Mac Wiseman."

So, the mystery remains. Was it A.P. Carter, Lester Flatt, or Mac Wiseman who added the two additional half verses to "Jimmie Brown, the Newsboy"? Even after all this research, the case remains far from closed. Will the real songwriter please step forward?

Mac Wiseman playing his Gibson Southern Jumbo banner guitar, ca. 1945 (John Edwards Memorial Foundation Records [20001], Southern Folklife Collection at Wilson Special Collections Library, University of North Carolina at Chapel Hill).

"Otto Wood, the Bandit"

Yesterday was July 10. It wasn't a day to watch the fireworks, have a picnic, wave a flag, or sing "The Star-Spangled Banner." Nope. Yesterday was the ninety-third anniversary of the day that the famed outlaw Otto Wood made his tenth and final escape from Central Prison in Raleigh, North Carolina.

Central Prison was not a place to have a tea party on the lawn. Completed at a cost of $1.25 million in December of 1884, it was the first prison built in North Carolina. It is said it took inmates fourteen years to construct the original castle-like structure from granite quarried just outside the prison's east wall. To this day, the prison is located west of downtown Raleigh on twenty-nine acres of land. Most of the complex is enclosed by a double-wire fence with razor ribbon on top. It's not the place they send you for an overdue library fine.

The life of Otto Wood was the stuff dime novels were made of. Born in Wilkes County, North Carolina, on May 9, 1894, Otto ran away from home at just seven years of age. After stealing rides aboard freight trains, he lived for a time in West Virginia with relatives of the infamous Hatfield clan, who were engaged in deadly feuds with their sworn enemies, the McCoys. From the Hatfields, Otto learned life skills that would soon become his stock and trade: moonshining, gambling, and shooting.

By the time Otto was thirteen, he had committed his first crime of stealing a bicycle, which he hadn't yet even learned to ride. While a teenager, Otto lost his left hand, either in a hunting accident or while working on the railroad in West Virginia (accounts differ). He was also plagued with a birth defect resulting in a clubfoot. When he was finally shot down at the age of thirty-seven, in a running gun battle with the sheriff of Salisbury, Otto had become the most notorious outlaw North Carolina had ever known. His exploits included no less than ten daring escapes from prison. He was wanted in at least five states for car and horse theft, moonshining, and murder.

Otto Wood, Central Prison, Raleigh, North Carolina, ca. 1927.

Otto was a man you didn't mess with. Once on the lam in the Southwestern deserts, he fought off a pack of hungry wolves and then captured a gang of Mexican outlaws who made the mistake of trying to rob him. Otto turned the surprised thieves over to the law but didn't stick around to claim the reward for fear of being recognized and sent back to prison. His most notorious crime was the November 3, 1923, murder of A.W. Kaplan, a Greensboro, North Carolina, pawnbroker. They apparently quarreled when Otto discovered that the store had sold his father's pocket watch, which he had pawned.

Not more than a month after Otto met his end in a fatal shoot-out with police, Walter "Kid" Smith and the Carolina Buddies wrote "Otto Wood, the Bandit" and recorded it on January 1, 1931. The song was frequently performed and recorded by Doc Watson in the late twentieth century.

"Stagolee"

His real name was Lee Shelton, but they all called him Stagger Lee or Stagolee. At birth, a fortune-teller was summoned because the newborn was double-jointed and had a full set of teeth. What worried the fortune-teller most was that the baby was born with a veil over his face, a sign that Stagolee would come to no good. The fortune-teller's warnings all came true. Legends say that the devil carried him off to the graveyard. Knowing his weakness for gaudy clothes and Stetson hats, the devil bought his soul in exchange for a magic oxblood Stetson made from a man-eating panther that the devil himself had skinned alive. If Stagolee wore that hat he had magical powers.

He could

> crawl into a bottle on a shelf;
> walk barefoot on a hot slag from a pig iron furnace;
> turn himself into a horse and gallop away;
> eat hot fire without getting singed;
> change himself into a mountain or a varmint; and
> wear no shoes, but his footprint would be that of a horse.

The devil, meanwhile, was growing impatient for Stagolee's soul. One cold frosty evening around Christmas, Stagolee was having a big winning streak down at the Jack O'Diamonds in St. Louis. In his haste of raking in all the money, Stagolee hung his magic Stetson on the back of his chair. The devil, seeing his chance, quickly turned himself into Billy Lyons, an innocent family man. Grabbing Stagolee's prized Stetson hat, Billy tore out the double doors toward the White Elephant Barrel House with Stagolee in hot pursuit. Stagolee pulled a pistol out of his belt and shot the devil, who instantly turned back into Billy Lyons. As Billy lay dying, Stagolee calmly claimed his hat.

The devil was sorely disappointed that the police did not kill Stagolee right then and there. The judge sentenced Stagolee to seventy-five years in the Jefferson pen. When the devil finally claimed his prize, Stagolee became quite popular in hell playing guitar in a jazz band, with the devil himself on cornet.

"Diamond Joe"

I've always been a sucker for a good ole cowboy song. In the early 1960s I got bit hard by the folk music bug that was sweeping the nation. One of my favorite performers was Ramblin' Jack Elliott. To me, he was the perfect combination of a cowboy and a folk singer. We frequently went to see him perform at the Ash Grove in West Hollywood. He told me one time that the reason they called him Ramblin' Jack was because he never stopped talking. On one of his long-winded introductions, his voice got lower and lower, and his speech got slower and slower until nothing was coming out of his mouth except the soft sound of him snoring!

Being a closet cowboy myself, my favorite Ramblin' Jack Elliott song was "Diamond Joe." Several years after I learned it, I heard a County LP of an old-time group called the Georgia Crackers doing a completely different song called "Diamond Joe." I always lamented the fact that Jack Elliott's song didn't have a chorus, so I combined the chorus of the Georgia Crackers' song with Jack Elliott's "Diamond Joe."

Ramblin' Jack Elliott playing his 1952 Gretch Sierra Sunburst guitar with a Hamilton capo, ca. 1959.

Yesterday I was singing my "Diamond Joe" around the house and my wife, Barbara, commented on the chorus ("Diamond Joe, come and get me, my wife now done quit me"). She asked, "Why did his wife quit him?" Since the song doesn't exactly explain it, I guessed that he was a shiftless, smelly, no-account cowpuncher and that she moved on to someone more appealing.

This made me remember that, several years back, I had done some research into the origins of the Jack Elliott version of "Diamond Joe." With the help of Nick Hawes, I traced the song back to his father, Baldwin "Butch" Hawes, the husband of Bess Lomax Hawes, who was the sister of Alan Lomax and daughter of the famed John Lomax.

Nick told me that in 1944 Butch wrote the song in New York City for a BBC radio program called *The Chisholm Trail*. Alan's wife, Elizabeth, wrote the script based on songs from the Lomax collections. The major character in the show was a tough hombre by the name of "Diamond Joe Chisholm." Elizabeth did not read music, so she inadvertently selected a rather stately melody in 3/2 meter that had been transcribed by Ruth Crawford Seeger, Pete's stepmother.

When Elizabeth realized that the tune wouldn't work, it was too late to rewrite the script. That's when she called on Bess Lomax Hawes, her sister-in-law, who was the music director of the program. Bess then asked her husband, Butch, to compose a new "Diamond Joe" song that would be more appropriate to the story. Since the song was to be performed by Lee Hays of the Almanac Singers, Hawes based the melody of his new song on "State of Arkansas," which he knew Hays had been singing for years.

Cisco Houston was also a cast member of *The Chisholm Trail*. Cisco, not realizing that Butch had composed "Diamond Joe," assumed it to be an old authentic cowboy song and recorded it for a 1952 Folkways album titled *Cowboy Ballads* (FA 2022). In 1954 those lyrics were printed in *Sing Out!* magazine. A few years later, a rodeo cowboy named George Williams apparently heard "Diamond Joe" from Cisco's record and taught it to Jack Elliott at a rodeo in Brussels, Belgium, in 1958. It then became a career song for Jack Elliott, and that's where I learned it.

Here are the lyrics that Cisco Houston sang (reproduced with permission of the Bess Lomax Hawes Trust):

> There is a man you'll hear about most every place you go.
> And his holdings are in Texas, and his name was Diamond Joe.
> Well, he carried all his money in a diamond-studded jaw,
> And he never was much bothered by the process of the law.
>
> Well, I hired out to Diamond Joe, boys, I did offer him my hand,
> And he gave me a string of horses, so old they could not stand.
> Well, I liked to died of hunger, he did mistreat me so.
> I never earned a dollar in the pay of Diamond Joe.
>
> Well, his bread it was corn dodger and his meat I could not chaw,
> And he drove me near distracted with the wagging of his jaw.
> And the telling of his stories, I'd like to let you know,
> There never was a rounder that lied like Diamond Joe.
>
> Well, I tried three times to quit him, boys, but he did argue so,
> That I'm still punching cattle in the pay of Diamond Joe.
> And when I'm called to Heaven, and it comes my time to go,
> Give my blankets to my buddy and give the fleas to Diamond Joe.

The other "Diamond Joe" song is a story in itself. It was first recorded for Okeh Records on March 21, 1927, by Paul and Leon Cofer, who were billed as the Georgia Crackers. I've always sung the chorus to this "Diamond Joe" as

> Diamond Joe, come and get me,
> My wife she done quit me.

After listening closely to their recording, I now realize that years ago I had misheard the recording and have been singing it wrong all along. Here's what they were actually singing:

> Diamond Joe, come and get me,
> My wife died and quit me.

So, this answers my wife's original question as to why she left him. She died!

But what is the meaning of the line in the chorus "Diamond Joe, come and get me"? There is conflicting evidence here. Fragments of the lyrics of this original "Diamond Joe" were published in the *Journal of American Folklore* as collected from African American sources in Mississippi from a Mr. Turner by Professor E.C. Parrow in 1909. The chorus goes:

> Diamond Joe, Diamond Joe,
> Run get me, Diamond Joe.

Several of these verses of Turner's version of "Diamond Joe" are almost identical to those sung by the Georgia Crackers in their 1927 recording. Here are those verses by Mister Turner. In parentheses are the Georgia Cracker's verses.

> Then I'll buy me a bar'el of flour
> Cook and eat it every hour.
> (Gonna buy me a sack of flour,
> Cook me a hoecake every hour).
>
> Yes, an' buy me a middlin' o' meat,
> Cook and eat it twice a week.
> (I'm gonna buy me a piece of meat,
> Cook me a slice once a week).

In 1911 Professor Howard W. Odum published an article in the *Journal of American Folklore* that included a version of "Diamond Joe" from a woman's point of view.

> Diamon' Joe, you better come an' git me'
> Don't you see my man done quit [me?],
> Diamon' Joe, you better come git me.
>
> Diamon' Joe he had a wife, they parted every night;
> When the weather it got cool,
> Old Joe he come back to that black gal.
>
> But time come to pass,
> When old Joe quit his last,
> An' he never went to see her any mo'.

And now, finally, we get to another possible origin of "Diamond Joe." Old-time music researchers Gus Meade and Lyle Lofgren dug up evidence that "Diamond Joe" was not a man at all. Instead, "Diamond Joe" was a steamboat line that ran from 1862 to 1910. According to this theory, the poor widower in the song wants the steamboat to come take him away.

Delving a little deeper, I discovered that there was a Chicago grain dealer named Joseph Reynolds (1819–1891) who used a logo of "JO" inside a diamond. He eventually built a steamboat, the *Diamond Jo*, to haul freight on the upper Mississippi River from St. Paul to St. Louis. So, this might be the Diamond Jo that the poor widower wanted to "come get him."

It should be noted that both Wilma Lee and Stoney Cooper and Bob Dylan recorded the Georgia Crackers' version of "Diamond Joe," while Joe Val and Laurie Lewis both learned the other song with that name from the recording of Ramblin' Jack Elliott.

"Run Mountain"

One of the signature songs of J.E. Mainer was "Run Mountain." It certainly ranks up there among the more bizarre songs in old-time and early country music. The song is curious both for the melody and because some of the lyrics are rather mysterious. The melody is set in the key of G, but it starts in the key of A. By the time the chorus comes around, it is in the key of G. Are you confused yet? If so, join the club! As if the melody and the key changes are not strange enough, what really takes the cake are the words to the chorus. More on this later.

"Run Mountain" seems to have originated with the North Carolina fiddler J.E. Mainer, who recorded it several times, starting as early as 1949. J.E. recorded it on April 7, 1963, for Arhoolie Records, with a spoken introduction: "Well, friends, here comes an old number called 'Run Mountain, Check a Little Hill.'" So, are we to believe it is an old song or a new one? The answer seems to be both. The melody is unlike anything else in the old-time repertoire, so it should be called new. At least one of the verses ("If I had a needle and thread") is common in any number of songs. The rest of the verses may come from blackface minstrel tradition, or they could be J.E. Mainer originals. The main thing that's so bizarre about the song is the chorus.

Sometimes he appears to sing it like this: "Run mountain, take a little hill, run mountain, take a little hill, Run mountain, take a little hill. There you get your fill." However, some of the verses sound like he's singing "Run mountain, chuck a little hill" or "Run mountain, shake a little hill." Any way you look at it, the chorus makes no sense. The line that says "There you get your fill" seems to suggest the song is about moonshine. But what does take, check, chuck, or shake a little hill mean? No one seems to know.

J.E. Mainer's Mountaineers, ca. 1937. Back row, from left: Daddy John Love, Zeke Morris; front row, from left: Wade Mainer, J.E. Mainer (John Edwards Memorial Foundation Records [20001], Southern Folklife Collection at Wilson Special Collections Library, University of North Carolina at Chapel Hill).

About thirty years ago I had the pleasure of being at an old-time music camp in Tennessee where Wade Mainer, J.E.'s younger brother, was sitting across from me at the lunch table. I took the opportunity to ask him exactly what his brother was singing on the chorus of "Run Mountain." Looking exasperated, Wade confessed that he didn't know what in the world J.E. was singing about. When Wade recorded it after his brother did, he sang "Run mountain, sugar in the hill." Without getting clarity on the meaning of the chorus from Wade, the mystery very much remains intact.

Here are the lyrics of "Run Mountain" as performed by J.E. Mainer's Mountaineers, 1949 (reproduced here with permission of Isaac Mainer).

> I went up on the mountain, to get me a load of pine,
> I put it on the wagon, I broke down behind.
> Run Mountain, check a little hill, run mountain, check a little hill,
> Run mountain, check a little hill, now you'll get your fill.
>
> When I's in the field, hard at work, I set down to play,
> Thinkin' of my old true love, she's many miles away.

Run mountain, check a little hill, run mountain, check a little hill,
Run mountain, check a little hill, and there you'll get your fill.

Me six miles from my home, and chickens crow 'fore day,
Me upstairs with another man's wife, better be a'gettin' away.
Run mountain, check a little hill, run mountain, check a little hill,
Run mountain, check a little hill, and there you'll get your fill.

I went up on the mountain and give my horn a blow,
I thought I heard my true love say, "That's comin' from my beau."
Run mountain, check a little hill, run mountain, check a little hill,
Run mountain, check a little hill, and there you'll get your fill.

If I had a needle and thread, as fine as I could sew,
I'd sew my true love to my side and down the road I'd go.
Run mountain, check a little hill, run mountain, check a little hill,
Run mountain, check a little hill, and there you can get your fill.

The above is partially based on personal interviews with Wade Mainer at various locations in North Carolina in 1979–1980.

"Fox on the Run"

In the early 1970s, "Fox on the Run" was among the most requested bluegrass songs. A bluegrass band could scarcely play a show without fans yelling for "Rocky Top" or "Fox on the Run." The song was written in 1968 by an Englishman named Tony Hazzard and first recorded as a rock song by the English group Manfred Mann in February 1969.

The first bluegrass band to record "Fox on the Run" was Bill Emerson, Cliff Waldron, and the New Shades of Grass. Listening to this bluegrass recording, a lot of

The Country Gentlemen, ca. 1959. From left: Eddie Adcock, John Duffy, Tom Gray, and Charlie Waller.

people were puzzled by one line of the lyrics that sounded like Cliff was singing "I fillustrate a girl." Of course, nobody had a clue what Cliff was singing about. When Charlie Waller sang it with the Country Gentlemen, he changed that line to "I see a string of girls."

Some years ago, I received an email from Cliff Waldron, who contacted me about playing his new CD on my bluegrass radio show. Armed with Cliff's email address, I seized the opportunity to get to the bottom of the "fillustrate a girl" question that had been bugging me for years. Here's what I wrote to Cliff:

> Hi Cliff: While I've got you on the line, I have a question that's been burning a hole in my mind for almost thirty years. On the second line of the second verse of your early recording of "Fox on the Run," you seem to be singing "I fillustrate a girl." What, pray tell, are you singing?

Here is Cliff's response.

> Hi Wayne, Regarding your question about THE FOX! My partner in music at that time, Bill Emerson, gave me the words to "Fox on the Run." You heard right, that is what I'm saying. I wanted to change that part of the song because it didn't make any sense to me. So later, after Bill went with the Country Gents I started saying "I see a string of girls," and that's what Charlie Waller is saying in their version.
>
> It was very hard to understand what Manfred Mann was saying on the original recording. But several years later, a good friend of mine told me the correct words were "I illustrate a girl." Believe me, that has haunted me for the past thirty-some years. I wish there was some way I could fix it but I can't, so I'll just have to live with it.
>
> I'll have to say, I learned a good lesson. Since then, I've tried to make sure the words are right, and I try and say them where folks can understand what I'm saying. Take care, Cliff

Tom Mindte smoking a Punch cigar while playing his 1924 Lloyd Loar Mandolin, ca. 2015 (photograph by Jim Scancarelli).

My friend Tom Mindte was on stage a while back when he had an exchange with an inebriated patron (hereinafter referred to as fan). Here's how Tom tells it.

> **Fan:** (Standing two feet in front of me.) "I wanna hear 'Fox on the Run.'"
> **Me:** "Buddy, we'll get that for you in a little while, we're in the wrong key right now."
> **Fan:** "I want 'Fox on the Dang Run' and I want it now!"
> **Me:** "I'll tell you what. I'm not gonna play 'Fox on the Run.' How do you like that?"
> **Fan:** "Well, to heck with you." (He storms out, gets in his truck, squeals wheels out of the parking lot.)
> **Me:** "She walks through the corn…."

Audience delivers a rare standing ovation.

"I've Just Seen the Rock of Ages"

"I've Just Seen the Rock of Ages" surely has the most chilling origin of them all. The composer was a little-known musician from Paris, Kentucky, named John Brenton Preston, who called himself "The Harmonica-Playing Man."

Preston spent many years of his adult life behind bars, and his rap sheet was said to be rather long. While out on parole sometime in the 1970s, Preston became acquainted with Ralph Stanley, and they traveled together to several festivals in Ralph's bus. One time while they were on the road, they stopped for lunch and Preston visited a Western store that was next to the restaurant. The story goes that when he emerged from the store, he was wearing a fancy pair of cowboy boots. Apparently, he had neglected to pay for the boots, so he was in hot water again!

During one period of incarceration, Preston landed in solitary confinement. As he sat on the cold, damp cement floor, the inspiration for a song came to him. It turned out to be "I've Just Seen the Rock of Ages." Afraid that he would forget the words,

Ralph Stanley, ca. 1971 (photograph by Jim Scancarelli).

Preston found a tiny pebble and scratched the words right onto the cement floor. If that image doesn't conjure up the setting for a lonesome song, I don't know what does!

When I first heard the story of this song and began to piece together some facts about the life of John Brenton Preston, I decided that I had to interview him. I spoke with David Freeman, owner of Rebel Records and publisher of the song. Dave guessed that Preston was still in prison, possibly in Kentucky. I immediately called the Kentucky Department of Corrections and got the name of the prison where he was being held. When I rang the main number, the operator transferred me directly to an actual cellblock. The phone call itself was rather chilling. Listening past my conversation with the correction officer, I could hear the sounds of prisoners echoing off the high ceilings and the cold, icy walls. It didn't take much for me to imagine being locked up there myself. Unfortunately, she told me that Preston had been transferred to another facility.

After several more attempts to track down Preston, the trail finally grew cold, and I wearied of the chase. I decided that John Preston did not want to be found. In one of my books, I did include this message to Preston. "John Preston, if you're reading this, please call me. I'd like to talk with you about this song." Of course, I didn't really expect to hear from him, but now I know one reason why—he died at age eighty on September 3, 2013, right around the time I was searching for him.

"I'm a Little Teapot"

I've always loved the song "I'm a Little Teapot." When I wrote my book *Painless Mandolin Melodies*, I naturally included it, thinking it was certainly in the public domain. One day I got a message on my answering machine from a New York lawyer who said he represented the song's composers, George Harold Sanders and Clarence Z. Kelley. He said that I had violated his clients' copyright and to call him back immediately. Before I returned his call, I did a little research and found that his clients did indeed own the copyright, but there were hundreds or people who also claimed the song. When I got the lawyer on the phone, he said he had purchased my book and found his client's

Painless Mandolin Melodies (photograph by the author).

song in there, uncredited. I thanked him profusely for buying my book, because almost no one else had done so. I admitted I had used the song but asked him how I was supposed to know which of the hundreds of claimants was the legitimate owner of the song. He paused and admitted it would be nearly impossible for anyone to figure that out. Then he asked me how many books I had sold and how much money I had earned on the book. I said, "Counting the one on your desk, we've sold about fifty books." When I added that we had barely broken even on that book, all I heard from his end of the line was a loud "click!"

Other Songs with Quirky Stories

"Banks of the Ohio"

"Banks of the Ohio" is one of a number of murder ballads that tells of a young man named Willie who proposes to his girlfriend on the banks of a river. When she refuses, he drowns or otherwise murders her. Such ballads go back to the early nineteenth century, with such titles as "The Lexington Murder," "Knoxville Girl," "Omie Wise," and "Pretty Polly." "Banks of the Ohio" has an odd twist. In one predecessor of the familiar song, while walking in the woods, a hunter happened on the new-made grave of the victim. Growing from the mound of dirt was a beautiful flower, which he picked to give to his wife. No sooner did he pick it, but a new flower suddenly sprang up in its place. When he picked that flower again, yet another flower sprouted up. Word spread and soon many local people went to the grave, where the same thing happened. When the accused murderer was asked to pick the flower, he refused. Finally, at the insistence of his friends, he reluctantly picked the flower, which instantly withered and died. After that, no other flowers appear on the mound.

"Buffalo Gals"

"Buffalo Gals" made a habit of changing its name. The original song dates to 1844 with the title of "Lubly Fan." But when minstrel bands took the song from city to city, they changed the name of the song to the name of whatever town they were playing. Thus, the song was sung under such titles as "Buffalo Gals," "Alabama Gals," "Charleston Gals," "Round Town Gals," "Browntown Girl," "Hagantown Girls," "Johnstown Girl," and "Maxwell Girls." The clincher is that John Hodges, who wrote the original song, changed his own name to "Cool White."

"Cumberland Mountain Deer Chase"

"Cumberland Mountain Deer Chase" is best remembered as recorded by Uncle Dave Macon on June 6, 1929. It was among his most popular songs. While growing up near Nashville, Tennessee, he once heard some workers from Czechoslovakia singing a song with a catchy melody, which he instantly memorized. Years later Uncle Dave added his own lyrics to that melody, calling it "Cumberland Mountain Deer Chase."

"Old Joe Clark"

"Old Joe Clark" is generally considered a Southern song, although verses have been found in Pennsylvania. Its origins are apparently from England, where it was collected in 1842 in *Nursery Rhymes in England*. Folksong performer and collector Bradley Kincaid recorded it in 1930. He was convinced that "Old Joe Clark" was based on a real person who lived in Manchester, Kentucky. He was said to carry a long knife at the back of his neck, so it would be within easy reach. Apparently, the Betsy Brown mentioned in the song was living with Old Joe Clark by force. One day some of Joe's hogs escaped and got into his son's garden on an adjoining farm. The son killed his father with a shotgun, which allowed Betsy to finally escape.

"Roll on Buddy"

"Roll on Buddy" possibly has the most misunderstood phrase in all of bluegrass. The first line is often mistakenly sung as "I'm going to the east pay road." Although the song is nearly always listed as "traditional," it was in fact composed by Charlie Bowman and recorded by Charlie

Tony Alderman (left) and Charlie Bowman, ca. 1928 (John Edwards Memorial Foundation Records [20001], Southern Folklife Collection at Wilson Special Collections Library, University of North Carolina at Chapel Hill).

Bowman and His Brothers on October 16, 1928. Researcher Bill Cox managed to get a copy of Charlie's handwritten lyrics to the song. What Charlie sang was "I'm going to that East Cairo." East Cairo (pronounced KAY-ro) is a town that no longer exists in Ballard County, Kentucky. It was across from Cairo, Illinois, in the southern part of that state, at the junction of the Ohio and Mississippi rivers. What truly is a mystery is what Charlie meant when he wrote, "You wouldn't roll so slow if you knew what I know." What in the heck did he know? Perhaps we'll never find out.

"Poor Ellen Smith"

In 1894 Peter DeGraff was accused of murdering Ellen Smith with a single bullet wound to her chest in Mount Airy, North Carolina. While legend has it that he composed the ballad "Poor Ellen Smith" while waiting in his cell for his execution by electric chair, there is evidence that the song is based on verses written by Charles Pepper in the 1890s. Be careful about singing this song around Winston-Salem, North Carolina. Forsyth County passed a law that made it a misdemeanor to sing "Poor Ellen Smith" in a gathering of any size, because it always fomented a riot. The melody was purloined from the eighteenth-century hymn "How Firm a Foundation." Since copyright laws were nonexistent in those days, DeGraff was apparently not charged with the crime of stealing that melody.

"Red River Valley"

"Red River Valley" has long been considered the quintessential American cowboy song. There have probably been more hot dogs and marshmallows cooked over campfires while it was being sung than any other song known to man or beast. I hate to be the one to break it

Jimmie Rodgers with his custom Weymann guitar, ca. 1928.

to you, but "Red River Valley" has its deepest roots in Canada. It refers to the river that flows into Lake Winnipeg, in the Province of Manitoba. My old friend and researcher Jim Bob Tinsley found that it was sung in the Northwest Territories of Canada as far back as 1869.

"My Rough and Rowdy Ways"

In 1929 Jimmie Rodgers recorded a song that has been covered countless times in country and bluegrass music. But one phrase, "and counted vile," was either too archaic or too obscure for later singers. Here's where it fits in: "I may be rough, I may be wild, I may be tough *and counted vile*, but I can't give up my good old rough and rowdy ways." Gene Autry, Jimmie Skinner, Webb Pierce, and the Hotmud Family sang it as written. Lefty Frizzell used "but that's just my style," and Hank Thompson and Merle Haggard copied him. Doc Watson sang "but it's just my style" and Billy Strings "'cause it's just my style," close variants of the Frizzell version. Hank Snow went in a different direction with "and out of style." The folk process in action!

"Please Pardon Me"

"Please Pardon Me" was composed by Huddie William Ledbetter ("Lead Belly") to try to persuade Texas governor Pat Neff to grant him clemency. On June 7, 1918, he had

Leadbelly playing his Stella Humungo 12-string guitar, ca. 1934.

been sentenced to seven to thirty years of hard labor for murdering his cousin, Will Stafford, over a woman. After seven years at Imperial Farm in Sugar Land, Texas, he was pardoned by the governor on January 15, 1925. It's not certain whether the song had an effect or not.

By 1930 Lead Belly was back in prison for attempted murder, but this time he was sent to Angola Prison Farm in Louisiana. Three years into his sentence, he was "discovered" by folklorists John and Alan Lomax. They returned with portable equipment and made extensive recordings, both in 1933 and 1934. With his good behavior, and the persuasive powers of the Lomaxes, Lead Belly was again pardoned, this time by Governor Oscar K. Allen. Upon his release in 1934 he became a driver for sixty-seven-year-old John Lomax on exhaustive field collection trips throughout the South.

Despite several additional scrapes with the law, Lead Belly became a fixture in the folk music revival in New York City and was friends with such figures as Woody Guthrie, Brownie McGhee, and Sonny Terry, as well as Charles, Peggy, Pete, and Mike Seeger. Lead Belly gave us such songs as "Bring Me a Little Water, Sylvie"; "Midnight Special"; "Goodnight Irene"; "In the Pines"; and "The Rock Island Line."

Appendix I: Miscellaneous

I've labeled this appendix "Miscellaneous" because it contains a wide variety of subjects from Hoss Cartwright's hat to my near-encounter with Bigfoot.

Cowboys in Bluegrass Music?

As a kid I desperately wanted to be a cowboy. I dreamed of owning a horse, riding the range, and doing what cowboys did. And why wouldn't I? Every night I slept under a cowboy blanket, and my lunch box was decorated with a decal of a handsome cowboy twirling his lariat. I grew up at the dawn of television, so all my heroes were cowboys: Hopalong Cassidy, Shane, Roy Rogers, Gene Autry, and John Wayne. I watched *Gunsmoke*, *Have Gun—Will Travel*, *The Rifleman*, and *Bonanza* while eating TV dinners. My favorite actor was Gary Cooper, whose riveting role in the movie *High Noon* knocked my socks off.

Back then, the entire country seemed to be smitten with everything cowboy. But we can't blame Hollywood and the Marlboro man for the popularity of the cowboy as a cultural icon. In 1893 noted historian Frederick Jackson Turner wrote an influential paper titled "The Significance of the Frontier in American History." Turner convincingly argued that the idea of the frontier was crucial

Wayne Erbsen as a young cowboy in California, ca. 1953 (photograph by John Erbsen).

in helping to define the American character. Since then, historians have been hotly debating the merits of Turner's claims of the importance of the West in American history.

We'll leave that argument to the historians. Stick with me as I outline some of the ways that cowboys and the Wild West took hold of our national consciousness.

Theodore Roosevelt. In 1884, New Yorker Roosevelt decided he wanted to live the life of a cowboy, so he bought a cattle ranch in the Badlands of the Dakota Territory and fashioned himself a cowboy. While having a friendly drink at a local saloon, Roosevelt was bullied by a man who thought the newcomer was a city-slicking sissy. In the fistfight that followed, Roosevelt proved his mettle and beat the man into believing that Teddy was as tough as the Rough Rider he would soon become. When Roosevelt eventually became president, politician Mark Hanna is said to have snorted, "Now look! That damned cowboy is president of the United States."

Dime Novels. As early as 1860, publishers Erastus and Irwin Beadle released a series of cheap paperback books called "Beadle's Dime Novels." These and other publications flooded the market with hair-raising stories of brave cowboys and frontiersmen fighting off wild Indians to save beautiful maidens.

Buffalo Bill Cody, a hero of many dime novels, started his own Wild West shows around 1883. These wildly popular Western extravaganzas helped to popularize the idea of the cowboy and the Wild West in America, England, and even in Europe.

Books. Owen Wister became known as the father of Western fiction with his many books, including *The Virginian* (1902). Zane Grey followed suit with a series of immensely popular books, including *Riders of the Purple Sage* (1912). Grey's success helped fuel an entire industry of Western books.

Movies. The first feature movie was a Western, *The Great Train Robbery* (1903). Westerns were popular throughout the silent film era. From 1915 to 1925, William S. Hart dominated Western films. Then came Tom Mix, who appeared in 291 Western films between 1909 and 1935.

Music. In 1925 Carl T. Sprague recorded an authentic cowboy song titled "When the Work's All Done This Fall." It sold a staggering 900,000 copies at a time when most people didn't even own a record player. Jimmie Rodgers, known as "the Father of Country Music," recorded at least seven cowboy songs in his short career and frequently performed in cowboy garb. His hits included "T For Texas (Blue Yodel #1)," and he built a home in Kerrville, Texas.

Gene Autry. Anyone looking for the single biggest reason why country music embraced the image of the cowboy quickly lands on Gene Autry. He singlehandedly changed the look of country music from the hillbilly in overalls to the cowboy in a white hat. As one of the most influential entertainers of all time, he played a vital role in popularizing the singing cowboy craze that took Hollywood and the nation by storm.

In brief, here's how the cowboy obsession caught fire. In 1924 Sears Roebuck, wanting to enhance its market visibility, launched radio station WLS in Chicago. A live country music broadcast, the *National Barn Dance*, soon became a beloved weekly feature. During the Great Depression, the country was in sore need of heroes, so the marketing department at Sears hit on the idea of promoting a clean, right-living cowboy hero to sell their products. Gene Autry, a member of the *Barn Dance* cast since 1930, was the obvious choice.

A likeable performer, Autry had been born in Texas and had started dressing as a cowboy for personal appearances shortly after he joined the *Barn Dance*. Interestingly, he

Appendix I: Miscellaneous

Left: Gene Autry, February 18, 1986 (Center for Popular Music).

bought his first cowboy outfit from Sears Roebuck. But ironically, his first big hit, "Silver Haired Daddy of Mine," was a mountain song, not a cowboy song. Sears soon produced a plethora of cowboy products, including the Gene Autry Roundup Guitar. In 1934, Gene Autry left WLS for Hollywood as star of *In Old Santa Fe*. Thus began the era when the singing cowboy dominated the silver screen.

Bill Monroe. In October 1939, Bill Monroe and His Blue Grass Boys joined the Grand Ole Opry. His first recording for RCA Victor subsidiary Bluebird Records was Jimmie Rodgers's "Mule Skinner Blues" (1940). In a 1980 interview

Above: Bill Monroe with his "The" mandolin, ca. 1979 (photograph by Charles Thomkins).

with the author, Blue Grass Boy Cleo Davis remembered that the Blue Grass Boys were the first performers to play the Opry dressed in white shirts, ties, and Stetson hats. Monroe's choice of attire for his Blue Grass Boys wasn't exactly the full-on "cowboy look," but it was close.

Two Meatballs in the Sand and Other Mondegreens

My love affair with words began almost before I learned to talk. Since moving to North Carolina from California in 1972, I've learned that a minner dipper is a mandolin, a scratch box is a fiddle, and a starvation box is a guitar. I've learned that a cathead is a biscuit, a ballet is a ballad, and that catawampus means crosswise. I've met fleshy (overweight) people and those who could hide behind a straw (skinny). I've seen people who cootered around aimlessly while being bumfusticated, flummoxed and flustrated. I've been told haint (ghost) stories by knot-headed (dumb or stubborn) folks who put stuff in pokes (sacks). I've grown and shaved a soup strainer (mustache) and got hitched (married) but have yet to visit a yarb (herb) doctor or grannywoman (midwife).

The words to bluegrass songs have been a source of particular fascination to me. Back in 1965, while still living in California, I went to a bluegrass show in a small club in Berkeley called the Jabberwock. On stage was Joe Val, a member of the Charles River Valley Boys. I remember that the banjo player, Bob Siggins, joked about the lyrics of the Bill Monroe song "Goodbye Old Pal." Siggins suggested that instead of "to me, boys, it was sad," he always thought it was "two meatballs in the sand."

Recently I got to wondering how other singers have accidentally mangled the words of other bluegrass songs. Come to find out, there's actually a word for mangled lyrics: mondegreens. Who knew?

When I asked some of my bluegrass buddies, students, and friends what mondegreens they have heard or sung, here's what they contributed.

> Are your varmints washed? (Are your garments washed) from "Washed in the Blood."
> With a naked horse (With an achin' heart) from "Doing My Time."
> My feet stink on the mantel (I'm feasting on the manna) from "Beulah Land."
> I fought the green creature (I fought the grim reaper) from "I've Lived a Lot in My Time."
> It is a whale that is hurt upon the shore (It is a wail that is heard upon the shore) from Stephen Foster's "Hard Times Come Again No More."
> The ants are my friends (The answer, my friend) from "Blowin' in the Wind."
> Feta cheese and hair (faded cheeks and hair) from "Wandering Boy."
> May I walk on your lawn every day (May I walk in your light everyday) from "Lord Have Mercy."
> There'll be no detours in heaven, Nora froze along the way (There'll be no detours in heaven, no rough roads along the way) from "I'm Using My Bible for a Roadmap."
> Hold back the Russian menace (Hold back the rushing minutes) from "My Baby's Gone."
> The mandolin player ate Cheese Whiz (The man in the middle is Jesus) from "The Man in the Middle."

They call me by a number of naughty names (They call me by a number, not a name) from "Doin' My Time."
Oh, beautiful and spaceship skies (O beautiful for spacious skies) from "America the Beautiful."
"Lonesome Light Bulb Waltz" ("Lonesome Moonlight Waltz").
Although your love was even colder, I'll wear your underwear tonight (Although your love is even colder, I wonder where you are tonight) from "I Wonder Where You Are Tonight."
"Big Spy Camera" ("Big Spike Hammer").
Bright day will turn to night, my love, the elephants will mourn (Bright day will turn to night, my love, the elements will mourn) from "The Blackest Crow."
Can I get you now or must the hen I take (Can I get you now, or must I hesitate) from "Hesitation Blues."
She'd row t'church a Sunday, she'd pass me on by, I saw her mind was changing bada-ol-bing on her eye (She'd go to church on Sunday, she passed me on by, I saw her mind was changing, by the roving of her eye) from "Handsome Molly."
That's the way I giddy my gnome (That way I'll get him I know) from "Feast Here Tonight."
Don't get a fuzzy raisin ("Don't get above your raising")
Poison tomatoes are taking our loved ones (Wars and tornadoes are taking our loved ones) from "The Family Who Prays."
My time on earth is buttered Spam (My time on earth is but a span) from "A Beautiful Life."
I saw your ass while you were leaving (I saw you last while you were leaving) from "I'll Just Stay Around."
"Nine Pound Hamster" ("Nine Pound Hammer").
"She Thinks I Steal Cars" ("She Thinks I Still Care").
"Bake a Little Longer, Cheese Pizza" ("Wait a Little Longer, Sweet Jesus").
I'm a stillborn man (I'm a freeborn man) from "Freeborn Man."

If you're like me, you might find these mangled verses more interesting than the "real" ones. Big thanks to everyone who contributed to this collection! If you'd like to contribute your favorite mangled lyrics, by all means, send them my way!

The Secret Signals of Bluegrass

It's Saturday night. Instead of relaxing safe at home, plopped comfortably in front of your big-screen TV, you've got your hind quarters parked squarely on a hard folding chair. If that's the case, chances are you're either at a festival watching your favorite bluegrass band, or you're huddled under a tarp in the pouring rain, jamming with friends or total strangers at a fiddlers convention. Either way, you often witness baffling signals and cues from one musician to the rest of the group. This will help you decode secret signals that are commonly used at bluegrass and old-time jams and performances.

The most likely place you'll see such signals or cues is at large jams. Sometimes, the size of the jam will help determine which signal is used.

The bluegrass jam leader. In a bluegrass jam, it's normally the lead singer who becomes the "jam boss." He or she makes it their business to send signals to the rest of the group. If a bluegrass instrumental is being played, whoever kicks off the song usually helps guide it to a smooth ending by sending a clear signal to the other musicians.

The old-time jam leader. Nearly always, it's the fiddler who selects the tune, sets the tempo, decides how long it will last, and when it will end. If there's more than one fiddler, whoever starts the tune will take ownership of that tune and will signal the ending to the other jammers.

The shout. You often hear the bluegrass jam boss speak or shout commands like "one more," "one more time," "last time," "take it home," or "take it to the barn." In Irish sessions, the fiddler is likely to yell "hup!" Many people rely on non-verbal signals because they find it difficult or impossible to speak while they're playing. One young lady was leading a jam, and I could tell she wasn't comfortable speaking and fiddling at the same time. Instead of using one of the more wordy shouts, through clinched teeth she managed to grunt the word "end," and then the tune suddenly stopped!

The nod. This is a common method of communicating that it's someone's turn to take the next break or that the song is about to end. Confusion about the meaning of the nod can sometimes result in a train wreck.

The eye. Making eye contact when the end is in sight is a common signal that's used both in bluegrass and old-time jams.

The eyebrow. Be alert to the "eyebrow shrug," a sure sign that something is about to happen.

The look. If the jam boss gives you "the look," either the song is going to end, your instrument is out of tune, or your zipper is unzipped.

The leg. The most common secret signal is now so common that it's no longer a secret. If you see the jam leader lift one leg, you can count on the song ending very soon. Sometimes called "the dogleg" (for good reason), this method does have its risks, particularly for old-time musicians who sit close to each other in a tight circle. More than once I've witnessed someone suddenly raise their leg and accidentally kick the person across from them. Ouch!

The foot. Instead of raising their leg, some people simply raise their foot. Depending on the session, this signal could easily be overlooked or confused with normal foot tapping. (Earl Scruggs looked askance at foot tapping on stage. He was known to stand on a Foggy Mountain Boy's shoe that was making audible sound.)

The pause or gap. This is my personal favorite. When I'm playing a tune, I will leave a quick pause or gap in the music right before I play the final tag or ending. This never fails to bring the session to a comfortable stop.

The instrument. Occasionally someone will raise the neck of their instrument to communicate that the tune is ending. Watch out for whirling ceiling fans!

The tag. Near the end of a tune, many musicians will play a series of notes that are sometimes called a "tag." These notes can vary, depending on the instrument and the style being played. The tag sometimes resembles the old phrase (well known to *Roger Rabbit* fans) as "shave and a haircut, two bits."

The accent means that you play a strong or loud note or chord just before the end.

The finger. When the end of a tune is fast approaching, sometimes the jam boss will waive their right index finger in a circle, like a flag. The problem with this method is that it's often confused with "the turnaround."

The turnaround. On slower, country-type songs, musicians often play a turnaround. This simply means repeating the last line of the chorus instrumentally. Many times, the leader will signal a turnaround by waving their index finger in the air.

Two fingers are a signal to play the tune twice more.

The middle finger. If you see the leader extend the middle finger of their right hand toward you, it means "that ain't no part of nothin'," as Bill Monroe once said.

The Birch Monroe. Speaking of Bill Monroe, the most sudden stop I've ever witnessed was signaled by Bill's brother Birch at Monroe's Bean Blossom festival in 1971. Best I remember, I was in the thick of a huge jam at the old barn with six or seven of us wailing away at ninety miles an hour on "Little Girl in Tennessee." I was singing lead and there was a crowd of thirty or forty people gathered around our little circle, five deep.

Birch Monroe, ca. 1972.

Out of the corner of my eye I noticed Birch Monroe, the no-nonsense manager of the park. I detected a fierce determination in his eyes as he marched headlong into the crowd while the song was going full blast. Since I was playing guitar and singing lead, Birch stepped directly in front of me and, without saying a word, wrapped both his hands firmly around the fingerboard and neck of my guitar. The song stopped so suddenly that we practically got whiplash! In all my days of jamming, I've never seen anything stop so quickly.

Not known for the subtly of his signals, Birch then ordered us to move our jam to the stage, which was empty at that time. Since we didn't want to tangle with Birch any more than we already had, we obediently followed his orders, and we continued the jam from the stage of the old barn.

The white hat. If you're watching a bluegrass band that's used to playing together, you might not see any signals at all. I was chatting with Bobby Hicks, a long time Blue Grass Boy and fiddler. I asked him how Monroe signaled to the band when a song was supposed to stop. He said Bill never used any kind of signal. He explained that after you played night after night on the road with Bill, you knew exactly where and when a song was going to end. He did point out that, after the song was over, Monroe often raised his white hat in the air while the audience wildly applauded.

Now that you know the secret signals, get out there and jam your guts out.

The Lester Flatt G Run

Bluegrass hero Lester Flatt had a lot to be proud of. The G run that bears his name has been attributed to Lester Flatt for three quarters of a century. You can hear this distinctive guitar run in practically every classic bluegrass song that can be played using a G-shaped chord on the guitar. Lester used several variations, but in the simplest version it is basically two notes played at the end of a verse or chorus. It consists of playing the D string of the guitar at the second fret followed by the G string open. It punctuates the song and serves the same purpose as an exclamation point at the end of a paragraph.

In the mid-seventies I was lucky enough to become friends with the legendary fiddler Jim Shumate, who joined Bill Monroe's Blue Grass Boys in 1945, just weeks after Lester Flatt joined the band. In a 1976 interview Jim explained, "I remember that Lester always had a funny run on the guitar, and we used to kid about that run. I accused him of doing it just to let people know that he was still there. That's about the truth, because we'd be going so fast, he'd just hit one string here and there, and then every chance he'd get, why he'd run something in there."

That "something" was Lester's signature guitar run. The Blue Grass Boys may have kidded Lester about his little run, but Lester's G run is no laughing matter to died-in-the-wool fans of traditional bluegrass.

We can trace the origins of Lester's G run back at least as far as the mid–1930s, when Riley Puckett played a version of it on the August 8, 1935, recording of "Blue Ridge Mountain Blues." On June 15, 1936, Zeke Morris played his version of the guitar run when he and Wade Mainer recorded "If I Could Hear My Mother Pray Again." If you listen closely to the Monroe Brothers' October 12, 1936, recording of "Roll in My Sweet Baby's Arms," you can hear Charlie Monroe playing something that approaches the Lester Flatt G Run.

On November 25, 1939, in his very first appearance on the Grand Ole Opry, Bill Monroe amazed the audience with his performance of Jimmie Rodgers's song "Mule Skinner Blues." For this number, Blue Grass Boy Cleo Davis chorded Monroe's mandolin while Bill

Bill Monroe (left) and Lester Flatt in front of WSM microphone, ca. 1946.

Appendix I: Miscellaneous 167

played guitar, using a run very similar to the Lester Flatt G run. Bill also played it when he recorded the song with the Blue Grass Boys on October 7, 1940, for RCA's Bluebird Records.

Comparing early versions of the G run, they are commonly played at the end of a verse or a chorus and culminate with the open G string of the guitar. Lester apparently streamlined it down to as few as two notes, a D and a G, which he was able to hit when the band was going 90 miles an hour. So, while Lester didn't actually invent that run, no one can argue that he gave it its biggest audience when he played it week after week at live appearances and on most Saturday nights on WSM's Grand Ole Opry. As Brian Sutton once said, "It was Lester Flatt who put it on the map." And for that, we are grateful. Thanks, Lester!

We Almost Played on the Grand Ole Opry

In the mid-seventies, I played fiddle and mandolin with the Black Mountain Bluegrass Boys out of West Virginia. We appeared at some of the big festivals, including one in Ottawa, Ohio. I remember it was hot as blue blazes, so as soon as we got off stage, I changed into old blue jean shorts with fringes hanging down and did not put on a shirt. Harley Carpenter was on guitar and lead vocals and Richard Hefner was our banjo picker and tenor singer. Together, they sang with so much power that they could peel paint off a barn door. Bill Monroe's bus was parked nearby, and he heard us singing from inside his

Black Mountain Bluegrass Boys, ca. 1976. From left: Wayne Erbsen, Richard Hefner, Dwight Diller, and Harley Carpenter (photograph by Lois Workman).

bus and came over to listen. He was wearing a white, three-piece suit and his signature white cowboy hat. He said he loved our singing, but that we should back off and not sing so loud. Someone took a snapshot of the band. I was standing next to Monroe dressed like a hippie.

I asked Bill if he would like to hear a song I wrote, and he said he would be glad to hear it. The song was named "The Old Virginia Moon," but I made a quick decision to change it to the "Old Kentucky Moon." I figured that Bill would like it better because he was from Kentucky. Bill said he really liked the song but said he couldn't use it because he already had "The Kentucky Waltz." Argh! This time I had really shot myself in the foot.

The one big thing that came out of our meeting with Monroe was that he invited us to be his guests on the Grand Ole Opry, which was quite an honor. We settled on a date and Monroe went back to his air-conditioned bus.

To prepare for our first Opry appearance, the band went to a Western shop, and each of us bought a light blue Stetson hat. I also bought a pair of black Western pants with the little arrows for belt loops. The night before driving from Hickory, North Carolina, to Nashville, I carefully laid out my pants so they would be ready for the trip. Before I went to bed, I got a call from Harley, who said that Richard had pneumonia and was in a hospital in Elkins, West Virginia. I told Harley how bad I felt that Richard couldn't go, but I could switch from fiddle to banjo and we could carry on our show. Harley said if Richard couldn't go, none of us were going. I begged and pleaded but Harley kept saying, "No, we ain't a-gonna go." Harley said he had tried calling Bill but was not able to reach him. So basically, we stood up Bill Monroe.

The next time I saw Bill, he had not forgotten and was standoffish and cold to me. And those Western pants that I had laid on the bed? They never got worn.

Curly Ray Cline (left) and Charlie Cline, ca. 1941 (courtesy David Davis).

Charlie Cline, Powerful Snorer

Charlie Cline was a powerful fiddler who played both with the Stanley Brothers and with Bill Monroe. He was perhaps best known as the loudest snorer who ever played with Monroe. It was on a snowy winter's night in 1954 and the Bluegrass Boys were sleeping in one of the little rustic cabins at Bean Blossom, Indiana. One night the band was sound asleep when Charlie started to snore so loudly that he woke all the boys up. One of them came up with the solution. Very quietly, they gently picked up the cot that Charlie was sleeping on and carefully set it outside in the snow. Then they came in, locked the door, and threw a big log on the fire. When Charlie awoke, he found himself covered with snow and freezing to death. He noticed the smoke coming out of the chimney and hatched a plan to pay back his bandmates. He climbed on the top of the cabin and stuffed some old rags down the chimney pipe. In a few minutes, the door flew open, and the band came pouring out, coughing smoke. When Charlie was sure everyone was out, he ran inside, then closed and locked the door—leaving the band to beat on the door with their fists to no avail. And that, my friends, is the gospel truth.

Hoss Cartwright's Hat

Years ago, I was hired to teach at Camp He Ho Ha in Edmonton, Canada, by Ron Mercer, who was quite a character. His daytime job was as a dispatcher with the Royal Canadian Mounted Police. When he picked me up at the airport, his car sported brightly colored orange flames painted on its side. He admitted that his sergeant made him park several blocks away from the police station.

Ron picked the banjo and was craving one with carving and fancy inlays on every fret. I mentioned that I was a banjo dealer and could order him a fancy banjo, which I did several weeks later. Ron liked to dress up in super flashy clothes, and he ordered a fancy country western suit from Nudy, the creator of the ostentatious suits worn by some famous country music stars.

Ron Mercer, ca. 2001 (courtesy Ron Mercer).

To complete his outfit, Ron needed a western hat, but not just any hat. He admired the big hat worn by Hoss Cartwright on *Bonanza* and managed to find the retired hat maker who had originally made Hoss's famous hat. The hatmaker asked Ron what size of a man he was, so he could make a proper hat that would fit his frame. Here's where things got interesting. Ron told the hatmaker that he was a really big man, even bigger than Hoss himself, who was 6'4" and 300 pounds. And that's what he got: a ginormous hat that only a giant could wear.

"Winning" the Folk Song Competition at Galax

Recently, my old friend Dale Morris complimented me for my rendition of that old song "I've Been All Around this World," which he heard it on an album of the winners of the Galax Fiddlers Convention for 1974. I laughed when he told me that but had to tell him, "That wasn't me."

Here's the story. I was a frequent competitor at Galax since 1972. The following year, I won first place in the clawhammer banjo completion. The next year I pre-registered

Plank Road String Band, Charlottesville, Virginia, ca. 1973. From left: Michael J. Kott, Al Thorp, Brad Leftwich, Andy Williams, Steve Gendron (photograph by Patrick Hinely).

to sing in the folk song competition but couldn't attend because my wife had booked our family at a beach house. At Galax, to compete, you must register a month or so in advance. Michael J. Kott, cello player and wild man from the Plank Road String Band, showed up at the convention raring to sing in the folk song contest, only to be turned away because he had not registered. My friend Tina Liza Jones told Kott that I wasn't going to be using my registration and for him to go ahead and sing in my place.

He got up there and sang a dandy version of "I've Been All Around This World." When it came time to announce the winners, they called "Wayne Erbsen" to the stage to accept his first-place blue ribbon and cash prize. Michael hooted and hollered and leaped up on the stage without even using the stairs. He reached to accept his prize, but the official said, "I know Wayne Erbsen, and you're not him." Kott said, "No, I'm not, but I sang the song." They reluctantly handed over the ribbon and prize money and Kott danced triumphantly off the stage. Turns out, Kott's performance under my name was released on the Galax LP for that year and I also got in the Galax record book as winning the folk song contest that year. When my good friend Wayne C. Henderson heard that I had won, he said, "That danged ole Wayne Erbsen. He wins when he's not even there!"

Jamming with David Grisman

In 1970, the name David Grisman barely registered on the bluegrass-meter. However, my friend and pickin' buddy Brian Lappin had heard him pick the mandolin and

Davis Grisman, ca. 1972 (courtesy Center for Popular Culture, Murfreesboro, Tennessee).

was convinced that he was the real deal. Somehow, Bryan knew someone who know someone who arranged for us to jam with him in San Francisco. On that day, we showed up at an upstairs flat in the Mission District with our instruments in hand, and there he was, David Grisman. Our band was called Stony Lonesome and consisted of me on mandolin and lead vocals, Brian Lappin on banjo, Nellie Levin on fiddle and tenor vocals, David Satterfield on vocals and guitar and Willy Lindler on bass.

We all got out our instruments and tuned up. Just as we raised our picks to chomp down on our strings, we heard a loud noise coming from downstairs. We looked down at the street below and saw a wild-haired guy trying to break into one of our cars. David Satterfield put down his guitar and was the first to rush downstairs, with the rest of us right on his tail. David reached the guy, who was obviously stoned on drugs. Instead of hitting him with his fists, David threw his arms around the fellow and proceeded to hug him. (This was the hippie days of peace and love.) The rest of us stood nearby assessing whether to call the cops. The guy assured us, "Everything is cool, man," so we let him be and we went back upstairs.

We got out our instruments and were about to play our first song when we suddenly hear a "BAM" coming from downstairs. We ran downstairs and the same guy was still trying to break into one of our cars. We realized that some hugs and a few kisses had no effect on him, so we decided it was time to pack it up and we all got in our cars and drove off. We never did get to pick a single note with David Grisman.

Bigfoot's Gone Away

Once I got a call at my company, Native Ground Books & Music. The caller (we'll call him John) asked if we were a printer. I explained that we were a publisher, not a printer. While I had him on the line, I offered to help him find what he was looking for. A long-winded fellow, he explained that he had written a book about a family of Bigfoot that was living in his yard in Haywood County, North Carolina. Intrigued, I urged him to tell me more about it.

He said he was a landscaper and that a family of Sasquatch made their home in the trees around his house near Lake Junaluska, North Carolina. He said he talked with them every day. When I pressed him about what kind of conversations they had, he said that they would stand so close, he could hear them breathing, but he admitted he had never actually seen them. He said he communicated with him using telepathy.

When I voiced skepticism, he invited me to come out and personally meet the family of Bigfoot. I told him I would get back to him on that. When I hung up the phone, I immediately told my wife, Barbara, about the most interesting phone call I just had. As a family counselor, she assured me that the caller was Looney Tunes and to forget all about it. I had to agree with her, but I also really wanted to meet his so-called "family." She firmly told me that I was *not* going out there alone, and she certainly wasn't going. With that, I called my three best friends, John, Dudley, and Ralph. John said he was a believer and to count him in. Dudley wasn't buying it and wouldn't be going. Ralph said he was a skeptic like me but would go along for the ride. With two of my friends going with me, Barbara couldn't say no, but she was plenty nervous about the whole thing.

I called him back and we set a date. His directions included turning right at a place where he said that UFOs frequently landed. He said to arrive about dusk, so as not to scare the family of Bigfoot. We arrived just as the sun was going down and were met by

Bigfoot, ca. 2020 (courtesy Jessica Jwill).

a normal-looking fellow in his early forties. His small house was on a bold creek, and he invited us in. Before we were to meet Bigfoot, he said that he had a microphone set up outside and said we should come into his house and listen to the tapes he had made. We started listening but mainly all we could hear was the bold creek. Every minute or two, he'd stop the tape and back it up. "Now, listen," he said. "Hear that click? That's him!" He continued playing the tape and we'd hear some other kind of little noises, and he'd say, "Right there. That's him!" Then he asked us, "Don't you hear it?" I said I didn't really hear anything, and Ralph agreed that he couldn't hear anything either. John, the semi-believer, said he thought he heard something. This went on for about an hour when he asked if we wanted to see visual proof. We all agreed, so he began showing us photos he had taken of the woods behind his house where he claimed they lived. "See those trees that are down? That's their boundary. They don't want anyone going in their territory." Still skeptical, he asked if we wanted to go behind his house and "meet" the teen-aged Bigfoot. We all nodded vigorously.

We went around to the back of his small frame house and sat in three chairs. Then he started talking to the most approachable of the Bigfoot family, a teenager. He told the bigfoot not to be afraid, that these men were his friends and would not hurt him. A non-stop talker, John was trying to soothe the beast, to convince him to make his presence known. Then John said, "Smell that? That musky smell is him!" As a matter of fact, we did smell something, and John said that the smell was sure proof that Bigfoot was close to us. Ralph then shone his flashlight over to the left and we all saw a coon. Ralph laughed and said that as a kid back in Texas, he had a pet coon and certainly knew that smell.

At that point, we had more than enough of our Bigfoot adventure and said it was time to go. The fellow knew he hadn't convinced us and reluctantly bid us goodbye. Our ride back to Asheville was quite interesting. Ralph and I felt like the whole thing was a hoax, but John insisted that it still might be possible that Bigfoot exists. The next day, I told our friend Dudley about our Bigfoot adventures, and he laughed so hard that he about fell on the floor. So much for Bigfoot.

Arthur "Guitar Boogie" Smith

I moved to Charlotte, North Carolina, in 1972 to teacher bluegrass music and American history at Central Piedmont Community College. A famous musician named Arthur "Guitar Boogie" Smith was a local living legend who wrote "Dueling Banjos." In the 1950s he had such a hit with his original composition called "Guitar Boogie" that he had his name legally changed to "Arthur 'Guitar Boogie' Smith."

Soon after I landed in Charlotte, I called his studio to see if Smith needed me as a

Arthur "Guitar Boogie" Smith in Charlotte, North Carolina, ca. 1969.

studio musician. He told me to come over the following Monday. I showed up with my banjo and he instructed me to sit in front of a mic and to read the charts on the music stand. The session went well, and when I started to put my banjo in its case, he asked me to play him something. I remembered that Don Reno used to perform with him. I gulped twice and dashed off a fast version of "Banjo in the Holler." He seemed satisfied with my playing and said he'd be in touch.

About a week later, I got a call from Smith, telling me to be at his studio in an hour. I tried to explain that I was teaching a class at the college then but could be available later that afternoon. He abruptly hung up on me and I never heard from him again. I guess I wasn't "Johnny on the Spot" enough for him.

Jim Bob Tinsley—Cowboy Singer and Mountain Lion Hunter

One of the most interesting people I ever met was Jim Bob Tinsley. He had been a cowboy, a teacher, and an author and he had once played guitar and sang in Gene Autry's band. An expert researcher, he once told me, "I could have found the Rosetta Stone, but I didn't know they were looking for it." Jim Bob was also a skilled tracker. In the 1940s, word got out that a Colorado mountain lion was killing scores of sheep, tearing up fences, and posing a risk to farmers. Jim Bob was called in to assist the tracking party. They headed out on horseback, with the hounds leading the way. On the ground was a foot of snow. About halfway up the mountain, the dogs picked up the scent and treed the mountain lion. With the hounds baying from below, the lion climbed out on a dead limb, which suddenly broke, hurling the lion down on the dogs below. Just as the fur was starting to fly and several hounds were already hurt, Jim Bob jumped off his horse and grabbed the mountain lion by the tail with his left hand. With his right, he pulled his Western-style six-shooter from his holster and killed the lion with a single shot to the head. After telling his harrowing true tail, I quipped, "And then you all went out for lunch." We had a big laugh on that one.

Jim Bob Tinsley in Brevard, North Carolina, ca. 2003 (courtesy Dottie Tinsley).

The Ghost of Scotty Stoneman

Such fiddling I had never heard when I first laid my ears on the music of Scotty Stoneman. The entire Stoneman family had relocated to the Los Angeles area in the early sixties and I got to see them perform frequently at the Ash Grove in West Hollywood. When the Kentucky Colonials hired Scotty to fiddle with them, I was able to soak in his fiddling nearly every week, as they hosted an open mic on Mondays.

While I've never been good at copying another fiddler, I was able to capture Scotty's feel or his fire. He had enough of that to burn the place down.

Years later, I joined a pick-up band to compete at the Grayson County Fiddlers' Convention in Elk Creek, in southwest Virginia. On the song we played, I just improvised a break. Just as we got off the stage, I saw Roni Stoneman from *Hee Haw* come running up all out of breath asking who was doing the fiddling. When I explained that it was I, she looked like she had just seen the ghost of her brother Scotty. She said she heard us from way across the field and said she heard Scotty's fiddling in my playing. Pretty spooky.

My Radio Career

Soon after I started teaching old-time and bluegrass at Warren Wilson College in 1982, I got the idea of starting a radio show at the local university, the University of North Carolina Asheville. It was strictly a campus station, and with five watts, it only reached about six blocks beyond the campus when the wind was blowing the right way. I remember being there alone on a Sunday night when I started to smell something like burning rubber. Smoke was coming up through the cracks in the mixing board and the room was filling with smoke. The mixing board was on fire! I rushed out of the control room coughing smoke and called the station manager, who alerted the fire department.

At that time my wife and I had three small kids, Annie and twins Wes and

Wayne Erbsen at WPAQ in Mount Airy, North Carolina, 2023 (photograph by Kelly Epperson).

Rita. When Annie got old enough, she would go to the radio station with me. We had a lot of fun together with her telling little stories about her pet worm. When she got a little older, she became "the weather girl," giving the latest weather forecast. When Wes and Rita got big enough, I brought all three kids to the station to give my wife a break. There was a long hallway at the station and the three of them would run up and down it, yelling and screaming as they ran. Luckily, the control room had a soundproof door.

One night Wes rushed into the control room all out of breath, being chased by the girls. He held the door shut with all his might while his sisters loudly beat on the door with their fists. At the time, I was back announcing the last song, so I had a live mic. My listeners must have thought a riot had broken out at the station.

When working as a performing musician was not enough to support a family of five, I decided to become a real estate agent. To advertise my listings, I had the bright idea of having a radio show on the local country station, WWNC. I called it *The Radio Realtor*. To promote a listing of a house I had for sale on Kenilworth Lake, the station engineer helped me record a radio spot, which I'd play on my show. He overdubbed some sounds of water splashing and I pretended I was playing my ukulele while paddling around the lake in my canoe. He overdubbed the sounds of ducks quacking, and the spot was popular enough that I soon sold that house.

Some years later I bought a log cabin not far from Mount Airy, North Carolina, home to legendary radio station WPAQ. I called and spoke with the station owner, Kelly Epperson. He said to come talk to him the following Saturday afternoon. I was super excited about the interview because I knew that WPAQ had been the station where many of the great bluegrass and old-time musicians had played. In fact, Mac Wiseman had been a DJ there in the fifties. Kelly was a wonderful man and was pleased that I had some previous radio experience. After chatting for a few minutes, he said that I would be on the air in ten minutes. "You mean I'm going to be doing a show right now?" "Yes," he replied. "In radio, you either have it or you don't, and you have it."

The only hard thing doing that first show was the fact that the board was so old that all the markings on the CD players had worn off from years of use. Kelly did attach some sticky notes to some of the buttons, so I'd know which buttons to push. I was gratified when many of my listeners would call up to tell me what a fine job I was doing. I knew one thing for certain: no matter which button I pushed, the board was probably not going to catch fire like it did during my previous radio show.

Gods and Generals

Soon after Ken Burns' famed documentary on the Civil War came out, I recorded five albums of music from that era. One day I got a call from the music director of the upcoming movie *Gods & Generals*. He was looking for authentic-sounding Civil War music and he stumbled on my recording of "Southern Soldier Boy" and wanted to use it in the film. He seemed like a rather slippery character, so I got in touch with the best New York copyright attorney I could find. He soon wrote up a contract that protected my rights and Ted Turner's attorney signed it.

Not only did they want to use my recording, but he asked if I could bring several musicians to play with me in the actual film. I rounded up my friends Larry Brown, Pete Vigour, and Jim Childres and we headed up to rural Maryland where it was being filmed. That morning we all got up, took showers, combed our hair, shaved, and reported to the outside wardrobe area. They gave us some filthy Confederate uniforms to put on. The hairdresser then approached me and said to get down on my knees. She took a can of what looked like axle grease and rubbed it in my hair, making me look like I hadn't washed or combed my hair since 1862. Then she took a bag of chimney soot and dusted my face with it. Finally, they stuck a bowler hat on my head and pronounced me fit for duty.

Once they had us in front of the cameras, the director's assistant came up close and looked me over from head to toe. I asked her, "How do I look?" She said, "You look good." Then as the cameras rolled, and the four of us played along with the original recording that was playing on speakers behind us. Once back in our hotel, the sleezy music director tried to pull a fast one. Since we had just recorded the tune, he said he wanted to use this recording, rather than my original version, that was bound by the contract. He tried tempting my friends with the promise that if they agreed, they would receive "fair" compensation. My friends had my back and saw through his ploy and refused to go along with the director's plan of cutting me out of the large sum I had been promised.

Months passed, and I never received a check. The director would not return my calls. With much effort, I finally got in touch with one of Ted Turner's team of lawyers, who gave me a "take it or leave it" deal which was considerably less than the large amount I had been promised. I took it.

Appendix II: Quickies

This appendix is titled "Quickies" because it's a patchwork of short facts, jokes, short stories, and whimsy.

Jethro Burns

"Why do cows wear bells? Because their horns won't blow!"

On Their Tippy Toes

Jethro Burns and Chet Adkins married twin sisters and frequently hung out together. One time they went to a ballet and noticed the young women were dancing on their tippy toes. Jethro said to Chet, "Why don't they just get taller people?"

Give Me a Break!

I'm addicted to brake fluid, but I can stop at any time.

Ralph and Stanley Carter

The Stanley Brothers were once announced as "Ralph and Stanley, the Carter Brothers."

Homer Haynes (left) and Jethro Burns, ca. 1948 (courtesy Terry Burns King).

Septic Music

I once got a call over at Native Ground Books & Music. The fellow on the phone asked if we have any "Septic music." I think he meant "Celtic music."

Making Stuff Up

After I had taken a few banjo lessons from a guy named Claude Reeves, I asked him, "Can I just make stuff up?" He said, "Yes," so I never took another lesson.

Hank Williams Said

"You got to have smelt a lot of mule manure before you can sing like a hillbilly."

Playing Pool

When I would play pool in the seedier parts of San Francisco in the sixties, I took the name "Stizie Slick," or "Stitz" for short.

Dimwits

In the 1950s Joe Maphis wrote the song "Dim Lights, Thick Smoke (and Loud, Loud Music)." I like to refer to it as "Dimwits Smoke Dope and Play Loud Music."

"Wee Wee"

When my granddaughter, Dora, came along, I hadn't yet picked out a nickname, so she started calling me "Wee." When it became "Wee Wee," I quickly decided on a name: "Poppy."

Fresh Picks

One time I played a show at an elementary school in North Carolina. One young boy saw me putting my picks away in a little tin box and asked, "Is that to keep your picks fresh?"

Ernest Tubb

"Smile when you call me a hillbilly."

Marshmallows

My first time on stage, I told this joke: "Last night I dreamed I ate a five-pound marshmallow, and when I woke up, my pillow was gone."

The Smoggy Mountain Boys

My first bluegrass band was naturally called "The Smoggy Mountain Boys," being from Los Angeles and all.

As Long as Yarn

I once had a Tommy Jarrell songbook that some folks put together by copying down the lyrics by listening to his records. They obviously were not from the South and did not always translate the words correctly. On "I Wish I Was a Mole in the Ground," when

Tommy sang, "I'll raise sweet taters as long as your arm," they translated it as "Raise sweet potatoes as long as yarn."

Bagels Ain't Sweet

While on tour in New York City in the sixties, Bill Monroe's banjo player, Steve Arkin, introduced Bill to his first bagel. After cautiously taking a little bite, Bill made a frown and said, "This donut ain't a bit sweet."

Bill Monroe on the Railroad Tracks

Former Bluegrass Boy Frank Buchanan once told me a story of the time they were driving in Monroe's car to a show when the front tires got stuck on a railroad track. The guy in the car behind impatiently started honking his horn and kept on honking. Monroe finally got out to have a word with him. Instead of yelling at him, Bill took the soft approach and said, "Why don't you get in my car and drive a while, and I'll get in your car and honk."

The Stanley Brothers in Florida

I overheard George Shuffler, a former member of the Clinch Mountain Boys, tell this amusing tale. When the Stanley Brothers were living in Live Oak, Florida, they would ride around in their black car in the hot Florida summer's sun with their windows rolled up, so people would think they had air conditioning.

The Smoggy Mountain Boys, Los Angeles, California, ca. 1964. From left: Larry White, Jamie Hooper, and Wayne Erbsen (photograph by John B. Erbsen).

The Stanley Brothers' Bass Fiddle

In the 1960s, when the Stanley Brothers had a full band, they would all cram into one car. The bass had to be tied to the top, so if it rained or snowed, they'd have to pour out the water before their show. Luckily, they used an aluminum bass.

You Ain't Comin' Back

A moonshiner had a still way up on the mountain. One day some revenuers came knocking at his door and his boy came out to talk with them. "Where's your pa?" "He's up making whiskey." "Can you show us where he's at?" "I sure can, but it'll cost you ten dollars." "OK, I'll pay you when we get back." "Sir, you ain't comin' back."

Bluegrass Motels

The owner of a North Carolina motel once told me that Bill Monroe and the Blue Grass Boys as well as Lester Flatt, Earl Scruggs, and the Foggy Mountain Boys stayed there when they were performing in the area. When Monroe's band slept there, Bill had his own room, but his four-piece band all had to share one room with two beds. However, when Flatt and Scruggs were guests there, each member of the band had his own room.

Leave Now!

Not long after learning the fiddle, I joined other friends who were also beginners and formed an old-time band. We certainly sounded scratchy, but we had enthusiasm. One time we landed a good-paying gig in a lodge up in the mountains in eastern California. Halfway through our first tune, the owner rushed up to me and stuffed some bills in my pocket and said to pack up and leave. Surprised, I said, "Well, let us at least finish this tune." "No! *Leave now*!!!"

Laying Out Pants

When I first moved to Asheville in the mid-seventies, I didn't know many musicians. I finally jammed with a good bluegrass guitar player, so I suggested we get together on Saturday to pick some. He replied, "Oh I can't possibly do that. I have to lay out my pants for church on Sunday." I took the hint.

Willie Nelson Look-Alike

One of my friends was a huge Willie Nelson fan. When she retired, she threw a big Willie-themed party and even rented a large hall with a stage so her many friends could help her celebrate. As a favor to her, I agreed to impersonate her idol. From Willie's website, she ordered me a bandana with braids. I certainly looked the part as I performed several of Willie's greatest hits. An old lady was sitting next to my friend and whispered to her, "I've always wanted to see Willie Nelson, and now I have!"

Senator Wayne Erbsen

I published my first four books with Carl Fischer, Inc., a firm whose origins date back to the Civil War. One time I called them to order some books to resell. The salesman asked, "Where should I sent it?" I replied, "Send it ta Wayne Erbsen." When I received the package, the shipping label said, "Senator Wayne Erbsen." I kid you not.

Nothing to Eat

In the early seventies, I met a talented bluegrass guitarist from Switzerland. During a picking session he asked if I knew a tune called "Nothing to Eat." I told him I didn't know a tune by that title, but he insisted that we play it. Finally, I realized he was talking about a tune that Doc Watson had recorded with Flatt and Scruggs. The title of that tune was actually "Nothing to It," but "it" became "eet" with his pronunciation.

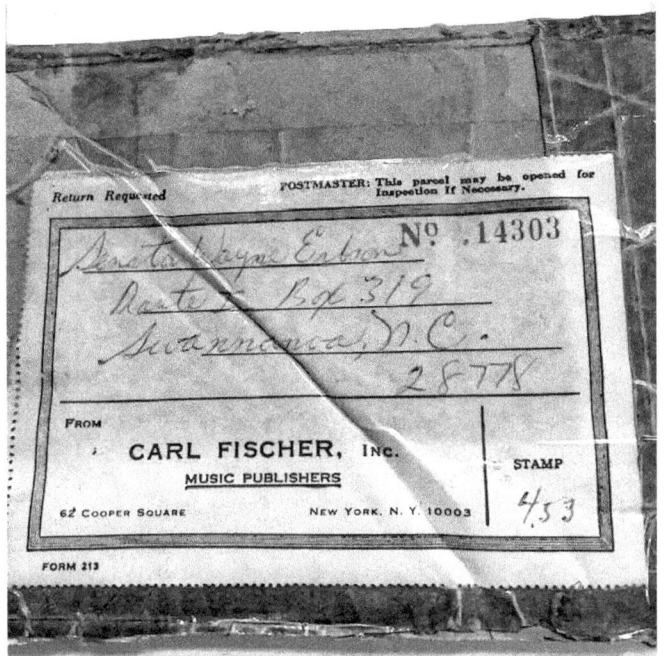

Senator Wayne Erbsen mailing label (photograph by the author).

Bill Monroe and Frank Sinatra

In 1982 Bill Monroe was invited to the White House to receive a National Heritage Fellowship Award to be presented by President Reagan. In the waiting room, Bill met another luncheon guest, Frank Sinatra. The two shook hands and Sinatra told Monroe how much he'd admired Bill's music when he listened to his performances on the Grand Ole Opry in the forties. Bill said, "Now, what did you say your name was?" "I'm Frank Sinatra." "And what do you do?" "I'm a singer." "I believe I've heard of you," Bill said. "Well, I hope so," said Sinatra, with considerable grace.

Runnin' Out of Memory

Trying to cash in on the new popularity of computers, Tim O'Brien once wrote a song called "Runnin' Out of Memory." Even as a boy, my son Wes was a master of the innerworkings of computers, so I played him that song. When it was done, he dryly said, "That man knows nothing about computers." Recently, I told this story to Tim, who laughed and said, "Your son was right. I still don't know much about them."

Jimmy Martin

I've always been a fan of Jimmy Martin. At one festival in the seventies, I approached Jimmy and asked him if he would like to hear several songs I had written.

Tim O'Brien, ca. 2019 (photograph by Scott Simontacchi).

He said to put them on a tape for him. So, that's what I did. At the next bluegrass festival, I handed the tape to Jimmy, and he thanked me. When I saw him the next time, I asked him what he thought of my songs. He coldly replied, "People give me tapes all the time. I throw 'em in a box and never listen to any of them."

Chicken Necks

In the mid-seventies, I shared a house with one of my bandmates, Uncle Ted White. He couldn't cook, and neither could I, but we still took turns "cooking." His mother bought him a crockpot but gave no instructions on how to use it. When it was his turn to cook, he went to the market and purchased a pound of chicken necks. He removed the scrawny necks from the package and dumped them into the crockpot along with some water and turned the thing on. When it was supper time, he proudly opened the lid to the crockpot to reveal what he figured would be a sumptuous meal. Once the steam had cleared, we hopefully peered into the crockpot, only to see some limp, withered, chicken necks. That night, we went out to eat.

Discovering Clarence Ashley

One of the more prolific old-time clawhammer banjo players in the 1920s was a man named Clarence Ashley. After his last recording, Ashley disappeared with no trace. In 1960 folklorist Ralph Rinzler attended the fiddlers convention in Union Grove, North Carolina, looking for old-time musicians who had dropped off the map. He approached an old man who was quite adept at the banjo and asked, "Have you ever heard of a Clarence Ashley?" The man paused to think and finally said, "I don't believe I'm acquainted with that individual." Rinzler thanked him and started to walk away. Seconds later, Ashley blurted out, "That's me!" Apparently, he'd been known as "Tom Ashley" for so long that he forgot that the name used on his records was "Clarence Ashley."

Showmanship of Mac Wiseman and Lester Flatt

I was standing at the side of the stage at Bill Monroe's Bean Blossom bluegrass festival in 1971. This was the year that Monroe and Lester Flatt ended their decades-long feud of not talking to each other. For their grand reunion on stage, the musicians were all smiles. As the fiddles kicked off "Little Cabin Home on the Hill," Mac Wiseman leaned over to Lester and I could hear him whisper in Lester's ear, "I don't believe I remember the words to this song." Lester whispered back, "Tonight I'm alone, without you my dear." Still smiling broadly, Mac calmly leaned into the mic and confidentially sang that song.

"Lee Highway Blues"

Years ago, I was jamming at a fiddlers convention near Spruce Pine, North Carolina. I had just played a hot version of "Lee Highway Blues" when someone walked up and requested that I play "Lee Highway Blues." I demurred, saying that I had just played it. Without saying a word, he pulled out a five-dollar bill and stuffed it in my pocket. I played it again.

Ted White, Asheville, North Carolina, ca. 2023 (photograph by JC Lance).

The Carolina Tar Heels, North Carolina, ca. 1959. From left: Clarence "Tom" Ashley, Doc Walsh, and Drake Walsh.

Joe Maphis' Flatpick

One of the greatest flatpickers was Joe Maphis. These days, people make a big fuss over what kind of fancy flatpick to use. Some people pay exorbitant sums for a pick that soon gets swallowed up in the washing machine like lost socks. In 1963, I was at a guitar workshop at the UCLA Folk Festival that featured Doc Watson, Clarence White, and Joe Maphis. Someone asked Joe what kind of flatpick he used. He held his pick close to his eyes and looked at it like he had never examined one before. He said,

Joe Maphis, "the King of the Strings," Los Angeles, California, ca. 1966.

"Gee, I don't know. I just play with whatever pick my wife Rosa Lee hands me before we go on stage."

Charlie Poole

Charlie Poole, the legendary band leader and banjo player from Spray, North Carolina, had a problem with alcohol; he couldn't get enough. At one recording session in the 1920s, Charlie complained that he had a little tickle in his throat and said that he needed some whiskey and lemons. They quickly returned with a bottle and five lemons. Charlie impatiently replied, "No, no! You got it all wrong! I want five bottles of whiskey and one lemon."

Brad Keith

In 1971, I was backstage at Bill Monroe's bluegrass festival in Bean Blossom, Indiana. Brad Keith had just got off the stage, playing banjo with Monroe. Waiting for him as he walked down the stairs was a country fellow from Asheville, North Carolina, whom I had met the day before. He approached Brad and shyly said he was disappointed that Brad hadn't played "Sailor's Hornpipe" during his set with Monroe. In a situation like this, most musicians would have brushed off the fan and said that the song is available on his album titled *Living on the Mountain*. Instead, Keith graciously stood there and played the requested song to an audience of one, the man from Asheville. I guess it was really an audience of two, because I was secretly eavesdropping from a few feet away. My opinion about Brad Keith soared after that.

Professor Wayne Erbsen

I first moved to Charlotte, North Carolina, in

Bill Keith at Folkfestival auf dem Burg Lenzburg, Switzerland, June 21, 1975 (photograph by Lilly Pavlak).

1972 to teach at Central Piedmont Community College. The day before school was going to start, I went to a craft fair that was being held on the banks of a large pond. Since I had my fiddle along, I decided to play a few tunes on the far end of the pond, quite a way off from all the activity. I didn't put out a hat or my fiddle case and wasn't asking for money.

Pretty soon a mean security officer marched over and demanded that I stop playing and follow him to the security office. He then harshly interrogated me like I was a common criminal. Eventually, he let me go with a stern warning never to do that again.

The next day was the first meeting of my American history class. To my surprise, who should walk in but the security officer? You should have seen the look on his face when he realized that I was going to be his professor!

Dog Bit

Once a dog showed up at our door, so we adopted him. We named him Kindle. As a Christmas present, my son, Wes, submitted Kindle's DNA to an online ancestor service. When we got the results back, I was shocked to learn that Kindle is my third cousin, once removed.

One day Kindle was hanging around our garden by the street. Walking up the road was a well-dressed gentleman wearing a three-piece suit and a tie. Kindle had never seen anyone wearing a tie before, so he ran up and bit the man on the leg. My wife, who was working on the garden at the time, apologized profusely and brought him up to the house to wash out his wound. He explained that he was a stockbroker and was walking from one client's house to another. She suggested that he see a doctor. When the doctor asked the name of the pet's owner, as required by law, he said it was Wayne Erbsen. The doc smiled and

Kindle the Dog, Asheville, North Carolina, ca. 2006 (photograph by Wes Erbsen).

said, "Do you realize you've been bitten by a famous musician's dog?" The stockbroker must have started to feel it was somehow his fault, so he soon paid us a visit, bringing a bag of dog treats for Kindle, who was feeling rather smug about the whole thing.

Lost Cassette Covers

After LPs there were 8-tracks and then cassettes. I jumped on producing cassettes, and we used to sell thousands of them. We had a good relationship with a cassette manufacturing plant in Ohio, which stored the extra covers we had printed.

One day we called them to reorder, only to find that their phone had been disconnected. We emailed and snail mailed them with no response. Desperate to get our covers back, I randomly called a private detective in that area. To interview him, I started asking a lot of questions such as what his success rate was, how long it would take for him to track down someone from the plant and get my cassette covers, and the like. He bristled at my questions and suddenly burst out with a tirade of how I was wasting his time, and he said that if I didn't decide in two seconds, he was going to gouge my eyes out with a stick or some such.

I figured that anyone who was that mean and threatening to a client must be a scary dude to deal with, so I hired him and wired him $300 as a retainer.

Within a week, he found our cassette covers and even arranged to have them shipped to another facility. There's a lesson in there somewhere, but I'm not exactly sure what it is!

How I Bought My Martin Guitar

I graduated from the University of California, Berkeley in 1967. One day I happened to be in a music shop in Berkeley and I couldn't help but notice a fine new Martin D28 hanging on the wall. After trying it out, I impulsively decided to buy it right then. I asked the owner of the guitar why he was selling such a fine instrument. (Remember, this was at the height of the hippie days of drugs, free speech, and free love.) He said he wanted to save the world. His plan was to take the money and move to one of the remote Hawaiian Islands. There he would spend years perfecting the best weed that had ever been smoked. Such a high grade of marijuana would certainly change the world by spreading peace, love, and harmony.

Several weeks later, I was surprised to see him slowly walking down the street in Berkeley, looking dejected and depressed. He recognized me and I asked him why he wasn't in Hawaii. He reluctantly said, "Oh, I spent all that money on drugs and never left Berkeley."

Ry Cooder and Donna Stoneman

I was sitting in the back row of the Ash Grove in West Hollywood in the mid-sixties watching the Stoneman Family perform. Sitting next to me was Ry Cooder, who must have been sixteen at the time. I had known Ry for some time, and we even went surfing together. After Donna Stoneman had taken a flashy mandolin break, Ry elbowed me and pointed out the difference between Donna's style of playing and that of Roland White, who later played with Bill Monroe and Lester Flatt. He said, "Roland plays what he has in his head," meaning he finds the notes on the mandolin that match what he is thinking. Donna, on the other hand, "thinks" with her fingers, meaning she plays the notes within easy reach of the chord she is holding down. I agreed with him but reminded Ry that Roland wasn't dancing in white go-go boots while playing the mandolin.

No Such Thing as Time

For thirty-eight years I taught Appalachian music at Warren Wilson College in Swannanoa, North Carolina. Warren Wilson had the reputation of being the biggest hippie school in America. One semester, I had the quintessential hippie in my fiddle class. He had the bare feet, the tie-dyed shirt, the holes in his pants, the beard, and the hair. Always late, he would merrily waltz into class ten or fifteen minutes after it had started, disrupt-

Donna Stoneman, ca. 1959 (John Edwards Memorial Foundation Records [20001], Southern Folklife Collection at Wilson Special Collections Library, University of North Carolina at Chapel Hill).

ing the class and interrupting my flow. More than once I scolded him for his tardiness. Nothing worked. Finally, I asked him why he was always late. "Don't you carry a watch?" He got this far away look in his eyes and said, "Time. Time doesn't exist. It's just a concept made up by evil bureaucrats. I don't believe in time. I flow with the winds, the seasons, the earth." I said, "That's fine, but at five minutes after the start of class I'm locking the door." The next day he didn't show up, so I locked the door at the appointed time. After a few minutes I looked through the window in the door and there he was, sitting on the floor in the hall. He really wanted to learn the fiddle, so after our little talk, he was always right on time.

Outrageous Old-Time Band Names

Many of the old-time bands from the 1920s and 1930s came up with some hilarious names for their bands. Some of these included the Skillet Lickers, the Fruit Jar Drinkers, and Seven Foot Dilly and His Pickles. Following in their footsteps, bands registering for the contest at the Old Fiddler's Convention in Galax have taken pride in registering the most outrageous names imaginable. Some registered funny band names without any attention of attending the festival. A few of these include the Hickory Stemp Marsh Marmots, Too Wet to Plow, Three Stripped Gears, Amish Power Company, Hoover Uprights,

Chester Drawers and the Lowboys, Frog Stranglers, Slopjar Serenaders, Too Hot to Cook, the Slugs, Another Boring Day in Paradice, Pizza Mormons, the Wabash Cannibals, Hen Cackle Sweet Serenaders, Digital Worms, Swami Tommy and the Round Peak Zen Boys, Foggy Bottom Howdy-Doers, Grayson County Jumper Cables, the Hypnotones, the Yard Apes, the Greasy Run Toad Trompers, the New Lost Memory Mumblers, the Newly Evicted Expo City Rounders, the Bush League Sand Pounders, the Dutch Cove 'Baccer Hoes, and Colonial Sanders and the Southern Fried Chickens.

Don't Touch My Suit!

Doyle Lawson has always been a snappy dresser. His fancy suits were often embroidered with sequins, rhinestones, and other flashy stuff. During one of his shows, he made a big deal of the band members not touching his suit. He went on and on about that until he nearly wore that joke out. After his show, I approached him backstage, asking if I could give him a demo of songs I had written. He said he would be glad to give it a listen. As I handed him the envelope, I casually touched the arm of his suit. "You did what?" "I touched his suit!"

Doyle Lawson (left) and Wayne Erbsen, Mount Airy Fiddlers Convention, ca. 2014 (photograph by Dudley Wilson).

Water Bottle

At that same Doyle Lawson show, I had forgotten to bring a chair but noticed some empty armchairs near the front, so I sat down. A few songs into the show, someone bumped me on the back to say those were his chairs. I apologized and went to get my own chair. While back at my camp, I grabbed a bottle of water from my cooler and stuck it in my back pocket. I took my chair and sat down right in front of the guy whose chair I had been sitting in. I guess I sat down too hard, because the water bottle that I had in my back pocket burst and squirted cold water all over the poor guy sitting behind me. I took off running because I didn't know how much more abuse he could stand.

Strange Names

During my teaching career, I've often had trouble remembering the names of new students. When teaching at Warren Wilson College it was particularly difficult because it was a hippie school, and many of their names were made up. For example, I was calling roll one time and I called out one student's name, "Grace." She explained that she was conceived at a Rainbow Gathering event and wanted to be called, "oola-eela-meela-weela." I tried writing it down in the margin of my roll but gave up in frustration. "I'll just call you 'Grace.'"

Is Hair Here?

In that same class, I needed some way of remembering students' names, so in the roll I would write down their nicknames and any distinguishing quality, as silly as they might me. For example, if a student had a nose ring, I would write down "nose" next to their name. In this class there was a boy with sticky-up hair swaddled with a rag, so I privately gave him the name "Hair." The following week I was calling roll. When I came to his name, I accidentally called out "Hair." No response. It wasn't until I yelled out "Is Hair here?" that I realized my mistake.

Thornton Spencer

In the early 1970s I was hanging out with my friend John Scofield at Thornton Spencer's small grocery store on Whitetop Mountain in southwest Virginia. Thornton was a master old-time fiddler but not much of a shopkeeper. He pretty much never stopped fiddling. When someone came in to buy a jug of milk or a loaf of bread, he would just yell over his shoulder, "Just put the money in the cash register and make your own change."

White Bread and Cold Beans

On one visit to Thornton's store, John Scofield and I were playing music with Thornton for most of the day and into the night. John and I were starving to death. Thornton must have heard our stomachs growling and said, "Are you boys hungry?" We nodded furiously, so Thornton took a loaf of white bread off the shelf along with a can of pork and beans. He proceeded to show us the art of eating bread and cold beans. First, you take a piece of bread in your left and kind of fold it in half. Then you pour in the beans. Well, I was raised in California, and only ate wheat bread. But I'll tell you what. The folded-bread cold-bean sandwich was the best thing I ever ate!

Thornton Spencer, Grayson County, Virginia, ca. 1972 (photograph by Mark Sanderford).

Zeke Morris, the Body Shop Man

Not only was Zeke Morris a legendary figure in old-time country music, but he also ran an auto body shop in Black Mountain, North Carolina. I brought my 1964 Volvo over to his shop one time because the driver's door wasn't closing right. Zeke took one quick look and left to get a tool. Now, Zeke was not a big man, but he was tough as nails. He came back with the biggest hammer I'd ever seen. After barely looking at the door, he reared back and hit that door jam with all his might. *Pow!!!* After that, thanks to Zeke's fine tuning, the door worked perfectly.

Wiley Morris, Another Body Shop Man

Years after Wiley Morris had passed away, I was doing more research on the Morris Brothers, so I called his oldest son, Ralph. After I had asked him a few questions about his dad, he stopped me and said, "Son. You know far more about my dad than I ever did."

Bill Monroe's Mandolin

It's well known that Bill Monroe once sent his mandolin back to Gibson for a re-fret job. Instead of doing only that, Gibson also refinished it. Bill was furious because he thought refinishing it hurt the tone of his instrument. In response, he took his pocketknife and gouged out the name "Gibson" on the headstock, leaving only "The."

One time someone was hanging around Monroe, trying to see the name of the mandolin that had been inlayed in the peghead. He asked Bill the name of the mandolin, and Monroe simply said, "It's a 'The.'"

The Biggest Bull in the World

Lester Flatt was introducing the audience to Cousin Jake, the bass player in the Foggy Mountain Boys. Lester said, "Now, I'm going to tell a story on you, Jake, so just hang back and listen. I'm sure you remember the time your fourteen kids wanted to go to the circus. They were advertising the circus by saying they had on display the world's biggest bull. His fourteen kids all begged to go to the show, and Jake finally said he'd take them if it wasn't too expensive. So they went to town and Jake went to the ticket window to ask about the prices. His fourteen kids were standing in line behind him. 'Ten cents each,' said the ticket man. Jake said he couldn't afford that and started to walk away. The ticket man called out at him and said, 'Are you really the father of all fourteen kids and want to see the bull?' When Jake assured him that they were all his, and that they all wanted to see the bull, the man said, 'Come on in, it's all on the house. I'd like for the bull to see you.'"

Bill Monroe's "The" mandolin peghead overlay, ca. 1960.

Playing for a Mobster's Funeral

My first musical instrument was the trumpet. I chose that instrument because I wanted to see how it would be possible to play all those notes with only three buttons. I started taking lessons from a man in his seventies named Leon Russell. He drove an original Model T Ford that he had bought new in the twenties. My first tune (that you could recognize) was "Lightly Row." After I had been taking lessons for several months,

Mr. Russell said, "Wayne, we're going to start all over, back to the beginning." With that, I got discouraged and decided to quit the lessons.

In middle school, I joined the school band. Even though I couldn't read the score, I just made stuff up. The band was so bad that no one noticed. My school was particularly rowdy, and the guys in the band behaved like a bunch of hoodlums and were very disrespectful to our poor teacher. One boy was really acting up, so in frustration, the teacher said, "OK, you get up here and conduct the band." That turned the boy around right on the spot. With his new responsibility, he started to act right. Then all the other rowdy boys started to shape up, because they also wanted to conduct the band. I didn't even come close to be chosen for that august position because I must have been a "goody goody."

Because I more or less played the trumpet, my Scout master bought me a bugle so I could play "Taps" at the end of every meeting. He insisted I bring my bugle on camping trips. The trouble was, I have always hated to get up in the morning, and as hard as my scoutmaster would try, he couldn't roust me up in the morning in time to get the other boys to wake up. He even resorted to grabbing my leg and shaking it, but still I slept.

On one camping trip in the High Sierra mountains, we were awakened by what felt like a strong earthquake. The ground shook so much that it rolled me over in my sleeping bag. Come to find out, what we felt was not an earthquake, but it was the first underground nuclear test conducted on September 19, 1957, in nearby Nevada. No wonder I'm a little "off."

During my Boy Scout years, my mother got a telephone call. A local mobster had been murdered and they wanted me to play "Taps" at his funeral in Hollywood. It was front-page news in all the newspapers. My mother told the man in no uncertain terms, "My son is *not* playing 'Taps' at that funeral." "But, Mom," I begged, "this might be the biggest gig I ever get to play." It was.

Wayne Erbsen as a Civil War soldier at the Vance birthplace, Weaverville, North Carolina, ca. 1995 (photograph by Martin Fox).

Index

Abernathy, Will 94
Acuff, Roy 49, 101, 102, 117, 121, 126
Adcock, Eddie 150
"After the Ball" 129
"Alabama Gals" 154
Alderman, Tony 155
"All the Good Times Are Passed and Gone" 127
Allen, Geary 83
"America the Beautiful" 163
"Angeline the Baker" 15, 16
"Apple Blossom" 56
"Are You from Dixie" 47
"Are You Waiting Just for Me" 65
"Arkansas Traveler" 56
Arkin, Steve 181
Arnold, Eddie 134
Ashley, Clarence "Tom" 34, 184
Atkins, Chet 39, 101, 179
Austin, Lonnie 29
Autry, Gene 135, 160, 161

Bailey, Brothers 74
Baker, Kenny 77, 80
Ballard Branch Bogtrotters 17, 18, 19
"Banks of the Ohio" 154
Barker, Dwight 68
"Beaumont Rag" 55, 124
"A Beautiful Life" 163
Berline, Byron 56
Berry, Hunter 83
"Beulah Land" 142
"Bill Cheatham" 62
Black Mountain Bluegrass Boys 167
"Black Mountain Blues" 70, 77
"Black Mountain Rag" 124
"Blackest Crow" 163
Blue Sky Boys 46, 74, 112
"Blue Ridge Mountain Blues" 127
"Blue Yodel #9" 116
Bolick, Bill 36, 46, 74, 112
Bolick, Earl 36, 46, 74, 112
Bond, Johnny 134
"Bonnie Blue Flag" 88
Bowman, Charlie 155
Boyette, Andy "Bijou" 96
"Bring Me a Leaf from the Sea" 26, 34, 94
"Bring Me a Little Water, Sylvie" 158

Brockman, Polk 57, 58
Brooks, Rex 95, 97
Brown, Larry 177
Brown, Milton 134
"Browntown Girl" 154
Buchanan, Frank 101
"Buckin' Mule" 44
"Buffalo Gals" 154
Bumgarner, Samantha 8
Burnett, Anissa 83
Burns, Jethro 179
"Bury Me Beneath the Willow" 21, 22, 140
Bush, Roger 123

"Cabin in Caroline" 69, 82
"Cacklin' Hen" 77
Callahan, Homer 43, 44, 45
Callahan, Walter 43, 44, 45
Callahan Brothers 113
Campbell, Archie 102
"Can I Sleep in Your Barn Tonight, Mister" 28
"The Cannonball" 24, 25
"Can't Yo' Heah Me Callin' Carolina" 11
Carlisle, Bill 115
Carolina Blue 79, 83
"Carolina in the Mornin'" 55
Carolina Tar Heels 26
Carolina Twins 94
Carpenter, Harley 167
Carson, Fiddlin' John 22, 57
Carter, A.P. 20, 21, 23, 24, 142
Carter, Gladys 21
Carter, Joe 21
Carter, Maybelle 20, 21, 137, 139
Carter, Sara 20, 21
Carter Family 15, 20, 21, 23, 40
Cash, June Carter 20, 22
Cassidy, Hopalong 159
Charles River Valley Boys 162
"Charleston Gals" 154
Charlie Bowman and His Brothers 155
Childre, Lou 96, 97
Childres, Jim 177
Chuck Wagon Gang 131
Clark, Roy 136
Clifton, Bill 125
Cline, Charlie 168, 169
Cline, Curly Ray 168

Cody, Buffalo Bill 160
Coe, Campbell 124
Coleman, Fiddlin' Joe 87, 88
"Coleman's March" 88
"Come Home, Father" 128
Cooder, Ry 189
Cook, Shane 80
"Cool Water" 73
Coon Creek Girls 45
Cooper, Stoney 148
Cooper, Wilma Lee 148
Copas, Cowboy 40
"Corrina" 94
"Cotton Eyed Joe" 77
Country Boys 123
Country Gentlemen 151
Cox, Bill 155
"Crazy Blues" 62
Crazy Water Barn Dance 30
"Crooked Creek Blues" 94
Crow, Mack 89, 93
Crowe, Wallace (Josh) 102
Crowe, Wayne 102
"Cumberland Mountain Deer Chase" 154
"Curly Headed Baby" 44

Dalhart, Vernon 11, 12
Darby and Tarlton 131
"Darling Little Joe" 140
Davis, Cleo 10, 107, 108, 109, 110, 111, 112, 113, 114, 115, 116, 117, 118
Davis, Doc 17, 18
Davis, Gussie L. 31, 130, 131
Davis, Jimmie 89
Davis, Walter 31, 34, 89, 91, 92, 93, 94
DeGraff, Peter 155, 156
Delmore Brothers 101, 110, 112
"Devil in the Strawstack" 53
"Devil's Dream" 53
"Diamond Joe" 5, 145
"Did You See My Daddy Over There?" 126
"Dim Lights, Thick Smoke (and Loud, Loud Music)" 124
"Dixie" 88, 131
Dixon Brothers 131
"Do Not Turn Me from Your Door" 133
Dodson, Tiny 29, 31, 32, 41, 48, 49
"Doin' My Time" 163

197

Index

"Don't Go Out Tonight My Darling" 13
"Don't Let Your Brew Run Down" 27
"Don't Let Your Deal Go Down" 27, 28
"Down by the Deep Sad Sea" 133
"Down Yonder" 108
"Driven from Home" 133
"Drummer Boy of Shiloh" 22
"Drunkard's Hell" 77, 78
Duffy, John 150
Duncan, Buck 101
Duncan, Perry 74
Dunford, Uncle Eck 15, 16, 17, 18, 19
Durham, Hal 102
Dylan, Bob 148

Earl Johnson's Clodhoppers 28–29
"Earl's Breakdown" 100
Elliott, Ramblin' Jack 145, 146
Erbsen, Wayne 52, 159, 167, 176
Erbsen, Wes 183

"Faded Coat of Blue" 128
Fairchild, Raymond 90, 100, 101, 102, 103
"The Fields Have Turned Brown" 78
Fincher, Harold 35
Fincher, J.W. 30, 47
"Fire on the Mountain" 75, 116
Flatt, Lester 41, 65, 66, 69, 96, 97, 126, 139, 146, 166, 194
Flatt & Scruggs 41, 50, 59
"Flint Hill Special" 100, 139
"Foggy Mountain Breakdown" 41
"Foggy Mountain Chimes" 139
"Foggy Mountain Special" 139
"Foggy Mountain Top" 115
Foley, Red 45
"Footprints in the Snow" 115
"Forked Deer" 56
Forrester, Howdy 64, 68
Forrester, Sally 96
Foster, Gwen 26, 31, 91, 93
Foster, Stephen 16
Fox, Curly 63
Fox, Martin 87
"Fox on the Run" 150, 151
"Freeborn Man" 163

Garren, Amos 10, 107, 116
Georgia Crackers 147
Gid Tanner and His Skillet Lickers 28
Gilliland, Henry 55
"Go Feather, Go Feather Your Nest" 34
"God Loves His Children" 69
"Going Back to Coney Island" 94
"Going Down the Lee Highway" 14
"Going to Georgia" 26
Goins Brothers 102
"Gonna Lay Down My Old Guitar" 113

"Goodbye Old Pal" 162
"Goodnight Irene" 130, 158
Grammar, Billy 102
Grand Ole Opry 32
"Grave Upon the Green Hillside" 40
Gray, Tom 150
Grayson, G.B. 13
Green, Archie 15
Greene, Clarence 34, 91, 93
Greer Sisters 13
"Grey Eagle" 62
Grey, Zane 160
Guthrie, Woody 158

Hall, Kenny 16, 96
Hall, Oscar 17, 18
Hamilton Gerald 80, 81
Hammett, Smith 97
"Handsome Molly" 13
"Hangman's Reel" 54
"Hard Times Come Again No More" 162
Harvey, Roy 28
Hash, Albert 54
Hawes, Baldwin "Butch" 146
Hay, George D. 167
Hays, Lee 146
Hays, William Shakespeare 22, 58, 131, 140
"He Will Set Your Fields on Fire" 116
Hefner, Richard 167
"Hello Stranger" 25
Henley Fisher 13, 30
"Her Name Was Hula Lou" 26
"He's Coming to Us Dead" 30
"Hesitation Blues" 163
"Hey, Hey, Hey" 78
Hicks, Bobby 79, 83
Hill, Joe 138
"Hills of Roan County" 47
Hodges, John 154
"Home Sweet Home" 128
Hooper, Jamie 181
Horton, Roy 142
Houston, Cisco 147
Howard, Clint 124
Howard, Randy 81

"I Am Dying, Mother, Dying" 133
"I Have an Aged Mother" 140
"I Have No Home" 133
"I Have No Loving Mother Now" 140
"I Love No One But You" 78
"I Wish I Could Shimmy Like My Sister Kate" 55
"I Wonder Where You Are Tonight" 134
"If You See My Savior" 24
"I'll Remember You, Love, in My Prayers" 22, 133
"I'll Twine 'Mid the Ringlets" 22, 136
"I'm a Little Teapot" 153
"I'm Going to Make Heaven My Home" 69

"I'm Lonesome for You" 25
"I'm Motherless Now" 134
"I'm on My Way to Canaan's Land" 142
"I'm the Man That Rode the Mule 'Round the World" 28
"I'm Thinking Tonight of My Blue Eyes" 116
"In the Baggage Coach Ahead" 130
"In the Pines" 158
"In the Sweet By and By" 138
"Is Mother There?" 134
"It Ain't Gonna Rain No More" 108
Irving, Maud 136
"I've Just Seen the Rock of Ages" 152
"I've Lived a Lot in My Time" 142

"Jack and Mae" 130
James, Sonny 77
Jarrell, Tommy 180, 181
Jefferson, Blind Lemon 23, 34, 89, 91, 92
Jenkins, Dewitt "Snuffy" 31, 94, 95, 97
Jenkins, Hoke 38, 50
JFG Coffee Boys 48
"Jimmie Brown, the Newsboy" 5, 22, 133, 138
"Joe Coleman's March" 88
Johnson, Daner 26, 27
Jones, Grandpa 40
Julian, Ralph 172

"Katy Hill" 114, 117
Kazee, Buell 128
"K.C. Stomp" 62
Keith, Leslie 187
Kentucky Colonels 176
"Kentucky Waltz" 148
Kincaid, Bradley 131
King, Pee Wee 40, 117
"Kingdom Coming" 128
Kirby, Fred 49
Krise, Speedy 50

Lambert, Curly 78
Lambert, Pee Wee 71
Lathum, Billy Ray 123
Laughlin, Tim 83
Lawson, Doyle 191
Layne, Bert 92
Ledbetter, Huddie William ("Lead Belly") 157, 158
Ledford, Steve 31
"Lee Highway Blues" 70
"Let Me Be Your Salty Dog" 39, 40
"Let Me Love You One More Time" 128
"Let the Church Roll On" 24
Lewis, Jerry Lee 136
Lewis, Laurie 148
"Life Is Like a Mountain Railroad" 134
"Life's Railway to Heaven" 134
"Lights in the Valley" 32

Index

"Listen to The Mockingbird" 77
"Little Cabin Home on the Hill" 142
"Little Darling Pal of Mine" 25
"Little Girl in Tennessee" 165
"Little Glass of Wine" 75
"Little Joe the Wrangler" 134
"Little Log Cabin in the Lane" 22, 93
"Little Maggie" 13
"Little Old Cabin in the Lane" 58, 89, 125, 133, 134
"Little Old Log Cabin in the Lane" 89, 133
"Little Old Sod Shanty on the Claim" 134
"Little Red Caboose" 134
Lofgren, Lyle 148
Lomax, Allen 49
Lomax, John 158
"Lone Grave by the Sea" 133
"Lonesome for You" 24
"Lonesome Moonlight Waltz" 163
"Lonesome River" 78
"Lonesome Road Blues" 26
"Lorena" 128
"Lost Indian" 56
Louvin Brothers 73
Love, Daddy John 35
"Love Grown Cold" 134
Lynn, Loretta 101, 102
Lyons, Billy 145

Macon, Uncle Dave 117, 126, 154
Magness, Tommy 62, 63, 117
Mainer, J.E. 29, 30, 32, 35, 95, 96, 121, 148, 149
Mainer, Julia 30
Mainer, Wade 9, 29, 30, 35, 49, 101, 121, 149
"Make Up and Be Lovers Again" 130
"Man in the Middle" 144
"Man of Constant Sorrow" 78
Maphis, Joe 123, 124, 125, 126
"Maple on the Hill" 31, 35, 130
"Marching Through Georgia" 128
Martin, Benny 77
Martin, Jimmy 103, 183
"Mary's Waiting by the Window" 133
"Maxwell Girls" 154
McCarthy, Harry 88
McCool, J.C. 94
McFarland, Lester 131
McGee, Kirk 56, 60, 61, 117, 126
McGee, Sam 59, 60, 61, 117, 129
McGhee, Brownie 23, 24
McMichen, Clayton 92, 110
"McPherson's Farewell" 53
McReynolds, Jesse 127
McReynolds, Jim 127
Medlin, Julian "Greasy" 96
"Meet Me by the Riverside" 135
"Meet Me in the Moonlight" 25
Melody Mountain Boys 74

Mercer, Ron 169
Messer, Wilford 101
"Midnight Special" 158
Millard, Tommy 9, 10, 114, 116, 118
Miller, John 172
Miller, Lost John 97
Mindte, Tom 151
Mix, Tom 160
"Molly and Tenbrooks" 76
"Molly Darling" 22, 133
Monroe, Bill 7, 8, 9, 10, 32, 56,, 63, 64, 65, 68, 73, 76, 96, 97, 101, 102, 103, 107, 109, 111, 112, 113, 114, 118, 122, 126, 161, 165, 166, 168, 180, 183, 193
Monroe, Birch 67, 68, 165
Monroe, Charlie 9, 10, 32, 65, 73, 110, 111, 112
Monroe Brothers 32, 46, 73, 110
Morris, George 31, 34, 35, 93, 96
Morris, Wiley 9, 31, 32, 33, 34, 35, 36, 37, 38, 39, 40, 41, 42, 43, 93
Morris, Zeke 9, 31, 32, 33, 34, 35, 36, 37, 38, 39, 40, 41, 42, 43, 49, 50, 93, 97, 149, 193
"Mother's Not Dead, She's Only Sleeping" 129
"Mule Skinner Blues" 115, 116
"My Dear Old Home" 133
"My Dear Old Sunny Home" 133
"My First Bicycle" 17
"My Grandfather's Clock" 128
"My Little Girl in Tennessee" 142
"My Long Journey Home" 10
"My Old Pal of Yesterday" 100
"My Rough and Rowdy Ways" 157
"My Southern Sunny Home" 132

"Nashville Blues" 113
Nelson, Willy 182
"Nine Pound Hammer" 10, 14
"No Letter in the Mail" 115
"Nobody's Darling on Earth" 133

Oberstein, Eli 10, 40, 46, 47
O'Brien, Tim 183, 184
"Old Hayseed's Railroad Train to Heaven" 134
"The Old Home" 78
"Old Joe Clark" 154, 155
"Old Love Letters" 134
"Old Virginia Moon" 168
"Omie Wise" 14
"On a Hill Lone and Gray" 24
"On Jordan's Stormy Banks" 124
"One Kind Favor" 24
"One Little Word" 130
"Orange Blossom Special" 70, 77, 102, 103, 117
"Otto Wood, the Bandit" 143
"Over in the Gloryland" 75
"Over the Waves" 33

Page, Zenie 72, 73
Parker, Byron 94, 96
Parrow, E.C. 147
Payne, Leon 118

"Peach Picking Time in Georgia" 117
"Peacock Rag" 62
Peer, Ralph 21, 24, 25, 57
Penny, Hank 118
Plank Road Stringband 170
"Please Pardon Me" 155, 156, 157
Poole, Charlie 26, 27, 28, 93, 187
"Poor Ellen Smith" 155, 156
"Poor Little Orphan Boy" 140
"Poor Orphan Child" 140
Pop Moore and His Oklahomans 135
Porchak, Aynsley 79, 80, 81, 82, 83, 84
Potter, Dale 77
"Precious Jewell" 49
Presley, Elvis 42
Preston, John Brenton 152, 153
"Pretty Polly" 78
Price, Fred 124
"Prisoner's Song" 12
Pruett, Marc 103
Puckett, Riley 92, 108

Rainwater, Cedric 7, 68
Rampy, Gene 115
Randolph, Vance 51
"Randy Lynn Rag" 100, 139
Rector, Red 39, 119
"Red and Green Signal Lights" 130
"Red River Valley" 156, 157
"Red Wing" 36
Reinhardt, Django 124
Reno, Don 41, 102
Riddle, Lesley 22, 23, 24
Rinzler, Ralph 184, 185
Robertson, Eck 54, 55, 56, 57
Robison, Carson 11
"Rock Island Line" 158
Rodgers, Jimmie 109, 156, 157
"Roll in My Sweet Baby's Arms" 115, 117
"Roll On Buddy" 155
Roosevelt, Theodore 160
Rorer, Posey 27
"Rose Conley" 13
Rothman, Sandy 124
Rouse Brothers 117
"Roxann Waltz" 80
Ruby, Texas 63
"Run Mountain" 5, 148
Ryan, Buck 70

"Sally Gooden" 36, 56, 57, 75
"Salty Dog" 93, 94
Sandburg, Carl 134
Satherley, Art 44
Sauceman, Carl 119, 121
"Savingest Man on Earth" 17
Scruggs, Earl 7, 41, 68, 69, 96, 97, 98, 100, 139, 140
Seckler, Curly 97
"Send Back the Picture and the Ring" 131
Shane 159
Sharp, Cecil 8

Index

Shelton, Curly 9, 29, 47, 48, 49, 50, 121
Shelton, Jack 9, 29, 47, 48, 49, 50, 121
Shelton, Lee 145
Shelton Brothers 47
Sherrill, Homer 31, 36, 38, 42, 47
"She's My Curly Headed Baby" 44
"Ship That Never Returned" 128
"Short Life of Trouble" 13
"Shucking the Corn" 139
Shuffler, George 71, 72, 78
Shumate, Jim 59, 62, 63, 64, 65, 66, 67, 68, 69, 70, 71, 75, 82, 96, 97, 166
"Silver Haired Daddy of Mine" 161
Sims, Benny 41, 50
Sinatra, Frank 183
Skillet Lickers 75, 92
Slaughter, Marion Try 11
Slim, Carolina 74
Smiling Rangers 36
Smith, Arthur "Guitar Boogie" 174
Smith, Carl 50
Smith, Fiddlin' Arthur 58, 60, 61, 62, 63, 93, 110
Smith, Fred 39
"Smith's Rag" 62
Smoggy Mountain Boys 180
"Soldier's Joy" 124
"Somebody Loves You Darling" 40
"Somebody Stole My Gal" 55
Sons of the Mountaineers 49
Sons of the Pioneers 47, 48, 73
"Southern Moon" 113
Spencer, Thornton 192, 193
Spiker, Buddy 83
Sprague, Carl T. 160
"Stagolee" 145
Stanley, Carter 71, 75, 76, 78, 89, 102
Stanley, Ralph 13, 71, 75, 76, 78, 89, 102, 152
Stanley, Roba 13
Stanley Brothers 71, 75, 76, 89, 127, 128
"Steel Guitar Rag" 103
Stokes, Leonard "Handsome" 31, 96
Stone, David 116
Stoneman, Donna 14, 189, 190
Stoneman, Ernest V. "Pop" 12, 14, 15, 97

Stoneman, Jimmy 14
Stoneman, Scotty 76
Stoneman, Van 14
"Storms Are on the Ocean" 24
Story, Carl 45, 50, 122
Stringbean 64, 67, 68, 96
"Sunny Side of Life" 46, 47
"Sweet Thing" 102
"Sweetest Gift a Mother's Smile" 74
Swell, Barbara 52

"Taffee Pulling Party" 17
"Take Me in a Lifeboat" 31, 35
Tarter, Steve 23
Tennessee Bluegrass Band 83
"Tennessee Waltz" 103
Terry, Sonny 158
"There Ain't No Use Working So Hard" 26
"This World Is Not My Home" 110
Thompson, Ernest 131
Tinsley, Jim Bob 175
"Tom Dooley" 53
"Tomorrow Never Comes" 134
"Too Late to Cry" 77
"Tragic Romance" 40
"Train 45" 13
Travis, Merle 69
Tubb, Ernest 65, 102, 180
"Tumbling Tumbleweeds" 73
"Turkey in the Straw" 56

Val, Joe 142
Van Eps, Fred 26, 27
Vigour, Pete 177

"Wait a Little Longer, Please Jesus" 163
Wakely, Jimmy 63, 135
Waldron, Cliff 151
Walker, Frank 26
Waller, Charlie 150, 151
Walsh, Dock 25, 26, 89, 125
Ward, Fields 17, 18, 136
Ward, Wade 17, 18
Warren, Paul 97
Watson, Doc 123
"Way Down Yonder in New Orleans" 55
"Way Out There" 48
WBT 9, 96
WCYB 50, 76
"We May Never Meet Again" 133
"We Parted by the Riverside" 133

"We Sat Beneath the Maple on the Hill" 130
"Wednesday Night Waltz" 33
"We'll Be Sweethearts in Heaven" 77
"We'll Meet Again, Sweetheart" 69
WGST 112
"What Is a Home Without Mother?" 118
"What Would You Give in Exchange for Your Soul" 110
"When It's Time for the Whippoorwills to Sing" 113
"When the World's on Fire" 114
White, Clarence 123, 124
White, Cool 154
White, Eric 124
White, Larry 181
White, Roland 124, 189
White, Ted 184, 185
Whitter, Henry 12, 13, 15, 26
WHKY 74
Wilgus, D.K. 53
Wilkie, Grady 41, 97
Williams, Hank 180
Wills, Bob 55
Wills, John 56
Wilson, Dudley 191
Winston, Nate 101, 143
WIRC 74
Wise, Chubby 70
Wiseman, Mac 123, 127, 185
Wister, Owen 160
Wolfe, Charles 96
Wood, Otto 143, 144
Woodie, Lester 71, 72, 73, 74, 75, 76, 77, 78, 79
Woodlieff, Norman 27
Wooten, Art 10, 107, 113, 116
"Wouldn't Mind Dying" 24
WPTF 9
"Wreck on the Southern Old 97" 12, 13, 26
WSM 97
WSPA 96
WWNC 9, 48
WWVA 126

XERA 20

"Yakety Sax" 103
"Your Old Love Letters" 134
"You've Been a Friend to Me" 133

www.ingramcontent.com/pod-product-compliance
Lightning Source LLC
Chambersburg PA
CBHW060343010526
44117CB00017B/2951